Landmarks in the Development of the Contractual System

Landmarks in the Development of the Contractual System

Lajos Vékás

Akadémiai Kiadó, Budapest 1986

Translated by

MIHÁLY KOCSIS

Editorial assistance by

DENNIS CAMPBELL
and
ROLAND SALAMEH

ISBN 964 05 3666 8

Printed in Hungary

To my parents

CONTENTS

PREFACE

1. The role of contracts should not be underestimated in a socialist economic system: both the public and the cooperative sectors of a national economy, as much as the economic relationships of individuals, are interwoven by contracts significant fundamentally for the important function which commodity relationships continue to fulfill in an economic system based on a collective ownership of the means of production. This momentous economic weight of contractual relationships calls for a modern pattern of contractual jurisprudence while creating the need for a system devoid of contradictions.

As the socialist system of contracts developed, two basic sets of difficulties emerged regarding the systematization of legislation and practice.

One of these two sets may be said to involve problems of categorization. Frequently, the largely traditional types of contract can be difficult to delineate and the resulting legal solutions do not completely satisfy the requirements of productive forces and production relationships in order to meet the needs of modern economic life. These problems are deeply rooted in the historic past which, combined with the influence of additional circumstantial factors, namely the persistence of commodity relationships, gives some objective basis for the legal forms and for the patterns of categorization which were devised in earlier social formations to be retained and reshaped for use under a socialist economy. We therefore feel it indispensable to provide an overview of the principal stages of development in order to answer questions raised by contract categorization at the present time.

Another prevalent set of basic problems concerning the contractual system remains the establishment of a systematic structure of *inter se* contracts among economic organizations. This is exemplified for instance by the widely varying methods of codification adopted in the socialist countries of Europe, such as the approaches conceived with regards to economic law: full separation (Czechoslovakia, German Democratic Republic), differentiation (internally) by plan contracts (the Hungarian Civil

Code of 1959), and systematic homogeneity (mostly the Polish Code of 1964).

At the root of these problems of systematization the omnipresent contradictions are evident between the social ownership of the means of production and the persistence of commodity relationships.

2. The main purpose of this study is to summarize the theoretical quintessence of the principal phases in the evolutionary process of the contractual system. It is also designed to help formulate the principles of a contractual system as optimal as possible by uncovering the historical roots of present-day problems. We shall attempt to place into a theoretical context those phases of development which can be judged to have made significant contributions to the formation, evolution, and changes in the institutions and principles of the prevailing contractual system. The following salient points are considered by the author to be of relevance for this discussion:

(a) elaboration of the essential elements of the fundamental types of contract and the idea of typification, in Roman law;

(b) general legal recognition and sanctioning of contract (at different periods and in different manners under the common law and in the continental systems of law);

(c) impacts of the industrial revolution, the scientific-technical revolution, and the modern forces of production in general (standardized contracts, self-regulating agreements, etc.);

(d) implications of changes in social relationships, primarily of the socialization of the means of production.

3. Given its subject and purposes, this study embraces a large body of historical material, yet it cannot be regarded as a history of institutions because, on the one hand, it is confined to tracing and evaluating the development process of contract law from the perspective of its systematic evolution; on the other hand, it is concerned with putting to light the theoretical benchmarks of historical change and laying bare the underlying general laws presently still in motion. Hence it will only scratch the surface of some major issues (e.g. contracts in commercial law), not to mention a smattering of detail.

The focus of our study being on the landmarks in the development of the contractual system, the questions of categorization will be treated solely from the aspect of systematic evolution, while the ramification of the legislative and practical problems concerning the various types of contract will only be discussed in the form of references and brief propositions at least to the extent necessary for the main purpose of our study.

Comparison of laws plays an important role in our discussion. In addition to evaluating the principal approaches and solutions in the socialist countries of Europe, we shall devote considerable attention to the development of the major western laws and to the patterns emerging from them. We do so in the awareness that the area of civil law where the dogmatic problems and results of capitalistic law and those of its systematization may offer useful lessons to learn from since the further development of the socialist law of contract is made-up precisely by the law of contract.

It was not possible to rely on comprehensive scientific works to meet the task we had undertaken; the general principles governing the structure of the contractual system and its main evolutionary phases have not been summarized by the science of law, and further less can be said of a summary treatment of the subject under a Marxist approach. The greater merit goes to the existing works which have produced a number of partial results. We have relied on them as a safe guide regarding several of the issues. Likewise, it was firstly the condensation of a voluminous amount of literary material that required our study to take the form of a scientific essay.

Unfortunately, it was only after sending the manuscript to the printer that the author could read such excellent new publications of direct concern to the subject of this book as Gilmore's *The Death of Contract* and Atiyah's *The Rise and Fall of Freedom of Contract.* For this reason the present book should be read as one that appeared before these two.

Appreciation is due to Prof. Dennis Campbell and Dr. Jur. Roland Salameh of University of the Pacific, McGeorge School of Law, for their editorial assistance.

I. THEORETICAL ASSETS IN THE TYPOGENESIS OF CONTRACT

"Tief ist der Brunnen der Vergangenheit. . ."

---

1. Introduction

The wise counseling of our predecessors, who condensed as they have the toil of their quests, forewarn the researcher determined to trace the birth of types of contract to show sober self-restraint in his delving into the past and provide him with useful guidance in his task. The following passage from Rabel's work written in 1907 will be quoted preliminarily for the purpose of making a realistic assessment of the tasks and possibilities rather than "taking exception to competence": *"Überall steht am Ausgang der rechtsgeschichtlichen Erörterung das offene Tor der Wirtschafts- und Sozialgeschichte. Die Beharrlichkeit des Privatrechts gegenüber der fortschreitenden Wirtschaft, die konkreten Antriebe zur Bildung neuer Rechtstypen, die allmähliche Erkämpfung der Vertragsfreiheit – dies alles sind Grenzprobleme, die allein zu lösen der Jurist nicht berufen ist."*[1]

The intervening decades have naturally brought great research results in economic, social and legal history treated as an interrelated and integral whole. In particular the Marxist method of inquiry into the past has gained widespread use and has produced hitherto unprecedented scientific doctrinal results, mainly in disclosing broad interrelationships, sketching contours, and explaining numerous amounts of detail. Research into particular questions of institutional history has also cleared serious misconceptions, thus removing grey areas in the scientific arena. Let us mention as an example Kaufmann's monograph[2] on leases under the ancient Roman law which has been used here as well as basic material in the exposition of several issues in our present study.

Notwithstanding the results of historical research, we find it appropriate to quote, by way of a beginning momento, the warning of Bechmann 100 years ago in connection with the evolution of sales contract under Roman law: *"Das ist ja von vornherein klar, daß die sozialen Erscheinun-*

[1] Rabel, Ernst: *Nachgeformte Rechtsgeschäfte,* Sav. Z. rom. Abt. 28, 1907, p. 379.
[2] Kaufmann, Horst: *Die altrömische Miete,* Köln–Graz, 1964. p. 393.

gen einer fernen Vergangenheit niemals in einer Weise erklärt werden können, die mit mathematischer Sicherheit und Vollständigkeit bis in's Einzelnste ihren Dienst leistet: wer eine solche Erklärung verlangt, der verkennt das Walten freier und incommensurabler Mächte in der Geschichte, der verkennt, daß uns die Vergangenheit immer nur in einem getrübten Spiegel erscheint; und wer solche Erklärung gibt, dessen Methode entweder eine aprioristisch construierende oder eine einseitig pragmatische ist."[3]

It is time to define the objectives of this chapter before the reader's interest is cooled by our self-restricting remarks. We have made it our primary concern to elucidate, through the prism of historical analysis, the interconnections between commodity relationships, contracts and their categorization, and to verify the acknowledged linkage between the categories with the historical results of research and, where necessary, to present them more elaborately. The fact that few questions can be answered by taking trodden paths, nevertheless allows for no more than some partial and isolated scientific statements that call for synthesis and rendered this task both difficult and enticing. The first question to cope with has either not been asked yet or is quietly and timidly raised in science; it deals with the how and under what circumstances private law of commodity production had created the category of types of contract, to what economic background and legal environment had brought about the products of the private law doctrine that came to maintain the field of law over a span of thousands of years while changing function only a number of times.

Our aim, then, is not "mathematical accuracy" but the investigation to the greatest possible extent of the thrust of development and the attempt grasping "the historical reduced to the logical". During the investigations, attempting to tackle the task and to answer the questions, the author has enjoyed a thrilling experience in encountering once more the general laws which, like drops in an ocean, govern the development of society and the human mind, forcing their way through the maze of unpredictable and random details. We earnestly wish for our readers to the same rewarding experience in this demanding exercise!

The origins of the history of private law go back to Roman law, and it is only in a few instances that institutional roots can be traced further, more often than not to the Hellenic world.[4] At the present level of

[3] Bechmann, August: *Der Kauf nach gemeinem Recht,* I, Geschichte des Kaufs im römischen Recht, Erlangen, 1876, p. 150.

[4] For Greek effects on Roman law see Kaser, Max: *Das römische Privatrecht,* I, München, 1955, p. 160 et seq.; Pringsheim, Fritz: *Ausbreitung und Einfluß des griechischen Rechts,* Heidelberg, 1952; *Griechischer Einfluß auf das römische Recht,* BIDR 63, 1960; in older literature especially Mitteis, Ludwig: *Römisches Privatrecht bis auf die Zeit Diokletians,* I, 1908, p. 12 et seq.; on the hellenistic periods of Roman jurisprudence: Schulz, Fritz: *Geschichte der römischen Rechtswissen-*

science we can almost completely stop with Roman law insofar as the typification of contract is concerned, since the fully developed, closed system of typification is a progeny of Roman law. Max Weber says of the Jewish law of antiquity that it is characterized by a freer development of the types of legal transactions than the Roman law[5] system, whereas Wolff writes on the law of Athens that is does not appear to attribute any particular importance to the types of contract as such.[6]

2. Commodity relations as manifested in law

The fundamental connection between commodity relations and private law contracts has been commonly known since Marx: "*. . . um diese Dinge als Waren aufeinander zu beziehen, müssen die Warenhüter sich zueinander als Personen verhalten, deren Willen in jenen Dingen haust, so daß der eine nur mit dem Willen des andren, also jeder nur vermittelst eines, beiden gemeinsamen Willensakts sich die fremde Ware aneignet, in dem er die eigne veräussert. Sie müssen sich daher wechselseitig als Privateigentümer anerkennen. Dies Rechtsverhältnis, dessen Form der Vertrag ist, ob nun legal entwickelt oder nicht, ist ein Willensverhältnis worin sich das ökonomische Verhältnis widerspiegelt.*"[7] As is clear from this Marxian thesis, it would, from various points of view, be a mistake to think that the appearance of commodity relationships or even the fuller growth of simple commodity relationships was followed within a relatively short period of time by their legal recognition and regulation.

It would be a mistake to do so mainly because the appearance of the exchange of commodities goes back to much earlier times than the emergence of law itself: although the exchange of commodities played a subordinate role for long periods of time, is nevertheless a rather ancient form of exchange of activities; in fact, not only in dealings with "relatives" and "aliens" but also as a concomitant of the unfolding social division of labor. We must keep in mind the long formative stage of the exchange of

---

schaft, Weimar, 1961, p. 44 et seq., particularly p. 73 et seq. and, in the postclassical age, p. 373 et seq.; compare also Toynbee, Arnold J.: *A Study of History, Reconsiderations*, London, 1961, Vol. 12, p. 375 et seq.

[5] Weber, Max: *Rechtssoziologie*, Neuwied, 1960, p. 235.

[6] Wolff, Hans J.: *Die Grundlagen des griechischen Vertragsrecht*, Sav. Z. rom. Abt. 74, 1957. p. 33, fn16; compare also Pringsheim, Fritz: *The Greek Law of Sale*, Weimar, 1960. We may then safely stop at the Roman private law because we concur with the writer of the sentence chosen for the motto of this chapter that *"mit unserer Forscherangelegentlichkeit das Unerforschliche eine Art von foppendem Spiel treibt"*, but nevertheless believe that at the origins of our chosen topic Rome is no *"Scheinhalte, lehmige Dünenkulisse, hinter denen, wenn sie erreicht sind, neue Vergangenheitsstrecken sich auftun, . . .neue Weiten zu neuen Vorgebirgen vorwärtslocken."* Mann, Thomas: *Joseph und seine Brüder, Vorspiel: Höllenfahrt*, Frankfurt/M, 1974, p. 9.

[7] Marx, Karl: *Das Kapital*, Berlin, 1962 (Marx–Engels Werke, Dietz Verlag, Band 23), p. 99; *Grundrisse der Kritik der Politischen Ökonomie* Berlin, 1953 (Dietz Verlag), p. 153.

commodities, which Marx describes in the following terms: *"Der unmittelbare Tauschhandel, die naturwüchsige Form des Austauschprozesses, stellt vielmehr die beginnende Umwandlung der Gebrauchswerte der Waren in Waren als die der Waren in Geld dar. Der Tauschwert erhält keine freie Gestalt, sondern ist noch unmittelbar an den Gebrauchswert gebunden. . . Die Produktion selbst in ihrer ganzen Konstruktion ist gerichtet auf Gebrauchswert, nicht auf Tauschwert."*[8] This embraces a whole historical period which in part predated the emergence of law while, together with the intricate interaction of other factors, contributed to the birth of law, and in part was concurrent with the genesis of law. The origin of the exchange of commodities reach back to the middle stage of savagery,[9] and in the period of primitive communal commodity relations one cannot even speak of law in the juristic sense of the word.[10]

But barter did not appear nor could it appear – by its nature, we may say – even after the emergence of law immediately in the legal cloak of contracts as they existed at the advanced stage of commodity relations,[11] not even if the way for the evolution of new forms was being paved by the very emergence of commodity relationships. What did occur was that commodity relationships appeared probably in the guise of pre-existing legal forms.[12] We must find this natural, particularly if we consider that the so-called traditional societies prior to the capitalistic mode of production were generally and fundamentally dominated by subsistence economy, with the exchange of commodities in the market playing but an auxiliary though relatively widespread role, alongside other forms of exchange of activities (primarily the forms of reciprocity under feudalism and following the city revolutions of redistribution).[13]

On the other hand, the development of law is slow with large digressions in following socio-economic transformations. Commodity-centred

[8] Marx: *Zur Kritik der Politischen Ökonomie,* Berlin, 1961 (Marx–Engels Werke, Dietz Verlag, Band 13), p. 35.

[9] Cf. Engels, Friedrich: *Der Ursprung der Familie, des Privateigentums und des Staats,* Berlin, 162 (Marx–Engels Werke, Dietz Verlag, Band 21), p. 160 et seq. Compare also Mádl, Ferenc: *A deliktuális felelősség a társadalom és a jog fejlődésének történetében* (Delictual Liability in the History of Social and Legal Development), Akadémiai Kiadó, Budapest, 1964, p. 69 et seq.

[10] Engels: op. cit., p. 39 et seq. For the nature of socially sanctioned customs of a normative character in primitive society, see also Kulcsár, Kálmán: *A jogszociológia problémái* (Problems of Legal Sociology). Közgazdasági és Jogi Könyvkiadó, Budapest, 1960. p. 131 et seq. Eörsi, also contends that "during the earlier stages of communism the existence of law could only be observed at the time when the desintegration process had already goten under way. Prior to that, law did not appear as a distinct phenomenon, and rules of conduct did not have a legal character". Eörsi, Gyula: *Comparative Civil (Private) Law,* Budapest, 1979, p. 50.

[11] Mádl: op. cit., p. 75.

[12] Ibid.

[13] Marx: *Grundrisse der Kritik der Politischen Ökonomie,* Berlin, 1953 (Dietz Verlag), p. 367. For the forms of economic relationships, and the basic modes of the exchange of activities (reciprocity, redistribution) in traditional societies, see Polányi, Károly: *A gazdaság mint intézményesített folyamat* (The Economy as an Institutionalized Process), Magyar Filozófiai Szemle, XV. Nos 5 – 6 of 1971, p. 738 et seq.

private law, which gives rise to the contractual categories, cannot emerge except on the basis of private property of a commodity nature: *"Das Privatrecht entwickelt sich zu gleicher Zeit mit dem Privateigentum aus der Auflösung des naturwüchsigen Gemeinwesens"*[14] and "while natural communities are existing and when they start disintegrating. . ., private property does not apply in typical cases to commodity and appears jointly with common property. This signifies that civil law is then making its initial steps towards its development. Under such conditions, the distinct commodity-centred civil law is only an exceptional phenomenon, even if it includes the monumental private Roman law. . ., since in these societies exchange relations are marginal compared to the owner–slave relationships."[15]

It is in this double sense that commodity relations historically predate the legal category of contract: on the one hand, they precede law in general and on the other, private law as the mother of contract taken in the legal sense. All the more admirable is private Roman law which has evolved as a "monumental exception"[16] and as an unparalleled intellectual accomplishment of its kind has elaborated on the law of contract together with its system of types, which has relevance far beyond its own needs and is largely suited to meet the requirements of commodity production in classical capitalism. Of course, this did not occur overnight in Roman law either as it was equally impossible for private law, the latter of which rose to classical heights in governing simple commodity production, to skip certain phases of development. On the contrary, the development of Roman private law provides a splendid example in which the contractual system of commodity-centred private law comes to blossom forth from sprouts rooted in natural communities of remote times.

3. Delictual roots

Beginning with the period of ancient Roman law through the middle of the 3rd century B.C., Roman society still presented the picture of a community that was essentially based on a more or less closed peasant subsistence economy.[17] This should, in the main, be accepted as a valid description even if the traditional claims for the closed nature of the Latin and early Roman societies and economies seem to be exaggerated and one-sided in the light of latest research.[18] It is no wonder, therefore, that

[14] Marx–Engels: *Die deutsche Ideologie*, Berlin, 1962 (Marx–Engels Werke, Dietz Verlag, Band 3), p. 62.

[15] Eörsi: op. cit., pp. 50–51.

[16] Ibid.

[17] Cf. Kaser: op. cit., p. 18 et seq.

[18] Cf. Kaufmann: op. cit., p. 320 et seq.

the system of social customs and morals of a community in disintegration was still palpable in the legal forms of commodity exchange and increasing economic transactions. This can be perceived mainly in the delictual or punitive approach, as presently called, to the forms of transactions. The roots of ancient economic transactions that were legally guaranteed and generating liability are to seek in the concept of delict.[19] The settlement of blood-feud remained at that time a mark of the manner in which property relations were legally recognized.

In the economic transactions of ancient Roman law "performance" was not the object of legal obligation but merely a tool for avoiding the consequences of liability.[20] The purpose of strictly formal transactions entailing liability was to secure "performance" by giving the "obligee" mortgage-like power over the person assuming liability, of which the latter was to be relieved by discharge of his obligation. Upon failing in his performance, the person was not relieved of liability and was in earlier times killed or enslaved and then later on held in debtor's bondage.

Although at a higher level of its development, this legal device clearly followed the pattern of delictual liability when performance became a formal way of relief from such delictual liability. Just like mitigating circumstances that allowed for avoidance of corporeal distraint, the liability procedure was the same as in the case of delicts. The entire legal construction reflected a vestige of an approach whereby relieving the person who failed to effect performance from liability was regarded a wrongful act against the other person.[21]

Needless to say, ancient transactions governed as they were by the concept of delict, were cumbrous for their very formal rigorousness so typical of the period. So was the *stipulatio* itself, which later achieved a singular career, although it had by this time acquired a more general practical relevance. The most typical of ancient transactions was *nexum*, one of the *"per aes et libram"* transactions. Its past is lost in the mists of time and its nature is therefore highly disputed. According to one view, it was used only to perform the function of a loan with a delictual character: whereby the borrower pledged himself as "security" for repayment of the loan.[22]

It was under the delictual approach, then, that the exchange of commodities, growing and expanding, started its movement towards becoming the concern of the law. Later, most of the ancient economic transactions governed as they were by the delictual concept came to disappear (as did *nexum* also), but some of them (particularly *stipulatio*) proved suitable to

[19] This discussion relies on Kaser's remarkable monography, see op. cit., p. 128 et seq. and particularly p. 131 et seq.

[20] Ibid., p. 132.

[21] Ibid.

[22] Ibid., and p. 148.

meet the demand of rapidly developing economic and social relations, by shaking off their ancient formal rigidity.

The informal exchange of commodities took place outside the domain of law for a long time because the ancient Roman private law still in adolescence had no device for handling informal economic transactions of daily life. However, these spread their wings wider and wider. Kaser writes: *"Schon in sehr früher Zeit wird es vorgekommen sein, daß jemand res nec mancipi (mit Ausländern auch res mancipi) vor allem zum Verbrauch oder zur Verarbeitung bestimmte Sachen wie Salz, Metalle, später auch Geld, einem anderen formlos und endgültig hingibt, sei es im Austausch gegen andere Güter, sei es als Geschenk, als Darlehen usw."*[23] Thus, in a long process, there emerged the main channels of the growing exchange of commodities, fulfilling basic functions, such as barter and, after the advent of money, sale, loan, etc., outside the domain of law, without the protection thereof, but in simple and informal ways. Such informal "transactions" also came to receive legal recognition under the delictual approach in such a way that the acquiring party was no longer regarded a thief and could remain in possession of the thing for the "transactions" absolved him from the suspicion of theft.[24] This was another, uniquely ingenious way of bringing the exchange of commodities within the realm of law, one which, understandably, could not use other legal means than those available and could only result from the existing delictual approach. It was still a long time become until the informal exchange transactions of daily life entailed real obligations under the private law and extra-legal "transactions" grew into contracts, or in modern language, into facts creating obligations.[25]

How strong the delictual vein of the Roman law of contract was is further shown by the fact that the delictual approach of ancient Roman law can clearly be perceived in some of the later types of contract. In the case of *depositum* it is certain that, where necessary, the ancient law resorted to praetorian indictment based on embezzlement to secure return of the thing deposited. It is not impossible that a similar approach was taken in providing legal protection for the ancient sprouts of *commodatum, pignus* and other institutions of private law.[26]

One of the "miracles" of Roman law is that in the time of a few centuries, it developed to the point of abandoning the delictual approach to the legal regulation of bartering relations, and gave way to the full

[23] Op. cit., p. 120 et seq., Cf. ibid., p. 153.

[24] Kaser: op. cit., pp. 36, 110 et seq., 456.

[25] Cf. Kaser: op. cit., p. 132.

[26] Kaser: op. cit. pp. 399, 438, fn23: compare also pp. 443, 445, 446, fn5 and p. 447. Weber is also led by the findings of his historical and sociological studies to see in the artificial extension of "actions" one of the main avenues bringing economic and exchange relations (*Zweckkontrakte vs. Statuskontrakte)* into the domain of legislation. See op. cit., p. 116 et seq.

crystallization of the contractual approach in classical law. This included the consensual character of the obligations assumed in four cases of their legally binding force. That period already saw the edifice of the types of contract fully erected. This achievement is in itself worthy of admiration, and it becomes still more radiant when compared to the approach and institutions of the feudal era, such as the debtor's prison, which, viewed on a historical scale, prevailed up to the recent past.

A few words should also be said of the theoretical value present in some aspects of the delictual approach of the ancient Roman law. Our modern mind can hardly be switched back to imagine the legal regulation of bargaining relations other than by recognizing mutual obligations as facts of law. Given this mentality, it appears little short of unnatural for ancient Roman law to have seen a "delictual wrong" in non-performance and to have recognized "liability" without "obligation". Under the socio-economic conditions prevailing at the time, we must find this solution to have been not only natural but, in our view, also highly developed. In support of this statement we may refer to the development of the common law of contract, which for a long time upheld the same approach so peculiar and even "unnatural" to us. We shall have more to say on this score in the next chapter. It suffices to say that here, as Roscoe Pound writes, the concept which sees a theoretical explanation for the enforceability of a contractual promise in the delictual character (now certainly involving a civil-law delict) of the breach of promise continues to be present in the theory of common law.[27]

4. Practicable graduation

Ihering is right in saying that all systems of primitive law take account only the cruder incidents of relations, which in their externals penetrate the senses, but do not consider the finer ones.[28] The economical and thrifty use by primitive laws of their modest means stems from one and the same stock and is an equally typical feature of them. It is the economy of poor people but is made a virtue by necessity to serve a given case: the law did not seek totality, it did not care about the essential economic relations being handled outside its scope, it was capable of covering the most important aspects only and it weighted them accordingly. A known example of this approach is the distinction made between *res mancipi* and *res nec mancipi*: the former included the means of production most important for the peasant economy prevailing in the period

[27] Quoted by Zwiegert, Konrad–Kötz, Hein: *Einführung in die Rechtsvergleichung auf dem Gebiete des Privatrechts,* II. Tübingen, 1969, p. 7.
[28] Jhering, Rudolf: *Geist*, II. 2. p. 422.

of ancient Roman law. The outstanding economic function it performed amid the primitive forms of production required that the conveyance of these things should only be effected in ceremonial forms of civil law (*mancipatio* or *in iure cessio*) in public and in a manner susceptible of proof. The fate of things less important for production, such as *res nec mancipi*, was of less interest to the community, which took therefore no concern in their transaction and conveyance. Informal delivery of possession (*traditio*) remained sufficient for their acquisition in all periods of Roman law.[29]

This same sparing approach and, very often, the economic weighting of questions can be observed in the movement of contracts towards legal recognition and in the evolutionary process of the types of contract. By way of illustration, it will suffice to refer to the emergence of two consensual contracts: *emptio venditio* and *locatio conductio*.[30]

In the period of ancient Roman law most sales transactions were executed promptly by a mutual exchange of performance and counter-performance, so it is obvious and understandable that what the law grasped was, in modern terminology, not the contractual element, the effect of the law of obligations, but the consequence *in rem*, the acquisition of property. This is shown by *mancipatio*, an ancient formal transaction which fulfilled the function of sale between Roman citizens. The sale *res nec mancipi* had the same characteristic in that the decisive role was played by *traditio* as the general mode of acquisition of property in ancient times, although the contractual element became of relevance rather early, with the sale "given weight" as the commonest *iusta causa*.[31] The only effect *mancipatio* had in the nature of obligation was the *actio auctoritatis*,[32] which, again not incidentally, was likewise related to acquisition of property and served to reinforce the liability of seller in case of an action brought to obtain the property. Informal sale under the law of obligations stopped short of producing even that effect unless recourse was had to *stipulatio*, a separate undertaking.[33] Agreement as a contrac-

[29] Brósz, Róbert–Pólay, Elemér: *Római jog* (Roman Law), Budapest, 1974. pp. 189 et seq.; Ihering: op. cit., II. pp, 1, 155; Bechmann: op. cit., pp. 144 et sqq., particularly p. 154.

[30] Cf. Mommsen, Theodor: *Die römischen Anfänge von Kauf und Miete*, Gesammelte Schriften, III, Berlin, 1907. p. 32 et seq.; Cancelli, F.: *L'origine del contratto consensuale di compravenditta nel diritto romano*, Milano, 1963; Bechmann: op. cit.; Kaufmann: op. cit. For the origins of *mandatum* and *societas*, the two other consensual contracts of Roman law, see Arangio-Ruiz, Vincenzo: *Il mandato in diritto romano*, Napoli, 1949 and *La società nel diritto romano*, Napoli, 1950; Watson, Alan: *Consensual societas between Romans and the Introduction of formulae*, Revue internationale des droits de l'antiquité, 9. 3e sér., 1962. p. 431 et seq.

[31] Cf. Brósz – Pólay: op. cit., p. 420 et seq.

[32] Bechmann: op. cit., p. 230 et seq.; Marton, Géza: *A római magánjog elemeinek tankönyve. Institúciók* (Textbook of the Elements of Roman Private Law. Institutes), Budapest, 1963, p. 205. For the delictual origin of *actio auctoritatis*, see Marton: ibid., p. 207. For the "accontractual" nature of the origin of *mancipatio*, see Kaser: op. cit., p. 39 et seq.

[33] Bechmann: op. cit., p. 318 et seq., p. 374 et. seq.

tual element began to the concern of the law when mutual performances had been separated in the context of time. This was at first prompted by purchase on credit, probably prior to the Act of the XII Tables, but shortly afterwards even the object of sale was fulfilled very often at a time subsequent to the conclusion of contract (e.g. transactions concerning the sale of future crops or harvests were practically an everyday occurrence as far back as the 3rd century B.C.)[34] Even from this stage it was a long way, hard to trace clearly in history, to go to the actionability of contractual agreement (e.g. granting of credit for payment of the purchase price required a separate *vindicatio*).[35] Yet Bechmann's arguments convincingly show that Roman law was led by the peculiarities of *emptio venditio* and *locatio conductio* (separation of performances in time or its possibility) to recognize the legal relevance of contractual agreement and its actionability.[36] What matters is, in effect, not the exact period in which actionability was recognized,[37] but the fact that such recognition came to pass and gave rise to the modern contract of sale.[38] To know whether this process was influenced by *stipulatio, fides,* or both (or eventually other incidents) is perhaps of just as little importance to us.[39] What intrigues the modern mind is the practicable gradation which marked this process of development.

The process leading up to the legal regulation of actions involving tenancy, lease and contracting, as we call them today, was an equally cautious one phased out in the period of ancient Roman law. Particularly Kaufmann's research results give us a rather clear picture of this process, which came to a head with the appearance of *iudicium locati conducti* somewhere in the late 3rd and 2nd centuries B.C.[40] It is of interest to note however, that by contrast to sales transactions, this line of development does not appear to have been that practicable, not only with respect to *locatio conductio,*[41] its final outcome, but also to its intermediate phases. It cannot be our purpose to describe the dogmatic details of how the legal means were devised,[42] but rather to indicate merely the breaks

[34] Idem., p. 230 et seq., or Brósz – Pólay: op. cit., p. 421.

[35] Cf. Bechmann: op. cit., p. 342 et seq. Unlike Bechmann (p. 457 et seq. Marton (ibid.) finds mutual *stipulatio* to have played a more general role in the agreement of sale becoming actionable.

[36] Op. cit., p. 417 et seq. (sale), p. 427 et seq. (lease), p. 435 *(locatio conductio operis).*

[37] Cf. Bechmann: op. cit., p. 342 et seq. Unlike Bechmann (p. 457 et seq.), Marton (ibid.) finds *Obligations in the Later Roman Republic,* Oxford, 1965, p. 40 et seq. Comare also Marton: op. cit., p. 205 et seq. and Brósz–Pólay: op. cit., p. 421.

[38] Cf. Diósdi, György (Ed.): *A római jog világa* (The World of Roman Law), Budapest, 1973, p. 166; Brósz–Pólay: op. cit., p. 421.

[39] Bechmann: op. cit., p. 457 et seq.; cf. Brósz–Pólay: op. cit., pp. 421, 426; Marton: op. cit., p. 205; Kaser: op. cit., p. 438.

[40] Kaufmann: op. cit., p. 325 et seq.

[41] On the "type" of *locatio conductio* more will be said at the end of Section 10 dealing with the general appreciation of typification in Roman law.

[42] Kaufmann: ibid.

that seem to have occurred at several stages in the process of dogmatic approaches. The primitive remedy of ancient sacral law (*pignoris capio*), which survived to be inscribed in the XII Tables also,[43] was applicable only to the hire of draught animals. The cross-section of the coverage of the aspects of lease was too narrow for legal practice to draw conclusions from for the entire spectrum of leases, particularly if facts relating to manual labor are also included in this category.[44] Nor did the next stage of development – at which a surety (*praes*), by a special formal transaction, guaranteed one of the performances of lease – point towards classification, or towards the creation of legal remedies based on types of transactions. The suretyship *praes* served not only to secure the lease but also to furnish some indirect legal protection in respect to other classes of facts as well.[45] For this reason, and because its criterion was form rather than substance, it was unable to evolve in socio-typical facts and to foster the evolution of leases.[46] Hence, up to the appearance of *iudicium locati conducti,* the decisive role was played by *stipulatio,* the "jolly joker" of Roman law, in providing legal protection with respect to aspects of lease. As far back as the period of the XII Tables[47] (perhaps even before) there existed a possibility to sue for rent (as *certa pecunia*) by a separate *stipulatio* under the procedure of *legis actio* and, interesting enough, for the performance of a contract for doing of manual labor (as *certa res*), but no remedy was yet provided[48] either for the thing hired or for the service contracted[49] (as *in faciendo* and hence *res incertae*). Such remedy became available at a later time when *stipulatio* for *incertae res* was made actionable. This same development allowed the obligation for performance to be made conditional, by *stipulatio,* on the effecting of counter-performance, including the possibility for action against such a *stipulatio,* which actually covered the whole transaction of lease.[50] This stage of the facts of lease entering the domain of law was still short of inducing typification because the *stipulatio incerti* left much more room for the parties to determine the content of agreement and to coin its terminology.[51]

Nevertheless, as we look at it today, we should say that even in this class of facts, which entered the domain of law in a zigzag line and with dogmatic "failings", Roman law attained a respectable standard of legal protection and a relative degree of generality at a rather early stage.

[43] Cf. Gaius, pp. 4, 28.
[44] Kaufmann: op. cit., p. 326 et seq.
[45] Cf. Kaser: op. cit., p. 152.
[46] Kaufmann: op. cit., pp. 327, 329.
[47] Gaius, pp. 4, 17. Cf. Gaius, pp. 4, 19 et seq. For references see Kaufmann: op. cit., p. 329 et seq.
[48] Cf. Kaufmann: ibid.
[49] *Ulp. D.,* pp. 45, 1, 75, 7.
[50] Cf. Kaufmann: op. cit., p. 339 et seq.
[51] Ibid., p. 341.

5. Money, money, money

At the core of the ingenious solutions and occasional zigzags of regulation by Roman law we find the demands of rapidly expanding economic transactions. Analyzing the facts of lease in ancient Roman law,[52] Kaufmann among other writers gives a brilliant illustration of how complex and complicated a movement of economic and social conditions was behind the process of property relations entering the domain of law. In his view, the fact that evidence to support the existence of collective ownership of land among the original inhabitants of Central Italy had been lacking since the time of their settlement was basic to the emergence of facts characteristic of lease; the peasantry consisted of individual owners farming their land on their own.[53] Let us add forthwith that the private ownership of land played a more general role and was a most decisive factor in the decline of primitive production relations and in the consolidation of the newly emergent pattern of commodity relations. Kaufmann also notes that the upper crust relying on the private ownership of land found their complements partly in the local craftsmanship pursuing their trade by occupation and in the proletariat closely linked with them, partly in the lack of a slave class of any considerable extent.[54]

Among the economic motives directly making for legal regulation money played the overwhelming part. At this point we do not have in mind the qualitative impact exercised by the emerging function of money on economic transactions, the transformation of the direct exchange of products into an exchange of commodities,[55] although this process was as

[52] Kaufmann: op. cit., Chapter II, p. 28 et seq.

[53] Ibid., p. 320. Cf. p. 50 et seq.

[54] Ibid., p. 321. Among other economic and social factors of relevance to the growth and proliferation of the "facts of lease" Kaufmann makes an in-depth analysis of the rise of craftsmanship (p. 58 et seq.), state-assisted construction (p. 83 et seq.), the emergent social need for tenement housing and the construction of tenement houses (p. 54 et seq.), industrial forms of agricultural cultivation (p. 107 et seq.), etc.

[55] Marx writes on this process: *"Die Warenzirkulation ist nicht nur formell, sondern wesentlich vom unmittelbaren Produktenaustausch unterschieden. . . Einerseits sieht man hier, wie der Warenaustausch die individuellen und lokalen Stoffwechsel der menschlichen Arbeit entwickelt, andrerseits entwickelt sich ein ganzer Kreis von den handelnden Personen unkontrollierbarer, gesellschaftlicher Naturzusammenhänge. . . . Der Zirkulationsprozess erlischt deswegen auch nicht, wie der unmittelbare Produktenaustausch, in dem Stellen- oder Händelwechsel der Gebrauchswerte. Das Geld verschwindet nicht, weil es schliesslich aus der Metamorphosenreihe einer Ware herausfällt. Es schlägt immer nieder auf eine durch die Waren geräumte Zirkulationsstelle. . . . Die Zirkulation schwitzt beständig Geld aus."* Marx: *Das Kapital*, Berlin, 1962 (Marx–Engels Werke, Dietz Verlag, Band 23), pp. 126, 127; *Grundrisse der Kritik der Politischen Ökonomie*, Berlin, 1953 (Dietz Verlag), p. 110 et seq. A classical description of the ancient barter of products is to be found in Homer's familiar lines of verse:

"The rest they purchas'd at their proper cost,
And well the plenteous freight supplied the host:
Each, in exchange, proportion'd treasures gave:
Some brass, or iron, some an ox or slave.

The Iliad of Homer, London, 1857, pp. 137, 566–569.

mentioned earlier, an indirect motivating force behind the emergence of contract as a legal category. Here we refer to the historical aspects indicating that the specific commodity character and the various functions of money had from the outset raised problems for the law, thus providing direct stimulus for economic transactions to be brought within the domain of law. Money completed this process by furnishing a means and a lever for law. Kaser, too, points out that "performance" in dealings involving liability under Roman law – owing apparently to enforceability and also to the delictual model – consisted at all times in payment of money.[56] Bechmann sees the main cause of sales and lease agreements in their being transactions conducted through the medium of money as a general measure of value.[57] Rabel states that a sale being perhaps the earliest actionable contract besides a loan is a natural fact requiring no explanation.[58]

It is interesting to note on this score that the bartering agreement dispensing with money is a stepchild of Roman law. One might think (and indeed there exists at times such scientific belief) that barter is the most ancient type of contract to have entered the domain of law. It preceded both sale and loan as it offered itself as it were, in terms of legal regulation as the simplest and most natural form of handling commodity relations in the process of growth. Yet insofar as it can be inferred from insufficient records of ancient times, it was not the case.[59] It was perhaps due to its simplistic and relatively unproblematic nature that the law took so little interest in barter, for it can hardly be disputed that barter was for a long time the basic transaction practised on a mass scale. While it cannot be ruled out in applying the delictual approach noted earlier, the ancient law relieved the bartering partners from the charge of theft[60] when the need arose, just as it did the partners to other basic informal transactions (sale, loan, etc.). A real remedy under private law took much more time to develop in the case of barter.[61]

[56] Kaser: op. cit., p. 123.

[57] Bechmann:. op. cit., pp. 482 et seq., 485. Cf. the role of credit in the appearance of consensual sale: ibid., p. 230 et seq. and Kaser: op. cit., p. 459.

[58] Rabel: op. cit., p. 326 and Marton: op. cit., p. 196.

[59] In our view, the two transactions as discussed in the famous text of Paulus on the connection between barter and sale (d.18.1.1. pr.-2) are to be understood in an economic rather than a legal sense. It was argued with conclusive force already in the late 19th century that the famous property dispute between the schools of Proculianus and Sabinianus, now an oddity of legal history (Gaius, pp. 4, 141), can in no way be construed to imply that sale started to grow out of barter only at the time of the dispute (in the early imperial period). See Bechmann: op. cit., p. 5 et seq.; Kaser: op. cit. p. 484 et seq., with fns 1 and 8.

[60] A reference with no particular explanation is made by Kaser: op. cit., p 38.

[61] It is on record that, in the case of exchange, remedies other than *in factum actio* were not provided even by the classical Roman law to claim counter-performance on the basis of unilaterally effected performance. See Marton: op. cit., p. 205.

The significance of money in the evolutionary process of contract law has already been realized by Max Weber who said that often the entry of money into economic life played a decisive role in the development of actionable contractual obligations.[62] Though instancing *nexum* and mainly *stipulatio*, he arrives at a similar conclusion concerning the recognition of liability for loan in Roman law.[63] He regards exchange as a clearly economic category, asserting that the origins of the legal devices proper intended to cover exchange. He states that they are marked by the separate role of metals functioning as money, *viz.* the appearance of sale.[64] His discussion fails to clarify whether he considers the appearance of the function of money to have been of importance for the development of contract law as an indirect factor working through the emergence of commodity and money relations, or whether he thinks to have discovered a direct relationship between the two phenomena. In our view as set out earlier, a direct relationship may also be said to exist between the specifics of money and its various functions and the development of contract law,[65] although the indirect effect was determinant.

6. The "anti-types" of ancient law

The generally accepted view in the modern science of civil law appears to be that historically, legal recognition was extended first to individual contracts and then to the types of contract; the contract as a phenomenon productive of general legal effect coming to be recognized somewhat later.[66] This logically attractive assertion seems to be in need of modification in the light of research into legal history.

[62] Weber: op. cit., p. 117.

[63] Ibid., p. 116 et seq.

[64] Ibid., p. 112 et seq.

[65] The transformation of *mancipatio* from sale for money into symbolic sale is perhaps one of the best examples of how the legal forms were influenced by money. Whether this process of change is linked to the introduction of coined money or to the demands of purchase on credit and the appearance of coined money viewed as a complex, the peculiar possibilities of money are found to be lurking behind this highly important development affecting the evolution of Roman law. With the payment of purchase price having been made symbolic, one performance of the sales transaction remained outside the walls of *mancipatio* surrounded with strict formalities. The agreement came into prominence to cover both performances, albeit without legal consequences involved for a long time yet to come. Cf. Bechmann: op. cit., pp. 154 et seq., 202 et seq.

[66] Eörsi (Világhy – Eörsi): *Magyar polgári jog* (Hungarian Civil Law), II, Budapest, 1965, p. 7. It is emphasized at the outset that our discussion here takes issue with this scientific thesis solely from the aspect of the entry of contract into the domain of law and its historical growth. Accordingly we share the view that at a later stage, after the general legal recognition of contract, the types of contract emerge as a result of the recurrence of various contracts of a similar nature. Cf. Világhy, Miklós: *Gazdasági reform és polgári jog* (Economic Reform and Civil Law), Acta Fac. X, Budapest, 1968, p. 61.

It is of course incontestable that the recognition of contract as a general fact creative of obligation was the last stage in the development of contract law and that it occurred in response to the demands of capitalist development. This stage was reached only by bourgeois private laws, at different periods in different countries. Such is the case in spite of the fact that an amazingly early period, probably as far back as the 5th century B.C.,[67] Roman law had devised with the aid of *stipulatio,* the form which in the course of time enabled an action to be brought practically against any authorized substance of contract. It is absolutely necessary to make a theoretical distinction between this state of affairs and the recognition in principle of the legal effect of contract or agreement.[68]

As against this there is but little in the records of Roman law to buttress the first part of the foregoing argument, namely that legal recognition was extended first to individual contracts and then to their types. It is a general feature of primitive laws that strict legal form as manifest in sacral and even magic externals is decisive to the attainment of specific economic goals[69] and that a particular form is designed to discharge various economic function or even to fill various types of economic roles. The transactions governed by ancient Roman law are also facts of law "covering such types". This appears to be the case with *nexum* also, though its past was lost in the abyss of time. Kaser writes that at the beginning the much-discussed *nexum* was presumably of more general significance[70] (as is suggested by the very term *nectere* = to bind). Géza Marton is firmly of the view that the term *nexum* came to be reserved for loan transactions at a later stage; this form and the act incidental to it (*gerere per aes et libram*) originally covered both sale and loan, the two most important contracts of primitive people.[71] Somewhat romantic and unprovable but not entirely improbable is the concept under which as quoted by Kaufmann, *locatio conductio* is thought to have sprung from the decay of an ancient general transaction.[72] *Stipulatio,*

[67] Schulz: op. cit., p. 38; cf. Marton: op. cit., p. 197 fn2 and Gaius, pp. 4, 17. For *stipulatio* in general, see Kaser: op. cit., pp. 150 et seq., 450 et seq.; Watson: op. cit., p. 1 et seq., fn37; Marton: op. cit., p. 199 et seq.; Brósz – Pólay: op. cit., p. 403 et seq. For an interesting approach to the origin of *stipulatio* and its initial role, see Weber: op. cit., p. 117 et seq.

[68] The recognition of the general binding force of contract and its effect on the function of types of contract will be treated at greater length in Chapter III.

[69] For the formalism of Roman law and its evolution, see Schulz: op. cit., pp. 28 et seq., 91, 155, 371 et seq. Cf. Koschaker, Paul: *Europa und das römische Recht,* München – Berlin, 1953, p. 191.; Marton: op. cit., p. 196.

[70] Kaser: op. cit., p. 148, liberally documented with references to literature. For the ancient types fulfilling different economic functions, see ibid., p. 163.

[71] Marton: op. cit., p. 196. A contrary course was taken by *mancipatio,* which developed from sale into a general transaction widely used for transfer of property (see ibid., pp. 149, 199; cf. Kaser: op. cit., p. 39 et seq.), although it might have played various roles *ab initio* (see Marton: op. cit., p. 148), just like *in iure cessio* (see Marton: op. cit., p. 49; Brósz – Pólay: op. cit., p. 247 et seq.).

[72] Kaufmann: op. cit., p. 14 et seq.

though not identificable with contract, similarly played a comprehensive, not type-like role: "Its general form enabled it to give any agreement the force of contract. Indeed, this contractual form being empty in itself, served primarily that purpose. . . For the very reason that *stipulatio* went far to satisfy the needs of life, it was followed by a rather long interval in the growth of contracts."[73] "Precisely the fact that *stipulatio* did not require a statement of the title of obligation allowed an extremely wide scope for its application. The form of *stipulatio* is found to have been used widely such as for loan, *novatio,* transfer of obligation, security, gift, surety in the law of inheritance, for promise of dowry at marriage, etc. The popularity of *stipulatio* is further shown by the fact that, rather often sale itself among other transactions, continued to be effected by the use of *stipulatio* even after the consensual contracts (which may be regarded as contracts of the most advanced type) had emerged in the pre-classical age."[74]

What we have said will perhaps support our opinion that the legal recognition of commodity and money relations and the evolution of contract law did not follow, except in tendency at the most, the logical line of development of the particular-specific-general. Here too, real development – the "aurulent, green tree of life" – show a much more varied and complex picture: responding to the demands of economic relationships in its time, the primitive law rugged as it was, emphasized the formal side of facts and did not take the least interest in logical aspects. Along with "inter-type" formations it nevertheless succeeded in grasping the typical in some cases (e.g. loan[75]) and more than that, *stipulatio* had in it the germs, the prototype of the general.

7. Needs of a world empire

In order for the Roman law of contract to have created – in the course of a few centuries, namely the pre-classical age – a closed system of crystallized types of contract out of a state of conditions described above, two factors had to be present: first and foremost, a degree of economic development which was no longer adequately served by the formal rigidity of the devices of ancient law, originating from primitive roots and insensitive to subtleties; second, what we have lately been inclined to ignore, analytical thinking which has been a characteristic trait of the Romans from early on,[76] which prepared an appropriate dogmatic cradle for the

[73] Marton: op. cit., p. 197.
[74] Brósz – Pólay: op. cit., p. 405 et seq.
[75] For the appearance of *mutuum* in ancient law, see Kaser; op. cit.
[76] Weber: op. cit., p. 213.

entry of rapidly developing commodity and money relations into the domain of law.

We can refer only in broad outlines to the large-scale economic and social transformation which took place somewhere in the period between the first Punic War and the time of Augustus. In that process a world empire grew out of a city-state resting on an essentially peasant economy and based itself on commodity-producing slavery, while the ancient rustic law transmuted itself into secular law.[77] In the course of little more than 100 years Rome became the exclusive ruler of the Mediterranean basin and an empire stretching to three continents as a result of the three Punic Wars. Concurrently and not less due to constant warring, there was a major shift in the class stratification of society and in the mode of production: the patriarchal slavery of slight importance to production evolved into a commodity-producing workshop slavery of considerable scale, which was soon to become the main base of production, while large masses of free peasants found themselves ruined in the competition of latifundia. Those "having lost their ancient land, swarmed into Rome where they either found some job opportunities (wage labour, handicraft), or swelled the ranks of the antique proletariat".[78] The change in the ownership of the means of production, the class restratification of society and the alteration in the forms of production greatly increased the importance of commodity and money relations and resulted in a highly developed trade and money economy and in extensive business transactions. No wonder that the law of contract as the most direct legal regulation of commodity relations had to work out qualitatively new devices to meet the challenges of the economy. As Kaser writes in summary, in no field of private law did the changeover from an agrarian economy to a commercial and money economy bring so deeply penetrating and forward-oriented changes during the centuries between the Punic Wars and the time of Augustus as in the law of obligations. The old law did not satisfy the needs of economic progress; with its few types of transactions it was much too cumbersome.[79]

The large additions to the numbers of foreigners, and consequently the greatly increased role of economic transactions with foreigners in an empire that grew out of a city-state are of particular relevance to our subject became, as is commonly known, the economic relationships established with foreigners constituted a bedrock of commodity and money relations.[80]

[77] For a more detailed discussion, see Kaser: op. cit., p. 159 et seq. with specific reference to the law of obligations, p. 397; Brósz – Pólay: op. cit., p. 41 et seq., with relevant literature indicated.

[78] Brósz – Pólay: op. cit., p. 43.

[79] Op. cit., p. 397; cf. ibid., p. 160.

[80] The very phenomenon of commodity relationships is known to have germinated in incipient transactions with the foreigners. In a reference to Aristotle's assertion, Marx writes: "*In der Tat*

In underlining the significance of the large-scale and quick socio-economic transformation that occurred in Rome during the last three centuries B.C. one must not lose sight of the aspects of continuity in development, because the incidents of relative continuity have a rather important role to play in the development of legal forms. We agree with Kaufmann's view as quoted: *"Als grundsätzliches Ergebnis darf festgestellt werden, daß die überkommene Auffassung von der in mehrfacher Hinsicht strengen Geschlossenheit der lateinischen und frühen römischen Gesellschaft und Wirtschaft bis über die Zwölftafeln hinaus nicht mehr aufrechtzuerhalten ist. . . Die durch die historische Schule der Nationalökonomie im vergangenen Jahrhundert begründete Lehre von der diese Epoche bis in noch jüngere Zeit bestimmenden geschlossenen Hauswirtschaft, die nach dem gelegentlichen Eigenständnis ihrer Vertreter nur auf das Typische abstellte und an der die dogmatischen Vorstellungen der juristischen Romantistik dennoch weithin für Einzelfragen orientiert sind, schenkte einer Fülle von sozialen, wirtschaftlichen, juristischen und sprachlichen Zeugnissen, die auch auf ganz andere Züge deuten, keine Beachtung. Die seit der spätrepublikanischen Geschichtsschreibung genährte Sozialidylle von der völligen wirtschaftlichen und politischen Gleichheit einer Bevölkerung freier Bauern, die ausschließlich von der Bewirtschaftung im Individualeigentum stehenden Grundbesitzes mit Hilfe zahlreicher privater Sklaven lebte, steht schon mit der seit langem bekannten, fast schrankenlos herrschaftlichen Organisation der Familie in einem völlig unglaubhaften Gegensatz."*[81]

8. Analytical thinking and apprehension of the "specific"

Taking into account the element of continuity in economic and social development will help to explain how, around the 2nd century B.C., Roman private law achieved the level of analytical und abstract thinking that was indispensable for a dogmatic underspinning of tl types of contract. As is observed very aptly by Bekker, molding the types of transactions obviously presupposes a developed capacity for abstraction in addition to an understanding of the requirements of economic relation-

erscheint der Austauschprozeß von Waren ursprünglich nicht im Schoß der naturwüchsigen Gemeinwesen, sondern da, wo sie aufhören, an ihren Grenzen, den wenigen Punkten, wo sie in Kontakt mit andern Gemeinwesen treten. Hier beginnt der Tauschhandel und schlägt von da ins Innere des Gemeinwesens zurück, auf das er zersetzend wirkt." Marx: *Zur Kritik der Politischen Ökonomie,* Berlin, 1961 (Marx–Engels Werke, Dietz Verlag, Band 13), pp. 35–36; *Grundrisse der Kritik der Politischen Ökonomie,* Berlin, 1953 (Dietz Verlag), p. 109 et seq. The role of foreigners in the development of contractual dealings and consequently the law of transactions is also emphasized in more recent literature. See Jörgersen, Stig: *Vertrag und Recht,* København, 1968, p. 14; Eörsi: op. cit., p. 473. Compare also Section 9.

[81] Kaufmann: op. cit., p. 320 et seq.

ships.[82] It took a rather long time to reach this stage, perhaps longer time than the world empire took to emerge.

A characteristic example of this process is the differentiation of facts by sale and lease and of their corresponding terminology,[83] which took place during the period extending from the 5th to the 2nd centuries B.C. Human thinking and with it terminology were for a long time unable to distinguish whether a transaction aimed at the acquisition of a thing was in the nature of sale or lease.[84] Kaufmann offers the following explanation for this: *"Die ursprüngliche Gemeinsamkeit der Terminologie für Kauf und Miete findet ihre Grundlage mit in der Tatsache, daß beide Arten von Sachverhalten in eine Frühzeit zurückreichen, in der sie sich noch nicht gegen Geld vollzogen. Beide waren naturale Austauschverhältnisse. Bei dem einen stand Ware gegen Ware, bei dem anderen Ware gegen Mietleistung. Die Mietleistungen aber waren in Sachen- und Werkmiete teilweise selbst wieder den Warenleistungen sehr ähnlich. Für eine unreflektiert-naive Anschauung war also eine scharfe Grenzlinie zwischen Kauf- und Mietsachverhalten nicht sichtbar."*[85]

Yet, with no contours of them in sight, the law was equally unable to evolve into types of contract, it followed life, and legislative language followed popular usage. This too is lucidly demonstrated by Kaufmann with the facts of *locatio conductio* and the example of *merces,* a related counterperformance designated with a special term.[86]

The requirements of commodity and money relations increasingly permeating economic life and the demands of economic relationships based on commodity production, could in theory have been satisfied in many ways by the pre-classical Roman law, which gave birth to categories of contract. Among the theoretical possibilities it will perhaps suffice to mention *stipulatio* which also gained prominence at that time, and given its numerous advantages (simplicity, availability to *peregrini,* etc.), came into general use. Nevertheless, Roman law did not perceive the real purpose of further development in this institution: rather than take another step toward the "general" as signalled by *stipulatio,* it managed to meet the needs of economic life by grasping the "specific" and creating the types of contract through which to channel the typical economic transactions.

In our view, this option for a concrete dogmatic approach can be explained by the fact that Roman law arrived in that period at the "possibility of perceiving the specific" on the logical level but bogged

[82] Bekker, Ernst Immanuel: *System des heutigen Pandektenrechts,* II, Weimar, 1889, p. 121.
[83] Kaufmann: op. cit., p. 303 et seq.
[84] Ibid., p. 304 et seq. Cf. Bechmann: op. cit., p. 422 et seq.
[85] Kaufmann: op. cit., p. 317 et seq.
[86] Ibid., p. 358.

down there and did not reach the "general", although the door to it had, in the main, been opened by *stipulatio.*[87] This is clearly shown by the formulary system of *actiones,* the dogmatic cradle of the types of contract.

9. Actions of the formulary procedure: the dogmatic cradle of the types of contract

It is on record that the classical Roman law adopted a procedural approach to facts. This was even truer of the earlier phase of legal development: the question of legislative concern and regulation was always one of whether or not a given relationship was actionable, was provided with the remedy of action. This is a general feature of the origins of private law development. The law of obligations, more than any other field of law, was closely connected with *actiones* with a given *actio* remaining at the centre of the entire dogmatic approach.[88]

With respect to specific types of contract Bekker is known to have been the first to focus attention on the significance of the system of actions and to make a more systematic study of this subject.[89] Following in his steps, many other writers traversed a similar path[90], placing smaller or greater emphasis on the relationships between the *actiones* and the types of contract existing in Roman law. By contrast to Bekker, Betti backed down and was also inaccurate in conceiving the categorization of *actiones* as a phenomenon closely associated with the classification of legal transactions.[91] We maintain that going the right way are those who identify

[87] We think that Watson evades the most important question when he explains the introduction of *bonae fidei actiones* by their use to fill the gaps between *stipulatii,* because while we believe this to be a justifiable hypothesis, it fails to raise the problem of why the gulfs between *stipulatii* were bridged by the praetor in that way rather than by an extension or generalization of them, as would appear obvious to the modern mind. See Watson, Alan: *The Origins of Consensual Sale; a Hypothesis,* Tijdschrift voor Rechtsgeschiedenis, 32, 1964, p. 245 et seq.

[88] Levy, Ernst: *Weströmisches Vulgarrecht. Das Obligationenrecht,* Weimar, 1956, pp. 13, 17. A similar view is held by Bekker: Both in the praetorian edicts, its main source, and in the principal scientific conceptions, the classical Roman law appears as an ordered material derived from the fundamental concept of *actio* (op. cit., p. 122). Let us add at this juncture that we see no qualitative difference of any degree of significance between the procedural approach and that under substantive law, but compare Eörsi: op. cit., p. 121 et seq.

[89] Bekker: op. cit., p. 121 et seq.

[90] Hoeniger, Heinrich: *Die gemischten Verträge in ihren Grundformen,* Mannheim–Leipzig, 1910, p. 338 et seq.; Betti, Emilio: *Der Typenzwang bei den römischen Rechtsgeschäften und die sogenannte Typenfreiheit des heutigen Rechts,* Festschrift Wenger, I, München, 1944, particularly pp. 254 et seq., 259 et seq.; Pringsheim, Fritz: *Natura contractus und natura actionis,* In: Gesammelte Abhandlungen, I, 1961, p. 381 et seq.; Wolff, Hans Julius: *Prozeßrechtliches und materiellrechtliches Denken in rechtsgeschichtlicher Beleuchtung,* In: L'Europa e il diritto romano, Studi in memoria di Paolo Koschaker, II, Milano, 1954, p. 403 et seq.; Leenen, Detlef: *Typus und Rechtsfindung,* Berlin, 1971, p. 124 et seq.; Kaser: op. cit., pp. 197 et seq., 404 et seq., 438; Kaufmann: op. cit., pp. 110, 118 and particularly 207 et seq.

[91] Betti: op. cit., p. 259. We feel that Betti refuses to follow the path trodden by Bekker and to identify the types of contract and their causes with the *actiones,* if for no other reason, but to

the types of contract with the corresponding *actiones* in pre-classical and classical law. For instance Leenen, who states that "the types of transactions are to be defined as identical with *actiones*".[92] ; or Sundberg, who writes that, "The typification of Roman contract law depended upon the categorization of actions. The latter fell into decay towards the time of the lower Empire."[93] The contractual *actiones* of the formulary system expressed the same thing in a procedural approach as the types of contract did in the language of substantive law, namely in terms of subjective rights. As is aptly observed by Bekker, *"Solange es Aktionen gab, war die Definition leicht: alle Geschäfte. . . . welche dieselbe "actio" erzeugen, gehören demselben Typus an."*[94] This definition is inaccurate, being little short of tautology, but its inaccuracy is precisely the proof of the sameness of the two categories, the *actio* and the type of contract.

The *legis actiones,* the forms of action preceding the formulary system, were not yet capable of grasping and defining the types of contract in terms of procedural law as they were too general, flexible, and elastic. Kaufmann points out in connection with the *stipulatio* of lease: *"Der Stipulation oder der ihrer Durchsetzung dienenden actio waren keine formalen Kategorien eigen, welche auf die Relationsbegriffe der Miete wie merces und pretium, locare und vendere sowie conducere, emere und redimere eine formende oder selektive Kraft auszuüben vermochten. Die konturenlose Elastizität der stipulatio incerti räumte den Parteien vielmehr volle Freiheit in der sachlichen und terminologischen Ausgestaltung ihrer Abreden ein. Da die rechtliche Form der Beteiligten kein Material an die Hand gab, Mußten sie dieses aus der Gemeinsprache so nehmen wie es dort vorhanden war."*[95] Bekker, too, maintains that there is no way of knowing for sure how far the types evolved in the *legis actio* procedure; the all too general forms were little favourable to such evolution.[96]

In this domain too, it is perhaps right to suppose continuous development, which came to a head in the edicts on the formulary system. This appears to be supported by the book of formulas from the last centuries of the Republican period, which contained models of actions and transactions.[97] In the classical age the need for the collection of formulary

---

lay the historical foundation for the objective *cause* doctrine of the *Codice civile* (see ibid., p. 275 et seq.). One of the main reasons for the acceptance of the doctrine of *causa* is stated by the preamble of the Code itself is adherence to the traditions of Roman law: §.25, Nr. 79, quoted by Betti in op. cit., p. 276.

[92] Leenen: op. cit., p. 124.

[93] Sundberg, Jacob: *The Law of Contracts. Jurisprudential Writing in Search of Principles.* In: Skandinavian Studies in Law, No. 7 of 1963, p. 127, fn7.

[94] Bekker: op. cit., p. 124.

[95] Kaufmann: op. cit., p. 341 et seq.

[96] Bekker: op. cit., p. 121 et seq.

[97] Cf. Bechmann: op. cit., p. 526 et seq.; Bekker: op. cit., p. 122.

actions was eliminated by the edict which had emerged as a comprehensive official collection of formulas, but the need for a collection of contractual models remained.[98]

Keeping this in view we may be certain that indeed, the formulary action or more accurately the praetorian edict, was the highroad on which Roman private law arrived at the level of expressing legal recognition of contracts through the typical. It is at this point that all contracts productive of legal effects are furnished independent formulas of action which constitute the core of the edict and which the jurisconsults rely upon for their fruitful activity.[99]

The view may still be regarded as very common that the formulary action has issued from *ius gentium,* the separate law for *peregrini.* In his highly authoritative monography Kaser writes: *"Das römische Verfahren der legis actiones stand den fremdenrechtlichen Prozessen nicht offen, weil es den Bürgern vorbehalten war. Mit guten Gründen nimmt man an, daß der Formularprozeß, der sich gegenüber den Legisaktionen gleichfalls vom strengen Formalismus freimacht, von der Fremdengerichtsbarkeit ausgegangen ist. Es wird eingerichtet oder doch besonders ausgestaltet worden sein, seitdem für die Fremdenprozesse ein besonderer praetor peregrinus eingesetzt wurde."*[100] Also, there is common ground in scientific literature on Roman law that the new procedure worked its way from *ius gentium* to the settlement of legal disputes between Roman citizens. The point still in controversy, if any, being the role played in this process by *lex Aebutia* around the middle of the second century B.C.[101] There are some writers who claim that the formulary system, along with the old civil-law procedure, were extended by this *lex* to suits between Roman citizens also,[102] while others maintain that the formulary action had, by the power of the praetor, been used in disputes between Romans even before the *lex* was framed.[103] and that the role of *lex Aebutia* was confined to giving the new procedure the force of civil law within certain established limits prior to and in parallel with the *leges Juliae* on the procedural law of Augustus.[104] Watson expressly states that "I have now

[98] Schulz: op. cit., p. 185; cf. ibid., p. 106.

[99] Bekker: ibid. Betti's assertion that Roman jurisprudence was from the beginning concerned with the task of categorization in the field of legal transactions in particular, notably with the elaboration and delimitation of different types of transactions is superficial and inadequate. See op. cit., p. 252; cf. ibid., p. 260.

[100] Kaser: op. cit., p. 180 et seq.; Marton: op. cit., p. 98 et seq.; Brósz – Pólay: op. cit., p. 112; cf. Schulz: op. cit., p. 59 et seq.

[101] Brósz–Pólay trace the *lex* to the middle of the second century (op. cit., p. 71) and Watson ascribes it to the years 150–144 (op. cit., p. 40, fn37).

[102] Marton: ibid.; Brósz–Pólay: ibid.

[103] This view was already held by Mitteis. See Marton: op. cit., p. 99, fn1.

[104] Kaser: *Die lex Aebutia,* Studi Albertario, I, Milano, 1953, p. 25 et seq.; op. cit., p. 181.

been convinced that the *lex Aebutia* had nothing to do with the introduction of the formulary system between Roman citizens."[105]

In the light of recent research Kaufmann questions the role of *praetor peregrinus* in the introduction of the formulary action with regard to lease at least, and considers the emergence of the new procedure, in respect of matters of lease in any case, to be the outcome of developments in relationships between Roman citizens. He draws his conclusions from an analysis of social conditions and a survey of the elements of lease: *"Es läßt sich von der Sache her nicht der geringste Anhalt finden, welcher auf die Urheberschaft des Fremdenprätors hinwiese. Das Schwergewicht der Mietsachverhalte liegt vielmehr von Anfang an ganz eindeutig unter den römischen Bürgern. Es wäre sehr erstaunlich, wenn nur die Vergleichsweise wenigen Mietsachverhalte, an denen Peregrinen beteiligt gewesen sein mögen, zur Ausbildung dieses iudicium geführt haben sollten. Mindestens für die Miete wird man daher der ... Hypothese vom Fremdenprätor als Schöpfer des Amtsverfahrens nicht folgen können."*[106]

No matter how profound the research and convincing Kaufmann's arguments are with respect to lease, they do not justify tracing the origin of the formulary action in litigious matters other than those between *peregrini.* In our viewpoints, we think it to be the most probable assumption that the institutions of the new procedure which had sprung from *ius gentium* and primarily its underlying principles, had in a continuous process found their way to, and struck root in, the disputes of Roman citizens as well before the *lex Aebutia* was adopted: e.g. in the field of lease itself, the process being only sanctioned and canalized by the *lex.* This is further indicated by the most important fact for our purpose which is that *ius gentium* is no longer considered in the science of Roman law to have given rise to all major types of contract. Bechmann still held that the actionability of all consensual contracts had its roots in the law of *peregrini*[107] while Max Weber is of the same view regarding all *ex bona fide* transactions enforceable by action.[108] According to Kaser, consensual sale has one of its roots, if not that alone in *ius peregrini,* and this may also be assumed to be the case with *societas.* Such origin is to be ruled out in the case of the two other consensual contracts (*mandatum* and *locatio conductio*).[109] This is not altered by the fact that the law of contract received the first and strongest impulse from *ius gentium* in bringing about the new legal forms, primarily in evolving the types of transactions that were easy to handle as well as practicable and virtually

[105] Watson: op. cit., p. 147, fn37; cf. ibid., pp. 40, 126 et seq., 431 et seq. fn 30.
[106] Kaufmann: op. cit., p. 344; cf. ibid., p. 324.
[107] Bechmann: op. cit., p. 437.
[108] Weber: op. cit., p. 144.
[109] Kaser: op. cit., p. 455; cf. pp. 456, 477, 181 et seq.

informal.[110] It is quite another matter that the *ius peregrini*, rather than evolve its own transactions, often improved upon those adopted from the *ius civile*. By the *ex causa emptionis traditio* the *ius civile* recognized the informal purchase for cash in respect of *res nec mancipi*, whereas this same device was available for *peregrini* in respect of *res mancipi* as well. In other cases, transactions like *mutuum* of civil-law origin were simply transplanted to relationships between *peregrini*.[111] All these go to show that the evolution of types of contract was influenced by an active interplay of *ius civile* and *ius gentium*.

As it were, the formulary action was devised to express the "specific" in the law, and to serve as a dogmatic cementing medium of the types of contract. The intention of the formula (perhaps by *demonstratio*) specified the conditions of fact and and law to be proved for establishment of the grounds of suitor's claim. The corresponding instruction of the praetor to the judge had to use, by necessity such terms which, on the one hand, pointed beyond the concrete fact in litigation as being more general than the characteristics of the given matter, and on the other hand, were sufficiently distinct from other classes of facts, which is to say that the intention had to grasp the "specific".[112] By the time the formulary system came into being the major classes of facts and types of contract had become more or less separated in the usage of economic transactions. This was also reflected in popular language.[113] Credit is due to the new form of action or to the praetor for the law's apprehension and coverage of the different categories, which were at the same time moulded and refined with much assistance from the activity of *iuris consulti*. By the classical age most of them had even been "given final shape", naturally clothed in procedural law and recognized as *actiones*. This solution is described by Kaser as follows: *"Die einzelnen Aktionen werden durch ihre Klaggrundlage, das dingliche Recht oder den persönlichen Verpflichtungsgrund, individualisiert; zumeist haben sie davon auch einen festen Namen, der zu technischer Bedeutung erstarrt ist. Danach bildet jede actio eine scharf profilierte und gegen die anderen Klagen abgegrenzte Einheit. . . . Die Formeln der zivilen Klagen nennen die Anspruchsvoraussetzungen nicht im einzelnen, sondern verweisen auf das ius civile durch gewisse Stichworte. . . . Die honorarrechtlichen Formeln dagegen, die der Prätor.*[114] *aus eigener Macht schafft, lehnen sich zum Teil als 'actiones ficticiae' an die zivilen an, indem sie einzelne oder alle ihre Voraussetzungen als gegeben unterstellen, zumeist aber sind sie 'in factum'*

[110] Cf. Kaser: op. cit., p. 397 et seq.

[111] Ibid., p. 180.

[112] Cf. Weber: op. cit., p. 207 et seq.; Betti: op. cit., pp. 256 et seq., 261.

[113] The terminological separation of sale and *locatio conductio* is brilliantly presented by Kaufmann: op. cit., p. 303 et seq.

[114] Cf. Schulz: op. cit., p. 174 et seq.

konzipiert, zählen also die Verurteilungsvoraussetzungen ausdrücklich auf." [115]

The "primarily analytical nature"[116] of Roman law so admired by many, including Ihering and Max Weber, created a truly amazing possibility for bringing the "typical" into the domain of law through the institution of the formulary system. Today it is difficult to frame any hypotheses as to the details of this process. The forms by which the classical law tried to fill the lacunas of the contractual *actiones* as provided for in the edicts fell similarly into obscurity. A benchmark of some sort for a conception of this course of development is provided by the so-called *in factum actiones,* on which Kaser writes: *"Das Rechtsmittel, mit dem in solchen Fällen geholfen wurde, war zunächts die actio in factum, deren Formel in individueller Gestaltung die Kondemnationsbedingungen aus dem konkreten Sachverhalt entnimmt. Wo jedoch dieser Sachverhalt die Anlehnung an das Vorbild einer oder mehrerer anerkannter Kontrakte zuliess, besonders dort, wo die Vereinbarung nur einen Zwischentypus zwischen regulären Kontrakten bildete, wird auch die Klageformel die Annäherung an die bestehenden Kontraktsklagen gesucht haben. . . . Wie es scheint, hat sogar das Edikt, wenigstens für einen Fall dieser Art, die Klage aus dem Trödelvertrag, eine Musterformel proponiert, die mit unter dem Titel 'De bonae fidei iudiciis' stand und deren demonstratio in den übrigen Fällen durch andere, vom Prätor in factum konzipierte Klauseln ersetzt werden konnte."* [117]

We think that the process of crystallization of *actiones* and types of contract worked out in a somewhat similar way also in its origin: in the field of commodity and money relations and in popular usage as their reflection, certain classes of facts tended to be differentiated and separated from other classes of facts of a different type, with the praetor bringing into the domain of law each in its respective "type" within the framework of the formulary system and gradually defining their scope with greater precision. The whole process had practically been completed by thc carly imperial period.

[115] Kaser: op. cit., p. 198 et seq. For differences in the formulae of actions under the *ius civile* and the *ius honorarium,* see ibid. For essential differences between the system of *actiones* and the system of precedents, see Koschaker: op. cit., p. 94 et seq.

[116] Cf. Weber: op. cit., p. 209.

[117] Kaser: op. cit., p. 486 and fn9.

10. From *actiones* to approaches under substantive law

In its last period of development, Roman private law, which was on the decline in several respects, and there remained but one stage to be reached in the movement toward the types of contract: the procedural cloth to be dropped by the system of *actiones.* This, too, was a gradual process, which is described by Kaser in these words: *"Mit der Zeit nimmt 'actio' aber auch eine materiellrechtliche Bedeutung an und bezeichnet das Recht, vom Gegner das zu erzwingen, was mit dem Prozeßverfahren erreicht werden kann. . . . Dieses materielle privatrechtliche Klagerecht. . . ist aber kein vollentwickeltes Recht, sondern der bloße Reflex davon, daß das ius civile oder der Prätor unter bestimmten Voraussetzungen die Gewährung eines Rechtschutzes in einem mit actio einzusetzenden Verfahren verheißt. . . . Dieser nur im Keim entwickelte materiellrechtliche Aktionenbegriff läßt sich mit unserem 'Anspruch' vergleichen, wenn mann dabei die Eigenart des römischen Rechts gebührend berücksichtigt. . . Die Klassiker. . . kennen weder eine Theorie des subjektiven Rechts noch einen ausgebildeten Anspruchsbegriff."*[118] In other aspects as well, the typification of *actiones* – a clear demarcation of formulas – was helped and urged by the types of transactions that had been called into being by business dealings based on commodity and money relations, or, in other words, had emerged, in the final analysis, in response to the needs of substantive law. What was left for the praetorian edicts was "only" to see that the forms of transactions, created by life itself and indicative of demands similar to those of substantive law, were refined into real gems of law when they established a boundary between them on a procedural basis. From the beginnings however, we find the substantive law much like a "mere reflex" lying hidden beneath the procedural cloak: the formulas laid down more or less detailed conditions in the nature of substantive law to govern adverse judgements.[119]

The way of thinking in terms of *actiones* was dealt its least blow by the procedural reform of the imperial period. The imperial action, originally the *"extraordinaria" cognitio,* was taking on growing importance first in the provinces, and then in Rome *vis-à-vis* the formulary or "ordinary" action. There is data to show that in the province of Egypt for instance, the *cognitio* was applied in cases before professional judges practically from the early imperial period.[120] Under Diocletian, at the end of the 3rd century A.D., the use of *cognitio* became prevalent in Rome itself,

[118] Kaser: op. cit., p. 197 et seq.; cf. ibid., pp. 404 et seq, 438; Leenen: op. cit., p. 125; Kaufmann: op. cit., ibid.; Levy: op. cit., p. 13 et seq. .

[119] Cf. Kaser: op. cit., p. 404.

[120] Koschaker: op. cit., p. 95.

and the use of formulas was specifically prohibited in 342.[121] Indeed, the new procedure no longer required the formulas based on *actiones.* A phenomenon both interesting and perhaps paradoxical, but nevertheless explained by the hold of traditions, is that during and even following decay of the formulary system, the *actio*-mindedness continued to prevail for a long time, not only in the second part of the third century,[122] otherwise a century of transition marking the end of the classical age on the decline, but even beyond for some time. However, since the formulary action which was the breeding ground for such way of thought gradually ceased to exist, there arose a contradiction between the surviving old notions and the new action, making its mark on the 3rd century. . . From then on, the *actio* was preserved with respect to claims as sanctioned by substantive law only, and finally lost ground altogether.[123] The post-classical theory no longer proceeded from action but from substantive private law.[124] Scientific teaching in the eastern part of the Empire evolved the idea of *natura contractus* as the counterpart of formulary actions in substantive law to solidify and delimitate the types of contract, yet in a flexible way for any concrete contractual will to fit into them.[125]

One of the peaks of the evolutionary process of the types of contract and highly important for future development, is represented by Justinian's codification which revived the classical traditions in this question just as it generally did in others. In their essential feature the imperial digests are nothing else than modernized reproductions of praetorian edicts, and the collection of the Emperor's laws ("codex") is likewise modelled on the system of *actiones.* The system of the edict adjusted to the demands of the formulary action constitutes the basic scheme of the Pandects which the *Codex* also tries to follow in its order of titles. Most of the headings retained designations by *actio* (rather than transaction). Only a few included titles by transaction, such as *de contrahenda emptione.* The contents of the digests, mainly those composed of commentaries on edicts, followed in the main a pattern corresponding to the *actio*-mindedness of the authors, who even in the chief work of Justinian's legislation, commonly speak of the conditions for and consequences of *actiones.* However, since *actiones* no longer exist, it is necessary to have the facts and their consequences directly interconnected, which naturally calls for a modification and reformulation of numerous tenets.[126]

121 Cf. Marton: op. cit., p. 121; Brósz – Pólay: op. cit., pp. 118, 128.
122 Levy: op. cit., pp. 3, 13 et seq.; Kaser: op. cit., pp. 162, 197 et seq.
123 Levy: ibid.
124 Kaser: op. cit., p. 496.
125 Levy: op. cit., p. 32 et seq.
126 Bekker: op. cit., p. 122 et seq.; Betti: op. cit., p. 265 et seq.

As we have seen, this and nothing less is the spiritual legacy – the closed system of the types of contract casting off their mold of procedural law – which Rome has bequeathed to posterity in this aspect of contracts. The closed nature of the system signifies that amid the prevailing commodity and money relations, business transactions received assistance from the Roman law at all times in the recognized types of contract only. Roman law operated with compulsory types,[127] even if its rigour was largely eased above all by the broad possibilities of *stipulatio* and by a widening range and a flexible treatment of the facts pertaining to the different types.[128]

The impressive accomplishments of Roman private law stand out in sharper relief when we recall that concern with individual cases was all the time a hallmark of the approach taken by the framers of Roman law.[129] "The practice of law is centered around the individuality of the case and not the generality of the legal rule; . . . judges or arbitrators are reluctant to adopt legal maxims and to use generalizations."[130] This assertion by Eörsi is a general appraisal of the type of private law marking the prehistory of bourgeois private law, but it holds also for Roman private law, even if we bear in mind Rabel's warning' *"Daß die Tendenz der römischen Rechtsentwicklung zunehmend auf Kausierung, nicht auf Abstrahierung gerichtet sei, ist viel zu allgemein ausgedrückt, um ohne weiteres gebilligt werden zu können."*[131] What is certain is that in the realm of contract law the Romans arrived at their "threshold of abstraction" in categorization. They are in their overwhelming majority, classical marvels of legal classification, as is amply evidenced by their long persistence. Only the *locatio conductio* proved later to be a faulty construction,[132] although this can also be explained in view of the prevailing economic and social conditions of the Romans and of their procedural approach to them.[133]

Finally in searching for the principal and most enduring virtues of typification in Roman law we must point out that the homogeneity of the

[127] Betti: op. cit.

[128] Cf. Leenen: op. cit., p. 125; Diósdi, György: *Atipikus szerződések a bírósági gyakorlatban* (Atypical Contracts in Judicial Practice), Jogtudományi Közlöny, XXVI, 1971, p. 89 et seq. The questions concerning the free and compulsory use of types will be given detailed treatment in Chapter III.

[129] Cf. Kaser: op. cit., p. 200 et seq.

[130] Eörsi: op. cit., p. 52.

[131] Rabel: op. cit., p. 379.

[132] The vicissitudes of the after-life of *mandatum,* particularly as regards its out-of-date regulation in the BGB, are attributable not to the Roman law but to the bourgeois, mainly German, *Codification.* Cf. Csanádi, György: *A megbízási jogviszony* (The Contract of Agency), Budapest, 1959, particularly pp. 7 et seq. and 41 et seq.

[133] Kaufmann: op. cit., pp. 4 et seq., 332, 344 et seq., 353 et seq.; Kaser: op. cit., p. 471; cf. Weber: op. cit., p 212; Bechmann: op. cit., p. 430 et seq.

Roman's legal concepts expressing the typical is of a scale to cover extremely varied economic contents and a great diversity of economic functions; the uniform and workable legal concepts lend themselves to governing a wide range of concrete commodity and money operations.[134]

11. Appendix: reception of the types of contract on the Continent

How did posterity draw upon the legacy of Roman law? Did it accept or refuse as a passive and burdensome inheritance, the possibilities offered by the types of contract for the legal regulation of commodity and money relations? The answer to this question, just as to those regarding the after-life of Roman private law in general, is basically twofold: the type system of Roman law was received into the Continent, while in fact the common law of England hardly took notice of it and travelled its own path. The major continental laws followed and improved upon the constrained trajectories of the Roman law of contract and as a result of long development, erected in its system the cupola of the general binding force of contract by basing it in the contract rules of the bourgeois codes of private law as well. The common law evolved its own particular law of transactions, which led it to the general sanctioning of breach of contract well in advance on continental practice.

The relationships between the types of contract and the general binding force of contracts as well as the role of classification on the bourgeois codes will be treated in a separate chapter. Similarly, a separate chapter will be devoted to the development of the English law of contract, with special emphasis on the main economic and social causes behind the peculiarity of its separate development and on its constituent elements in the system of law. Therefore, in this section, the major aspects of the continental reception of Roman law that appear to be of relevance to the types of contract will be discussed in brief outline only.

It is known how the Roman private law which had been more than seemingly dead was revived; first on Italian soil and later in the rest of Western Europe, by the demands of vigorously expanding industry and commerce and of rapidly advancing commodity and money relations.[135] This process, which took place approximately from the 12th to the 15th

[134] Weber stresses this as a striking feature of the logic of Roman law, contrasting it with the concepts evolved by English law, which are also legally heterogeneous; op. cit., p. 213.

[135] Cf. Marx – Engels: *Die deutsche Ideologie,* Berlin, 1962 (Marx-Engels Werke, Dietz Verlag, Band 3), p. 62 et seq. For the economic, social, political and cultural conditions of the cities in Northern Italy, see Savigny, F. Karl von: *Geschichte des römischen Rechts im Mittelalter,* III, Heidelberg, 1822, p. 90 et seq.; Engelmann, Woldemar: *Die Wiedergeburt der Rechtskultur in Italien durch die wissenschaftliche Lehre,* Leipzig, 1938 (giving a detailed description of how and in which aspects the Roman law was surpassed by resurgent legal life).

centuries and which was essentially contingent on the dissemination of, and acquaintance with, the full manuscript of the Digests in the last third of the 11th century.[136] It has been recently described by Koschaker[137] with a lyrical touch and by Wieacker[138] with a fascinatingly profound knowledge of material.

Nor is it necessary to explain to any great length why achievements of contract law, gained such prominence namely the area of law destined to subserve business transactions in a direct way and elaborated at the highest level by Roman jurists in the preclassical and classical periods.[139] Additionally, the Roman types of contract came again into play, in the form established by Justinian, namely free from *actio* but governed by numerous provisions bearing the imprint of *actiones.*[140]

The continental advance of Roman private law in the Middle Ages peaked in the long process of reception. We are not concerned here presently except in rough outlines with this extremely interesting field of legal development and its causes. Further, our references will be confined to a few fundamental works from the abundant literature on the subject.[141]

Roman law was received mostly in German territories, where practicable reception entailed changes in the overwhelming part of the older German private law, similarly in the science of private law and in legislation and legal practice.[142] The take-off point was Justinian's law, albeit in a form adapted to the special medieval interpretation as described by Wieacker in these words: *"Rezipiert wurde nicht das (damals in seiner ursprünglichen Gestalt unbekannte) klassische römische Recht; auch nicht das geschichtliche justinianische Recht als solches, sondern das*

[136] Koschaker: op. cit., p. 62, with relevant literature indicated.

[137] Koschaker: op. cit., pp. 55 et seq., 87 et seq.

[138] Wieacker, Franz: *Die Privatrechtsgeschichte der Neuzeit,* Göttingen, 1967, pp. 60 et seq., 80 et seq.

[139] Cf. Kaser: op. cit., p. 400 et seq.; Wieacker: op. cit., p. 237; Eörsi: op. cit., p. 160. Interesting but unusual is the opposite view of Max Weber: *"An der Rezeption der materiellen Bestimmungen des römischen Rechts waren gerade die modernsten', also die bürgerlichen Rechtsinteressenten gar nicht interessiert; die Institute des mittelalterlichen Handels- und städtischen Grundbesitzrechts entsprachen ihren Bedürfnissen weitaus besser. Nur die allgemeinen formalen Quantitäten des römischen Rechts waren es, welche ihm mit unvermeindlich zunehmender Fachmässigkeit des Rechtsbetriebs überall da zum Sieg verhalfen."*; op. cit. p. 257.

[140] Bekker: op. cit., p. 123.

[141] Savigny: op. cit., I–III, Heidelberg, 1815–1822; Vinogradoff, Paul: *Roman Law in Mediaeval Europe,* Oxford, 1929. Valid in many other aspects, a very apt critical appraisal of the theories of German reception in the 19th century is made by Below, Georg von: *Die Ursachen der Rezeption des römischen Rechts in Deutschland.* München–Berlin, 1905. In more recent literature, Wicacker, op. cit., Part II, p. 97 et seq., Part III., p. 204 et seq.; *Zum heutigen Stand der Rezeptionsforschung,* in: Festschrift für Joseph Klein, 1967. p. 181 et seq.; Koschaker: op. cit., pp. 113 et seq., 141 et seq., and particularly 161 et seq., 212 et seq. For the principal causes of reception, for the differences in French and German reception, see Eörsi, op. cit., pp. 158 et seq. and pp. 39, 55, 565.

[142] Wieacker: op. cit., p. 124.

europäische jus commune, welches die Glossatoren und vor allem die Konsiliatoren auf der Grundlage des justinianischen Corpus Juris, aber mit wissenschaftlicher Verarbeitung der zeitgenössischen, vor allem oberitalienischen Statuten, Gewohnheiten und Handelsgebräuche einheitlich durchgebildet hatten,. . . in den Beschränkungen und Erweiterungen, die ihm seit alten die Schule von Bologna gegeben hatte."[143]

The revival and adoption of the Roman law of contract and of the types of contract themselves were rendered difficult by the fact that in in the *Corpus Juris,* the classical formulary action is mingled up with the procedural system of Byzantine times and thus the resulting overall picture is rather unbalanced.[144] An even more serious problem presented itself by the changed pattern of economic and social relations, for it had by then become necessary to have the received Roman law applied, as often as not, to facts that had been totally unknown in earlier times. The latter called for more advanced dogmatic approaches to be created. A more definite dogmatic complexion was imparted to the types of contract by the science of *usus modernus pandectarum,*[145] which linked up the legal science of the late Middle Ages and its German reception with the spiritual revolution of Natural Law – mainly on German soil, but also in Holland, Spain and Scandinavia – provided the current trend with a positive law dogma in place of the collections of sources, literature and maxims of the European *ius commune.*[146] It was in this period that the dogmatic armour of the types of contract was being forged, which defying criticisms from the science of Natural Law, was adopted by the codes based on Natural Law, and some refinement, was later passed on by the legal science of the Pandects to the codifications of modern times as well.[147]

As we have seen, continental law adopted the categorization of contracts through Roman law, without paying any heed to its appropriateness and applicability to the economic conditions prevailing in the early period of modern times.[148] The *usus modernus* merit the recognition of the general consensual contract and thus going beyond the categorization of contracts by Justinian's law and the formalism of the old German law alike.[149] This was a very significant step, one of making the rich more and more uncomfortably rigid. It also closed the type-system of Roman

[143] Ibid., p. 133 et seq.; cf. pp. 129 et seq., 417; Koschaker: op. cit., p. 223.

[144] Cf. Bekker: op. cit., p. 123; Wieacker: op. cit., p. 137. As is known, a truly reliable basis for obtaining full knowledge of the classical law was presented by the pieces of Gaius' works found at Verona in 1816; Bekker: ibid.; Wieacker: ibid., p. 417.

[145] Wieacker: op. cit., p. 213; cf. Dubischar: *Über die Grundlage der schulsystematischen Zweiteilung der Rechte in sog. absolute und relative,* Tübingen, 1961.

[146] Wieacker: op. cit., p. 214 et seq.; cf. Koschaker: op. cit., pp. 122, 253.

[147] Cf. Wieacker: op. cit., p. 205.

[148] Wieacker: op. cit., p. 237; cf. Weber: op. cit., p. 257.

[149] Wieacker: op. cit., p. 242.

law and made it suitable to a fuller extent to the demands of contemporary economic life. It completed the body of contract law material which served as a point of departure, and even served as a basis for the rules on contract as laid down in the codes that were framed at the turn of the 18th and 19th centuries.

The formulation of concepts and the pattern of systematization were indispensable for the work of codification, however, they were products of the theory of Natural Law: the necessity of systematizing the types of contract was first raised by Grotius, mainly Pufendorf. What is more, Pufendorf drafted the first special part of the law of obligations,[150] classifying the types of contract by the economic content gratuitous, onerous, and mixed contracts.[151] That helped the law of contract, which had outgrown Roman law, to ripen for codification by the 18th century.

We have to deal briefly with the distinctive features of the reception of Roman law in France, which according to Koschaker, stood midway between Germany and England with respect to its reception of the law.[152] In Southern France, Roman law was virtually "dormant" chiefly within the framework of the *Breviarium Alaricianum.* That territory was readily receptive to the effects of the Roman law of the 11th and 12th centuries after they had been revived in Northern Italy. As far back as the time of glossators, that part of the country came into contact again with Roman law, even experiencing some sort of incorporation but warding off and cushioning the impact of encroachments of Roman law, while learning to improve and refine most of the national law through reliance on the methods and approaches of Roman law. This is how the *droit écrit,* a special version of the Roman law received in Southern France came into being. In regards to particularly the French law of contract of the Middle Ages, there emerged a separate law of obligations partially of Germanic origin in the territories of the *"pays de Coutumes"*[153] yet it was neither long-lived nor significant. It is characteristic that, for instance, *Le Grand Coutumier de France* of 1514 had no rules regarding contract types, and Troncon's famous collection of customs (*Le droit Français et coutume de la coutume de la Prevosté et Vicomté de Paris*) from the 17th century also included but a few provisions on contracts, which at any rate clear originating from Roman law.[154] Thus the groundwork for the French bour-

[150] Cf. ibid., p. 310. For the formation of concepts and systems by natural lawyers and its significance, see ibid., pp. 275 et seq, 373 et seq.

[151] Pufendorf, Samuel: *De iure naturae et gentium,* libri VIII, 1672, Chap. V, p. 2 et seq. Cf. Wenn: *Das Schuldrecht Pufendorfs,* Göttingen, 1956. For Grotius' law of contract, see *A háború és béke jogáról* (On the Law of War and Peace), II, Akadémiai Kiadó, Budapest, 1960, p. 222 et seq.

[152] Koschaker: op. cit., p. 221 et seq.

[153] Planiol, M. – Ripert, G.: *Traité pratique de droit civil français* ,VI, Paris, 1952, p. 2 et seq.; cf. Esmein, A.: *Études sur les contrats dans le très ancien droit français,* 1883.

[154] Cf. Colin, A. – Capitant, H.: *Cours élémentaire de droit civil français,* I, Paris, 1947, p. 16; Zweigert – Kötz: op. cit., I, Tübingen, 1971, p. 82. For the career of Roman law in France in

geois law of contract was likewise laid by Roman law, or more specifically, the *droit écrit* relied on it. It is chiefly to the credit of the works of Dumoulin, d'Argentré, Domat and Pothier that at the time of preparations for the *Code civil* there already existed in French territories a uniform law of obligations derived from Roman law. Such uniformity is all the more noteworthy since as late as the 18th century the *droit coutumier* and the *droit écrit* continued to show a number of fundamental differences in other areas, i.e. personal, family and property law), requiring serious work of co-ordination to be done during the elaboration of the *Code civil.* Needless to say that the *droit écrit* was far from identical with Justinian's *Corpus iuris civilis,* whereas the French law of contract preceding the *Code civil* differed from Roman law in numerous aspects of great import. For example. by consistently abandoning differentiation between contract and mere *pactum* or rejecting any distinction between title and the mode of contracting, not to mention the superiority of systematization. Notwithstanding this, the contractual system of the French law has its roots entrenched in the Roman private law as deeply as the German or Austrian law does.

---

general, see ibid., p. 81 et seq. and, for a more detailed historical analysis, Viollet, Paul: *Précis d'histoire du droit français,* Sources, Droit privé, Paris, 1886, and Ourliac, P. – Malafausse, J.: *Histoire de droit privé,* I, Les obligations, Éd. Themis, Paris, 1957.

II. THE SEPARATE DEVELOPMENT OF COMMON LAW

"The life of the law has not been in logic;
it has been in experience."

1. General traits

The motto of this chapter, a well-known thesis of Holmes,[1] could be illustrated by the evidence of legal development in many countries, but one of the best collections of examples is offered by the history of English law.

Investigators of the common law of contract, bred in the legal thinking of continental law, may readily agree with this statement as quoted from the book of Zweigert and Kötz: *"Häufig stellt der Rechtsvergleicher fest, daß eine für selbstverständlich gehaltene Figur des eigenen Rechts, die geradezu durch die Natur der Sache gefordert zu sein scheint, nichts weiter ist, als ein ziemlich einmaliges, auf besonderen historischen oder soziologischen Bedingungen beruhendes Institut, welches – wie man dann meist ebenso verblüfft wie ernüchtert eingestehen muß – in anderen Systemen nicht bekannt ist, geschweige denn vermißt wird."*[2] The continent's experts in private law come under the spell of such "sobering amazement" when comparing the law of contract channelled into categories with the contractual institutions of the common law. The divergences are so large that they defy any comparison: ". . . The law of particular contracts offers one example of such a comparative-law difficulty. The ways of looking at this part of the law are certainly quite different. . . in common-law countries. . . and Roman law and. . . continental law systems."[3]

[1] Holmes, O. W.: *The Common Law*, 1881, p. 1.

[2] Zweigert–Kötz: *Einführung in die Rechtsvergleichung auf dem Gebiete des Privatrechts*, II., Tübingen, 1969, p. 118.

[3] Sundberg, Jacob: *The Law of Contracts. Jurisprudential Writing in Search of Principles.* In: Scandinavian Studies in Law, No. 7 of 1963, p. 125. The "structural" barriers to convergence between the continental bourgeois laws and the common law are illustrated also by Eörsi with examples of types of contract based on the differences between agency of representation and commission, or agency: "The divergence of common law and continental law is perhaps greater in the field of agency than anywhere else. Here the question is no longer one of divergent legal solutions as in the case of the sale of movables, but rather that the two law groups operate with different conceptual systems and different basic concepts of regulation. Each field has a structure

Comparing the present state of common law and its science to the Roman law of contract, Lawson makes the following pertinent observation: "We have a law of contract, while theirs was a law of contracts... English authors have concentrated their attention very much on problems connected with... matters which can be dealt with generally for all classes of contracts... The Roman law paid far more attention to the terms of contracts and very little to problems on a general level."[4] This comparison however, does not hold true for the several preceding centuries during which the common law of contract was evolving in slow degrees to a general sanctioning of breach of contract. Though the common law by-passed the level of development offered by Roman law and did not assimilate its closed system of types of contract, it nevertheless managed to surpass it after a long lapse of time, evolving through centuries to what became superior, and generalized: the contract of binding force regardless of type. It travelled its own separate and typical path preserving its primitiveness for some time, yet on the whole, tried to meet with a fascinating ingenuity and a peculiar juristic inventiveness, the needs of a more and more vigorous process of capitalist development.

What are the essential circumstances (economic and social aspects, "immanent" factors of legal development) which made the continental road, leading to the classification of contracts under the influence of Roman law, "impassable" for the common law and caused it to follow "roundabout ways" so peculiar to us? Among the moving causes we must refer largely to the general features of common law[5] as concretely manifested in the law of contract.

---

of its own. Basic distinctions prevail in both fields, although their lines of division cross each other." Eörsi, Gyula: *Comparative Civil (Private) Law*, Budapest, 1979, pp. 379–380. Cf. Zweigert –Kötz: op. cit., II. p. 120 et seq. and, in the context of Great Britain's entry into the Common Market and of legal harmonization as contemplated in Art. 100 of the Treaty of Rome. Chloros, A. G.: *English Law and European Law: The Problem of Harmonisation,* RablesZ. 36 of 1972. p. 601 et seq.

[4] In: Buckland – McNair: *Roman Law and Common Law, A Comparison in Outline,* Cambridge, 1952, p. 267 et seq. Failure to even attempt to seek the cause of such differences between common law and Roman law is a point of weakness in the correct distinction drawn by Lawson: "Why the Romans concentrated on the terms of contracts, rather than on the problems more closely connected with the general law of contract, we shall probably never know...". Ibid.

[5] In the abundant literature, for earlier works see in particular Blackstone, William: *Commentaries on the Laws of England,* London, 1774, I, p. 63 et seq., and for more recent ones see Allen C. K.: *Law in the Making,* Oxford, 1961. p. 128 et seq.; Kiralfy, A. K. R.: *The English Legal System,* Cambridge, Mass. 1963. Among the works projecting through the continental focus, see in particular Radbruch: *Der Geist des englischen Rechts* (a wonderful book rhyming to Ihering's), Göttingen, 1965; as well as Ehrenzweig, A. A.: *Das Common Law.* Z.f.R., 1960. p. 145 et seq.; Goldschmidt, W.H.: *English Law from the Foreign Standpoint,* London, 1937. Cf. Dainow, J.: *The Civil Law and the Common Law. Some Points of Comparison,* Am J. Comp. Law, 15 of 1966–67, p. 419 et seq.; Zajtay, Imre: *Begriff, System und Präjudiz in den kontinentalen Rechten und im Common Law,* A.c.P., 165 of 1965, p. 97 et seq.; Weber, Max: *Rechtssoziologie,* Neuwied, 1960. pp. 284 et seq., 101, 199, 215; Koschaker, Paul: *Europa und des Römische Recht,* München –Berlin, 1953. o. 172 et seq.; Wieacker, Franz: *Die Privatrechtsgeschichte der Neuzeit,* Göttingen, 1967. p. 496 et seq.; Eörsi: op. cit., pp. 121 et seq.

We agree with Eörsi who, after Engels, considers the early class compromises between the feudal big landowners and the surgent bourgeoisie to have been the most important determinant among the hardly discernible factors that made for the very peculiar development of the common law. That compromise allowed for the long survival of precapitalist elements in laws and due to the relative strength of the bourgeoisie, enabled the legal institutions which the bourgeoisie needed to be at a height equal to the demands of the period. They emerged and took root, with the result that England was the very first country to develop, even though in zigzags, its bourgeois law of contract marked with the imprint of its time.[6]

Most authors stress, not without justification, the judge-made character of common law (judge-made law) is one of its inherent peculiarities.[7] At every step, the law of contract was being moulded fundamentally by the casuistic system of precedents, a mediaeval form of "law-finding" in which the law appears as a phenomenon "discovered" by the judge. Judicial practice was not seeking a rational system (as is aptly stated by Max Weber, "handicraft-like empiricism" impeded from the outset the formation of a well-arranged system in common law),[8] but elaborate patterns of contract, and action were fit to be used in practice and suited to recurring individual needs.

With that method prevailing, it was not only impossible to devise a reasonable way of systematization and rationalization of the law, but even legal concepts of a relatively general nature were rather slow in evolving through intricate channels. The lack of a real common law theory was another contributory factor; the empirical doctrines of common law were elaborated exclusively or mostly in legal practice. It was due to the relatively stronger position of the bourgeoisie that the case-law approach as a natural concomitant of the judge-made law could not, even in the field of contracts, prevent altogether the emergence of generalized legal concepts (as it did in the service of feudal interests) and the development of a comprehensive doctrine of property and a modern law of damages.[9] Thus once it became stronger, the bourgeoisie prevailed upon the reluctance to, or forbearance from more general legal concepts, with a frame of mind that ensued from the use of precedents by the judge-made common law (and from its other peculiarities):[10] the general claim for damages for

[6] Eörsi: op cit., pp. 130–131. Cf. Engels: *Socialism*, Special Introduction to the English Edition of 1892. p. 97 et seq.

[7] Cf. Eörsi: op. cit., p. 123 et seq.; Wieacker: op. cit., p. 497 et seq. Ehrenzweig holds a different view: op. cit., p. 147.

[8] Weber: op. cit., p. 199.

[9] Eörsi: op. cit., pp. 123 et seq., 130 et seq.

[10] The aversion to general legal concepts, and the fact that legal thinking in terms of concepts has to this day been unable to establish itself in the ambit of common law is traced by Eörsi mainly

breach of contract had finally come into the open by the beginning of the 17th century.

This clearly shows that the established legal devices were far from determinant; the common law with its case-approach arrived at the threshold of the general notion of contract much sooner than the German law, which excelled in abstractions and had a strong philosophic charge. It shows also that "legal patterns and methods are not mechanically related to the law-determining, content-shaping socio-economic conditions. They are suitable to support a very different system if the particular historical progress attracts such a solution."[11] Eörsi relies on this statement as well.[12]

It is undoubtable that the interests and demands of the bourgeoisie, together with the implications of the commodity and money relations of capitalist development, played a decisive role in that common law "surpassed itself" in the field of contract law. We can hardly err in adding to this factor the effect exercised by the inner specifics of legal development and the working of its own set of laws. We refer in the first place to the "omission" of classification and the lack of categorization of contract. Failing as a system of types capable of satisfying the demands of economic transactions more completely, we might also say, more adequately and above all more simply that the English law of the Middle Ages, the common law was compelled, as it were, to take a step forward and give legal recognition to the more general. It may therefore be said that the system of contract classifying which was rooted in Roman law did not yet fit in with, and was of too high a standard for, the rather primitive material and approach of the contract law as conserved by the early compromise of the bourgeois and feudal classes. At the same time the need for introducing the coherent and comprehensive system of categories as adopted in the continent ceased to exist after the generally binding character of contract had been recognized.

Although somewhat simplified by necessity the introductory remarks about the general line of development of the common law of contract need to be developed in two aspects before we proceed to a more complete presentation of the contractual system of England. Consideration of these aspects will also serve a useful purpose in providing an added explanation for the omission and neglect of classification. These aspects,

---

to the "inhistorical historicity" of common law, namely to its centuries-old reliance on judicial decisions, embedded in and wedded to a completely different pattern of historical, economic and social conditions, in solving problems of the day at any point of time in history. See op. cit., p. 284.

[11] Engels: op. cit. p. 99.

[12] Eörsi: op. cit., p. 134.

which involve the distinctive features of the common law developing in the way of an "enfant terrible", are:

(a) non-reception of the Roman law,

(b) survival of the procedural approach based on a rather primitive system of actions, down to the second part of the 19th century.

2. The non-reception of Roman law

Just as the reception of Roman law in the Continent was of decisive importance mainly for the development of contract law, non-reception in England also made its effect felt primarily in the legal recognition of contracts. It is therefore appropriate to make a special point of this phenomenon incidental to the separate development of English law.[13]

Until the end of the 19th century common lawyers held and claimed that the development of English law had remained totally unaffected by Roman law. Research into legal history has since shown that this summary statement is not valid: while it is true that Roman law was not accepted or incorporated into English law, its effect did reach and even tempt the country of "splendid isolation" in two different waves. There is no doubt that Roman law bore an influence on England's development partly through judgements of the ecclesiastical courts and the Lord Chancellor, partly through legal education and jurisprudence,[14] not to mention the "reception" of *lex mercatoria.*

Roman law made its first encroachment on English law after (and in consequence of) the Norman Conquest during the 12th and 13th centuries: "It is very true that between the years 1150 and 1250 or thereabouts the old Roman law, in the new medieval form that it took in the hands of the glossators, exercised a powerful influence not only on the growth of legal theory in England, but also on some of our English rules."[15] Nor can we rule out some degree of influence exercised in that period by Roman law on the pattern of writs (judicial orders) which played a decisive part in the development of contract law.[16] Still, the most important aspect is a special, incipient need for systematization which arose in the wake of the activities of statesmen and professors of law

[13] Eörsi: op. cit., p. 118.

[14] Potter, Harold: *Historical Introduction to English Law and its Institutions,* 1958, pp. 23, 282 et seq.; Pollock, Sir Frederick – Maitland, Frederic William: *The History of English Law before the Time of Edward,* 1, 2nd ed., reissued by S. F. C. Milson, Cambridge, 1968. I. p. 131 et seq., II, p. 570 et seq.; Holdsworth, William Searle: *A History of English Law,* II, London, 1936, pp. 145 et seq., 176 et seq., 227 et seq., 267 et seq., IV, London, 1937, pp. 218, 228 et seq. Cf. Koschaker: op. cit., pp. 74 et seq., 82, 142, 144, 213 et seq.

[15] Pollock – Maitland: op. cit., Vol. II, p. 599; cf. p. 131 et seq.; for illustration of institutional effects of Roman law, see I, p. 146; II, pp. 46, 89, 114, 503.

[16] Cf. Vinogradoff, P.: *Roman Law in Mediaeval Europe,* Oxford, 1929, p. 98 et seq.

trained in Roman law (Lafranc, Vacarius, Glanvill, Bracton).[17] It is to the credit of their work (based on Roman law) that from the incoherent principles of ancient German law there emerged some sort of a system without any essential change in the contents thereof. Glanvill and Bracton drew heavily upon the phraseology and terminology of Roman law as well.

In his attempt to systematize the law of contract Glanvill borrowed terms from the Roman law in a way that they preserved the institutions and spirit of the ancient law. He used the terms *mutuum, depositum, commodatum, emptio venditio, locatio conductio,* but what he associated with them was not Roman law but ancient Anglo-Saxon law. Nor were his distinctions clear and unambiguous. Moreover, in the last analysis, he conceived all contractual relationships (designating them with terms known in Roman law) as being different forms of manifestation of debt, an institution of ancient English law,[18] as being variations of an institution which as will be seen, never fully assumed a contractual character, but carried marks of property and even delicts, although it was doubtless suitable for the legal enforcement of different contractual relationships. This example of Glanvill's attempt shows that in that period, at the end of the 12th century, the economic and social conditions of England were in many aspects a far cry from those reflected in Roman law. No wonder that Vacarius' disciple, who had been educated in the ideas of the school of Bologna, was unable to adapt the terminology of Roman law to the conditions of contemporary England, and to the ancient law embedded in them and preserved by strong traditions.

Practically the same pattern prevailed half a century later at the time of Bracton. "Though . . . Bracton has copied many more Roman rules than Glanvill, we are not surprised to find that the actual principles of the law are much the same as they were in Glanvill's day."[19] This accounts for the fact that Bracton's borrowings from the Roman law, probably in the continental practice of the time,[20] did not have so much to do with rules on institutions as with concepts and the system itself. His work was not, either in intention or effect, in any sense an imposture: his subject matter was honest, native, feudal law of England, though influenced, as it was

[17] Cf. Holdsworth: op. cit., II, pp. 147 et seq., 188 et seq., 232 et seq. Lafranc had been teaching law in Pavia and in Bec of Normandy before he set foot in England with William the Conqueror and became Archbishop of Canterbury Vacarius took with him the spirit of the school of Bologna to Oxford, where he introduced, and became a highly successful master of, the still famous teachings of Roman law.

[18] Holdsworth: op. cit., III, London, 1935. p. 414; Fifoot, C. H. S.: *History and Sources of the Common Law. Tort and Contract,* New York, Repr. 1970, p. 217 et seq.

[19] Holsworth: ibid., p. 415.

[20] Cf. Pollock–Maitland: op. cit., II. p. 196. It is, however, necessary to call attention, that Maine's opinion is gravely at variance with the facts established by the researches of Maitland, facts which were inevitably misunderstood in 1861. cf. ibid., p. 564.

bound to be influenced, by the accepted juristic method of the day – a method necessarily Romanistic. He was certainly indebted for considerable portions of his remarkable treatise to Roman law – not, however, the *Corpus Iuris* itself, but the revived Roman jurisprudence of the Bolognese glossators of the twelfth century.

Furthermore, when Roman law was first hovering over England, English economy and society, and hence English law (in particular the law of contract) were not like those in contemporary Northern Italy and were not ripe yet for the reception of Roman law. Industry and commerce of a scale large enough to need more advanced legal means or at least to live with them, were still to emerge in contemporary England. The primitive law of contract, rooted as it was in ancient personal actions, was perfectly suited to the feudal conditions of England in the 12th and 13th centuries, with some advantage seen at best in borrowing a partial system from Roman law. "In England Roman theories of contract never took root. Bracton's book shows us that they did not fit English facts" – writes Holdsworth.[21]

This is why and how the first attempt at Roman law was "repelled" by common law, which remained essentially intact in spite of its response to certain influences. After Bracton's time there was less and less talk of the Institutes, and the spell of Roman law practically melted away by the end of the 13th century. Following the short-lived and virtually ineffective attempt at the Romanization of common law, the English law of contract preserved its ancient Anglo-Saxon (Germanic) traits.[22] Roman law remained an abstract science, a nourishment of universities, which it had been for the most part even in the 12th and 13th centuries: the influence it had exercised on English law through Glanvill and Bracton became superficial and transitory. Although Bracton made a half-hearted attempt to inject the legist theory into the body of the English law of contract, the worst parts of his work are precisely the thin chapters dealing with contract but confined to scholastic practices which, though containing some truth here and there, are wanting in vigour for lack of practical experience to support them – sum up Pollock and Maitland[23] in an incisive but somewhat rough account of the chasmic contradiction between contemporary English reality and the attempts at the assimilation

[21] Holdsworth: op. cit., III, p. 412.

[22] Cf. Pollock – Maitland: op. cit., II, p. 570 et seq.; Holdsworth: op. cit., IV, p. 218.

[23] Pollock – Maitland: op. cit., II, p. 193 et seq.; cf. ibid., p. 570. Maine is outright depreciative of Bracton's forlorn attempt: "That an English writer of the time of Henry III should have been able to put off on his countrymen as a compendium of pure English law a treatise of which the entire form and a third of the contents were directly borrowed from the *Corpus Juris*, and that he should have ventured on this experiment in a country where the systematic study of the Roman law was formally proscribed, will always be among the most hopeless enigmas in the history of jurisprudence." See *Ancient Law*, London – New York – Toronto, 1946, pp. 67 et seq. It is, however, necessary to call attention, that Maine's opinion is gravely at variance with the facts established by the researches of Maitland, facts which were inevitably misunderstood in 1861. The more important appraisals of Bracton's work are cited and critically analyzed also by Fifoot: op. cit., p. 218 et seq.

of Roman law. Roman law was of too high a standard, and the type system of contracts much too refined, for the English society and law of the Middle Ages. This is the reason why the marriage of common and Roman law failed for the first time to take place in that period.

The second "attack" of Roman law in the 16th century was more powerful than the first: "in the middle of the reign of Henry VIII. . ., if ever, the common law was in a serious danger."[24] Nevertheless, according to more recent research, the threat of incorporation was not as strong as for instance Maitland[25] thought at the beginning of that century.[26] At any rate, early in the 17th century, there was a serious quarrel among the common law courts and the chancery as well as other newly established courts. The second failure of incorporation can definitely be traced to various factors.

The argument that non-acceptance was largely due to the influence of early Roman law, which, as if by way of "vaccination" acted to strengthen and protect the common law,[27] is attractive but, on the evidence of the facts mentioned earlier, less realistic. It is true that the invasion by Roman law in the 12th and 13th centuries was another contributory factor, mainly in creating a minimal need for systematization, to the advance of the common law of contract, yet, as we have seen, its role can hardly be overestimated. The significance of an independent and self-conscious society of lawyers[28] likewise showed itself, chiefly in an indirect way, in the moulding of the common law: a most flourishing period in the growth of common law was marked by the 14th to the 16th centuries, when English law underwent a great evolution and developed into a peculiar system governed by its own set of laws. This was to the credit of the legal profession.

Indeed, lawyers played a large part and carried an important social weight,[29] enjoying a veritable monopolistic position in the development

[24] Holdsworth, op. cit., IV, pp. 254, 283.

[25] Maitland, Frederic William: *English Law and the Renaissance,* Cambridge, 1901, in: The F.W. Maitland Reader, New York, 1957, p. 211 et seq.

[26] Vinogradoff: op. cit., p. 70 et seq.

[27] Vinogradoff: op. cit., p. 71 et seq.; endorsed and adverted to by Wieacker: op. cit., pp. 111, 152.

[28] Holdsworth: op. cit., IV, p. 252 et seq., particularly p. 285 et seq.; Weber: op. cit., p. 256; Koschaker: op. cit., 214 et seq.; Wieacker: op. cit., p. 152; Zweigert – Kötz: op. cit., I, Tübingen, 1971, p. 243 et seq. For the development and role of the legal profession in England, see Holdsworth: op. cit., I, London, 1938.

[29] As far back as the 14th century, the English lawyer was portrayed by Chaucer in this way:
"A sergeant of the lawe war and wys
That often hadde been at the Parvys
Ther was also ful riche of excellence
Discreet he was and of greet ruerence
He semed swich hise wordes weren so wyse
Iustice he was ful often in assise

of law. We agree with Eörsi[30] in that their commitment would have proved insufficient for the preservation of the integrity of common law as for the renewed rejection of Roman law. This would have been so had it not been for its coinciding with serious class interests (expressed in the compromise between the two major dominant classes of the time). The bourgeois interests were satisfied by the degree of development which the law of contract had reached during the 15th to the 17th centuries (when the common law, encouraged and complemented by equity, arrived at the door of recognizing the general binding force of contract) and by the assimilation of the legal material of the international merchant law (which, for that matter, reflected a strong influence of Roman law). In addition, acceptance would have handicapped the maintenance of pre-capitalist land ownership by its tendency towards the generalization of commodity ownership and its integration into a conceptual system.[31]

Thus among the several factors the dominant one behind non-acceptance was that at the turn of the 16th and 17th centuries Roman law was no longer needed by England. This is not only true of the lawyers but above all, of the ruling class too, because its interests were satisfied by the kind of law which had by then developed by its own impetus at home. Further despite its pre-capitalist features and methods, specifically in the law of contract, it began to surpass the continental solutions, including the closed system of types of contract, as derived from Roman law. This is why the marriage of common and Roman law failed to take place for the second time and definitively, and the peculiar common law of contract preserved an independent existence of its own.

3. The procedural development of law

(a) The procedural approach may be regarded as a general feature of the beginnings of legal development. For a long time the law did not govern social relations in the form of subjective rights but offered formal procedural remedies by providing for the right of action (*actio*, writ, etc.) where specific facts were present. In this domain the systems of law varied only in the length of time they bore the imprint of this infancy, together with its drawbacks and eventual benefits. ("Generally speaking, the procedural approach is more rigid and formalistic than the substantive law

---

By patente and by pleyn commisioun
For his science and for his heigh renoun
Of fees and robes hadde he many oon
So greet a purchasour was nowher noon"

The Canterbury Tales (Studies on the basis of all known manuscripts by John M. Manly and Edith Rickert), Vol. III, p. 15: 309–318.

[30] Eörsi: op. cit. p. 119 et seq.

[31] Op. cit., p 119.

approach. But contrary examples can also be found in the common law viewed in a wider sense. Frequently equity brings flexibility by applying procedural means into the strict law."[32])

As has been seen, it was not until the post-classical age that Roman law began to shake off its procedural cloth. Among the major systems of law in modern Europe the French took the lead in this field, the line being undoubtedly closed by the English, with the German standing somewhere in between. Cambacéres' first draft of the *Code Civil* was still intended to include the right of action under a separate section, treating this material as clearly constituting ways and means to enforce subjective rights that arise out of contracts and other titles. The rational of the draft therefore made a sharp distinction between the corresponding actions and their functions on the one hand, and the *actiones* of Roman law, their nature and role on the other, with the purpose of regulation stated to be that of laying the basis for a procedure which replaced the old procedural law of the feudal pattern. This would help to enforce material law and justice in accord with the needs of the new society. The subsequent drafts and the final text then completely omitted the part dealing with the law of procedure, and left its regulation to a separate code.[33] The procedural approach was far from playing so dominant and lasting a role in German law as in common law, although not least under the influence of Roman law and owing to reminiscences, it survived for quite some time. At the end of the last century Bekker wrote, precisely in connection with contracts, that some well-trained courts applying the ordinary law still examined all matters from the point of view of whether they could be brought within the scope of a *'species actio'* and, if so which one.[34] As is also noted by Eörsi, the vestiges of the procedural approach survived in German law for a long time, just as they did in Roman and English law, although the concept of subjective right (*subjektives Recht*), its greatest antagonist, played an essential role in German jurisprudence, and was given to abstractions. According to Coing, it was not until 1856 that Windscheid separated substantive law from procedural law and from the theory of claim.[35]

(b) From the very beginnings down to the second part of the 19th century, common law was characterized by the development of procedural law and by the procedural approach. More than that, the English concept of law has retained, until today, much more of its procedural character than the continental.

[32] Op. cit., p. 122.
[33] Cf. Charmatz, Hans: *Zur Geschichte und Konstruktion der Vertragstypen im Schuldrecht, Brünn – Wien,* 1937, Reprint edition, Frankfurt/M, 1968, p. 147 et seq., with sources indicated.
[34] Bekker, Ernst Immanuel: *System des heutigen Pandektenrechts* II., Weimar, 1889, p. 123.
[35] Eörsi: op. cit., p. 167.

As is graphically expressed by Maine, "So great is the ascendancy of the Law of Actions in the infancy of Courts of Justice that substantive law has firstly the look of being gradually secreted in the interstices of procedure."[36]

Glanvill's and Bracton's scholarly works, the first "books of authority", also discusses the law within the ambit of writs.[37] Again, the decisive significance of "procedural law-finding" was not lessened by the "freeze" on writs in the second part of the 13th century (Provisions of Oxford in 1250 and Statute II of Westminster in 1285). Moreover, new procedural forms of legal development (actions on the case, etc.) were devised afterwards,[38] although the inevitable spread of writs opened the door to the evolution of approaches under the substantive law as well.[39] The English law did not abandon the system of writs until the second part of the last century, when the Procedure Acts (1852, 1854, 1860) and the Judicature Acts (1873, 1875) broke with the system of actions and introduced a uniform civil procedure in place of the various procedural arrangements based on writs. Of course, this reform was likewise unable to give up the procedural habit of thought established by centuries-old traditions; traces of it are still to be found in the law in contract itself. Legal material is often arranged by forms of action even in modern manuals of contract law. While the "form of actions" lost its technical meaning in procedure, it retained a role in elaborating and systematizing the substantive law. "The forms of action have been buried, but they still rule us from their graves" – wrote Maitland a few decades ago.[40]

(c) There is hardly a better example than the very growth of contract law to show how little this characteristic, which is so important from a certain stand, revealed of the essence of common law. As was noted in the preceding chapter, the Roman law of the pre-classical and the classical age set the dogmatic stage for the long-lasting types of contract firstly procedurely in the formulary actions whereas the common law produced a quite different law of contract by a very similar approach. This is why it appears necessary for the common law method of legal development to be examined at some length in this study, first of all the system of writs, then the methods of improvement. It appears necessary to question the actual

[36] Maine, H. S.: *Early Law and Custom,* 1889, p. 389.

[37] Cf. Zweigert – Kötz: op. cit., I, p. 232.

[38] Cf. Pollock–Maitland: op. cit., II. p. 564; Zweigert–Kötz: op. cit., I, p. 233 et seq. The relationship between the "action on the case" and Statute II of Westminster is disproved by Fifoot: op. cit., p. 66 et seq.

[39] Cf. Pollock – Maitland: op. cit., II, p. 564; Eörsi: op. cit., p. 429.

[40] Maitland, F. W.: *The Form of Actions at Common Law,* p. 2; quoted by Zweigert–Kötz: op. cit., I. p. 250. Cf. Salmond, Sir John–Williams, James: *Principles of the Law of Contracts,* London, 1945, p. 29 et seq. (Contracts and Choices in Action). Compare also Rheinstein, Max: *Die Struktur des vertraglichen Schuldverhältnisses im anglo-amerikanischen Recht,* Berlin – Leipzig, 1932. pp. 129 et seq., 136 et seq.; Zweigert–Kötz: op. cit., I. p. 249 et seq.

similarity between the *actiones* of Roman law and the writs of common law and, in particular, the socio-economic conditions and conceptual abstractions presupposed by, and reflected in, the two institutions. Despite the similar form of legal development, they led the evolution of the two systems of law to different outcomes in the realm of contracts.

Most continental writers prefer the writs of English law to the system of *actiones* in Roman law,[41] but this affinity is pointed out by the English authors themselves.[42] Such comparison is not without justification:[43] by the 12th and the 13th centuries there had come about written formulas for different writs, making legal remedy subject to the presence of specified facts in a way which on its face was entirely similar to the praetorian formulary action. One ought not be surprised, then, if the common law procedure had evolved under the direct influence of Roman law, because, as has been seen, the law of the island country was first invaded by Roman law in the period between 1150 and 1250 or thereabouts, when the system of writs became prevalent. But that was not the case, if not for any other reason than the fact that the English lawyers of the time, who were trained in Roman law (or were reading it at least), were totally unaware of the essence of the formulary system. As the mediaeval Romanists of the Continent, they originated from Justinian's law since they had access to it. The Digests and Institutes, works of the great emperor-codifier, would have been the only sources of information available to them, even about the classical Roman law is, had they been able at all to distinguish between the classical, the post-classical and Justinian's law. They were however totally ignorant of those differences because as is noted by Pollock and Maitland, "they were not historians; they did not have any wishes to disinter the law of the republican or of the Antonine period. They were lawyers, and the Roman law that they sought to restore was the law of Justinian's last years. Unless it had been altered by some emperor of German race, that was for them the law which was still by rights the law of the Roman world. All that Justinian or any of his predecessors had abolished was obsolete stuff which no one would think of reviving. What they knew of the formulary system was that it had been swept away by imperial wisdom. Therefore their influence was all in favour of a simple system of procedure under which a magistrate would decide all questions of fact and law without any division of labour and without any formula. If they could have had their way in this country, the procedure of our temporal would have been similar to our spiritual courts: a libellary procedure which had no place either for the 'original

[41] Rheinstein: op. cit., pp. 10, 12 et seq.; Zweigert – Kötz: op. cit., I, p. 234 et seq.; Eörsi: op. cit., pp. 121, 132 et seq. Differences underlined by Weber: op. cit., pp. 99, 120.

[42] Pollock – Maitland: op. cit., II, p. 558 et seq.

[43] For an in-depth analysis of this problem by methods of legal history and comparative law, see Peter: *Actio und Writ, Eine vergleichende Darstellung römischer und englischer Rechtsbehelfe*, Tübingen, 1957.

writ' with its authoritative definition of the cause of action, or for the 'issue' submitted to a jury."[44]

Consequently, the long-lived English procedure of the Middle Ages emerged and evolved the way it did free from the influence of Roman law. Eörsi goes to the heart of the matter when dealing with "Roman-law-like" phenomena in common law, he states that "this follows not from reception, but to a great extent from the similarity of certain conditions. The coherence of an empire's law is of concern here; when lawyers' work had already become a distinct field, and when socio-economic conditions became much more complex than they were outside the empire, but the conditions for a distinct generally applied legal code were lacking although the rigidity of early practice had to be relaxed. The *actiones* and writs were expanding; moreover a *ius aequum* had to have a place beside the *ius strictum.*"[45]

This example of a "parallel in the social subconscious" between the Roman formulary action and the English procedure based on writs also explains why the mediaeval English law is more in step with the law of the republican period than with the ("classical") law of the imperial age,[46] while most laws of continental Europe grow congeneric to the Roman law of the imperial age.[47] The available source-books on Roman law were the works of Justinian in England as much as in Northern Italy, and, as has already been mentioned, even the effects of Roman law reached English soil through the schools of Pavia (Lafranc) and Bologna (Vacarius). However the economic and social conditions of those places were quite different, and in many aspects much less developed. Against this background it is understandable that "while the other nations of Western Europe were beginning to adopt as their own the ultimate results of Roman legal history, England was unconsciously reproducing that history; it was developing a formulary system which in the ages that were coming would be the strongest bulwark against Romanism and sever our English law from all her sisters."[48]

All these, we believe, substantiate our conclusion that the major part of the answer to our basic question does not lie in the technical differences[49] between the Roman formulary action and the English procedure

[44] Pollock–Maitland: op. cit., II, p. 560.

[45] Eörsi: op. cit., p. 133.

[46] Wieacker: op. cit., p. 498, fn26. Cf. Ehrenzweig: op. cit., p. 146 et seq.

[47] Eörsi: op. cit., pp. 132, 133, with relevant literature indicated.

[48] Pollock–Maitland: op. cit., II, p. 558..

[49] According to Pollock and Maitland, "the differences between the two formulary systems are at least as remarkable as the resemblances"; e.g. "while the praetor listens to both parties before he composes the formula, the chancellor when he issues the original writ has never heard the defendant's story, and in most cases the plaintiff obtains a writ 'as of course' by merely saying that he wants it and paying for it." Op. cit., p. 560. For this reason they say of writs: "We call it distinctively English; but it is also in a certain sense very Roman." Op. cit., p. 558; cf. Weber: op. cit., pp. 99, 120.

of writs, but in the particular economic and social conditions of the period in which the writs emerged and in the peculiarity of legal thinking related to them. These were not negligible but essential differences from several aspects. This general setting provides the explanation why the common law, with its manner of action "copying" of the praetorian procedure, evolved into a law of contract entirely different from the Roman.

(d) The writs, which are the core of legal development in England, came into being over two centuries (with rapid momentum between 1154 and 1272) following the growth of the central royal power.[50] That was in a period when, as was already noted in our reference to the first fruitless wave of Roman influence, both economic and social conditions and legal thinking in England stood at a very low level. England in the wake of the Norman Conquest can safely be called a model country of feudalism, with a strictly structured feudal pyramid of the land-owning nobility. Only the central power of the king, which was strong as early as the formative stage, gave a special course to the growth of English law. A peculiarity which, coupled with the centralization of the administration of justice and the unification of law, proved to be decisive to the evolution of law. In the prevailing environment of feudalism, commodity and money relations retained but a peripheral role during centuries which spanned the exact period of time in which writs were being issued or the foundations of common law were being laid. They helped determine the shaping of the legal development method. It is no wonder that the regulation of contracts found its way into this system through side doors and yet, we shall still see, as a mere reflex-phenomenon of remedy conceived under the lay of real property or of delicts, it was of greater significance for feudal conditions.

This pattern of conditions is reflected in the formulation of writs as well. In the so-called heroic age, writs were issued by the king's chancery, practically with nothing but fiscal and political considerations in mind, successively and on purely empirical basis, without scientific foundation or underlying abstraction. This accounts for the fact that the hundreds of writs issued until 1285 included no more than 30 to 40 commonly used actions that showed up considerable differences.[51]

For our subject, the most important feature of the whole system of English writs is the low level of abstraction derived from the early German law and preserved in later periods. Roman law is usually said (and not without foundation) to have been a long way from the conceptual habit of thought, yet the type system of contracts or more specifically *actiones,* which had evolved from Roman law in the pre-classical and classical

[50] Cf. Pollock–Maitland: op. cit., II, p. 559.
[51] Ibid.; also p. 564 et seq.

periods, was using legal terms (*emptio venditio, locatio conductio, mandatum, societas,* etc. or their respective *actiones*). As against this, the common law writs had no relation to legal categories but simply differed by the object of pleading with the essence being the object of the plaintiff's action (land, chattel, money, etc.). The level of abstraction in the system of writs is fittingly illustrated in Pollock's and Maitland's finely "wrapped" description: "The impatient student who looks down upon medieval law from the sublime heights of 'general jurisprudence' will say that most of our English actions are mixed and many of them very mixed."[52]

The English system of actions followed the pattern of the Roman formulary action only in its rigorous externals. As late as Blackstone's day, the plaintiff had to indicate in advance the form of action out of the existing 70 to 80 on which to base his claim. His choice could not be changed and everything from the applicable precedent to the form of evidence and execution was dependent on it.[53]

Such an arsenal of legal devices would have been incapable of giving birth to a law of contract equal to the standard of Roman law even if the prevailing economic and social conditions had required something more than the common law actually produced in this field. This is another indication that the similarity between the Roman system of *actiones* and the writs of medieval England was superficial in many respects since the two procedures were based on different tiers of abstract thinking. It was not therefore an accident that the former became the dogmatic cradle of the types of contract, while the latter was slow to evolve solutions to contract law more in keeping with the requirements of commodity production. The latter had been advancing from the 15th century onwards and later with the demands of capitalist development in England as well.

4. High points in the development of the English law of contract

In the light of the foregoing it is no surprise to find the early common law of contract,[54] if such existed at all, showing the level of the earliest Roman law: there were no signs except of partial solutions which, wrapped as they were in actions bearing marks of property law or of the delictual approach, provided legal remedy only for certain claims of a contractual nature.

[52] Op. cit., p. 571; cf. Rheinstein: op. cit., pp. 17, 20.

[53] Zweigert – Kötz: op. cit., I, p. 249.

[54] Of the major works dealing with the evolution of the English law of contract, see Pollock–Maitland: op. cit., II; Holdsworth: op. cit., III; Fifoot: op. cit., p. 217 et seq. Of the works taking the continental approach, see Rheinstein: op. cit.; David, René–de Kerstrat, F. G.: *Les contrats en droit anglais,* Paris, 1973. p. 13 et seq. Compare also Khalfina, R. O.: *Dogovor v angliyskom grazhdanskom prave,* Moskva, 1959; Eörsi: op. cit., p. 130 et seq.

(a) Debt

The first common law institution, at least partially contractual in nature is regarded to be the action of debt-detinue.[55] These two writs which had originally been uniform, or at any rate closely related, fell apart during the 13th century and their final parameters were established by the middle of the 14th century. Glanvill still tried to rely on categories borrowed from Roman law for describing the area in which remedy was provided by this double form of action and for stating that the *actio* of debt was used to enforce claims arising *"ex causa venditionis, aut ex commodato aut ex locato aut ex deposito aut ex alia justa debendi causa."* (Fifoot is right to note on this score that it is hard to believe that such terms were able to give an adequate definition of the common law embryonal as it was, in the time of Henry II.[56]) Once detached, debt was used to claim a specified sum of money or other fungible things, whereas detinue served to sue for a specific chattel or its value. Most of the modern English authors find that detinue was not of a contractual character, and it is also discussed by Fifoot as a tort.[57]

The nevertheless surviving debt concept initially showed rather amorphous characteristics. According to Holdsworth, debt in its early stage had predominantly property law features but it was also contractual in nature to a degree to serve as enforcement for pecuniary performance under some of the different classes of contract (loan, purchase price, rent, etc.). It had certain delictual elements as well, but it never acquired a fully contractual character.[58] It had a very wide scope of application extending for instance to settlement in court, or security of performance. In early times (13th and 14th centuries) it had to be drawn up mostly in the form of a sealed deed.

It was not until the early 15th century that the contractual character of debt began to be accentuated in its writ of a mixed function. This process of theoretical clarification was largely due to the widening uses of the action of debt, which by now came to cover claims for specified sums of money deriving from other facts (mainly doing of work), in addition to the traditional cases mentioned earlier. It was gradually extended to any

[55] Fifoot: op. cit., pp. 24 et seq., 217 et seq.; Pollock – Maitland: op. cit., II, pp. 169 et seq., 203 et seq.; Holdsworth: op. cit., III, pp. 318 et seq., 420 et seq.

[56] Fifoot: op. cit., p. 217.

[57] Ibid., p. 24 et seq.

[58] Holdsworth: op. cit., III, pp. 420, 425; cf. ibid., II, p. 368. Max Weber looks on the delictual approach to the contractual function as a general feature of primitive laws, and as an example makes special mention of the evolution of medieval English law. Among the most important characteristics of the erosion of the dividing line between the two sections of law, he refers in particular to the absence of incidents creating subjective liability and of differentiation between the two classes of facts in respect of legal consequences. Op. cit., p. 93 et seq. Cf. ibid., pp. 114, 117, 120, 214.

cases where pecuniary counter-performance stood against some performance. The term "debt on a contract" as widely as it was used in this period covered neither contract nor contractual promise in the modern sense of the word: the obligor's performance was founded not on the promise of performance, but the obligation to pay derived from the performance received. This element of mutuality is the first recognizable sign of contract law at the common law: the formula *"quid pro quo"* which was to be found as early as the 14th century, came to be a technical term expressing the necessary link and correspondence between rights (benefit) and obligations (duty) during the 15th century. It is not surprising that Holmes believes he finds the roots of the later theory of consideration in this phase of development.[59]

All this goes to further show that initially the common law did not sanction anything except real contracts. At the same time it is worth noting that the period from the middle of the 14th century was known to be another case in which the germs may be discerned regarding a sales contract transmuting it into one of a consensual nature.[60] By a process which came to a head in the middle of the 15th century the common law courts appear to have recognized the principle that seller may sue for the price by the action of debt and buyer may sue for the thing purchased by the use of detinue (particularly in the case of single things). They arrived at this conclusion by realizing that ownership may pass on without delivery.[61]

These traits of common law reveal its hidden possibilities almost beyond our grasp and signify a truly admirable development, even if the toleration of these "consensual" contracts as an isolated contrast to the real character of the principle *quid pro quo* is not to be seen as the outcome of some calculated logical process. All the courts did, within the bounds of medieval writs, was to respond to the pressure of commercial life.[62] The process could have been set in by some random factor just as well: in the beginning the courts allowed the seller to sue for the purchase price solely on the ground that the buyer guaranteed payment on the faith of seal, and subsequently they were never again able to get back to their primitive simplicity. Continuing insistence on deed in a relationship of a markedly commercial nature (like sale) amounted to undue amounts of meticulousness. The seller's writ of debt had to be balanced with buyer's writ of detinue, the latter's proprietary nature being substantial enough to suggest the need for, or at least the desirability of, recognizing ownership

[59] Fifoot: op. cit., p. 220 et seq.; Pollock – Maitland: op. cit., II, p. 207 et seq., particularly p. 212 et seq.; Holdsworth: op. cit., III, p. 421. In the last analysis, Fifoot argues against the existence of interconnections between the technical characteristics of debt and the consideration theory. Op. cit., p. 395 et seq.

[60] *Groome'Case,* 1348, Y.B. 21 Ed. III., p. 11.; pl. 2; cited by Fifoot: op. cit., p. 227.

[61] Ibid., p. 228 et seq.

[62] Ibid., p. 229.

in favour of the party who was seeking to obtain the use of a given thing. Thereupon the break from real doctrine, which was first motivated by convenience, came to be covered with the mask of rationality.[63] In any case, sale was the only, though very important, exception in medieval English law.

In other aspects, debt as a form of action was only available when and if the claim was formally proved or the plaintiff was able to show that he had a substantial benefit to demand from the defendant (or perhaps from a third person named at his request to receive such benefit). There were several other formalities, particularly the "technical" rule that did not allow debt to be founded on unspecified claims which restricted the scope of debt's application in medieval times.[64]

(b) Covenant

Another root of the common law of contract can be traced back to the early 13th century and can be found in the possibilities offered by the action of covenant for the enforcement of claims. This form of writ may be said to have originated from tenancy of land and other legal relationships connected with it: cases found in early registers of precedents, including those treated by Bracton, are all related to real property. At the same time Fifoot makes it clear that at least in the early period, the general view according to which the role of covenant was confined to real property cases, is unfounded.[65]

Of greatest relevance to the development of the theory of contract was perhaps a special case to which the writ of covenant was widely applicable. As early as Glanvill's day, giving security for settlements in court with the approval of judges was a natural and generally accepted use of covenant, the dispute itself being imitated and fictitious in large measure and aiming for the enforceability of a settlement concerning the conveyance of land. (Shortly after Glanvill's time, this form of covenant developed its appropriate formal requisites too: the settlement between the litigants as approved by the court, was written into a deed in three copies,

[63] Ibid.

[64] Ibid. For the role of debt today, see Salmond – Williams: op. cit., p. 589 et seq. The action of account which was partly used as a remedy competing with the action of debt, had played a large part in the medieval common law of contract then gradually faded into the background in the 18th century as it failed to remain competitive with the similar benefits of equity. Fifoot: op. cit., p. 268 et seq. Cf. Pollock – Maitland: op. cit., II, p. 221 et seq.; Holdsworth: op. cit., III, p. 426 et seq., II, p. 367. For this reason and because of its lesser relevance to the conceptual line of legal development, we do not deal with the evolution of debt, as it also fails to receive more complete treatment in the major continental accounts much like those of Rheinstein and René David's of the development of the English law of contract.

[65] Ibid., p. 255 et seq. Cf. Pollock – Maitland: op. cit., II, p. 216 et seq.; Holdsworth: op. cit., III, p. 417 et seq.

two were received by the litigants and one retained by the court. This arrangement which facilitated the use of evidence survived down to 1833.) The theoretical significance of this group of actionable cases derives from the fact that the promise of contract – the role of agreement at common law – came into play in them for the first time: the covenant was designed to realize the goal suggested by its name and to grow into a generalized contractual remedy.[66] That this hope failed to materialize and that the common law did not, on the plane of theory arrive at the idea of contract through the institution of covenant, is accounted for by the fact that originally the covenant was required to take the form of a sealed deed.[67] This was certainly the case by late 13th and early 14th centuries. This greatly restricted its scope of application. Even so, the action of covenant played a major role and English lawyers grew accustomed to the idea of contract.[68]

The parameters of the action of debt and the action of covenant appear to have been established by the end of the 13th century; debt was an exclusive remedy, and where it was allowed (namely in the case of an obligation concerning a specified sum of money) covenant was not available. For that matter, in the case of an action of debt a deed had only probative force, whereas in the case of an action of covenant it was the *conditio sine qua non* of writ. These formalities prevented the further development of covenant. Had they not existed the common law would have come across a general remedy for breach of contract by the early 14th century; that would have been based on unilateral promise rather than as on a bilateral deal[69] as it was in the end.

We feel it would hardly be possible to find a better example than this to illustrate the baffling by-paths of legal development, although here as well there appears to be an obvious explanation why the covenant, the promising legal remedy, ceased to develop. In the last analysis, economic and social conditions in the England of the 14th century had as yet no need for a law of contract at the relatively high level which covenant represented.

(c) The rivals of common law

The sprouts of common law ("toleration" of consensual sale, the said uses of covenant, etc.), which foreshadowed progress during the period from the 12th to the 15th centuries, were but exceptions proving the rule: a law of contract capable of meeting the demands of more extensive transactions was yet to emerge. The available devices as outlined above

[66] Fifoot: op. cit., p. 257.
[67] Ibid., p. 257 et seq.
[68] Holdsworth: op. cit., III, p. 420.
[69] Fifoot: op. cit., p. 258.

were but arrangements intended to cover individual cases and did not provided in anyway the adequate legal means for the protection of contractual relationships. While the writs at hand to enforce contractual elements (debt, covenant and account) covered rather broad areas, were nevertheless in part complementary and even competed with one another. They were in the main far from what could be called law of contract. The prerequisites for one to emerge were economic growth and considerable trade, which experience has shown tend to bring pressure on law to develop appropriate means in response to economic needs. This is the way it happened with English law as well.

Although the summary statement "that medieval England was all the while in an economically backward state"[70] is not borne out by more recent research into economic history, the fact is that the opposite was true in some areas.[71] Signs of really noticeable trade were to be observed from the 15th century when, on the other hand, the legal demands of gradually growing foreign and international trade were satisfied not by common law devices, but to a great extent within the ambit of Merchant Law – the English variant of the *lex mercatoria,* which had been developed on the Continent under strong Roman influence – and of urban (local) customary laws. Their methods were, in several aspects, more advanced and mainly more flexible than the devices of common law: as early as the middle of the 14th century they recognized the informal covenant and, where necessary, provided remedies even for infringements of oral agreements. They also relied on certain usages to protect merchants, granted procedural benefits to foreign merchants, etc. Understandably, priority was given to the development of the law of sales. The lead in giving legal support to commerce was taken by the so-called market courts, whose role began to decline in the second part of the 15th century and faded into the background in the 16th century. This not owing the least to the growth of the common law and its "stricter control" by which the local customary laws were partly absorbed and partly displaced.[72] (The vitality of common law is shown by its later ability to absorb even the principal rules of Merchant Law during the 17th and 18th centuries.)

From the second part of the 15th century the common law had to face a new rival, namely equity which emerged from the practice of the courts of chancery and recognized as independent forums for the administration of justice and exercised a marked impact on the evolution of contract law as well.[73] Equity played an important role by the recognizing the enforce-

[70] Holdsworth: op. cit., V, London, 1937, p. 113.

[71] Cf. Fifoot: op. cit., p. 289 et seq.

[72] Ibid., p. 293 et seq.

[73] Cf. Barbour, W. T.: *History of Contract in Early English Equity,* Oxford, 1914; Fifoot: op. cit., p. 301 et seq.

ability of unspecified pecuniary claims, especially in the easing of inequities resulting from the roughness of common law, and admitting suretyship to secure claims based on deed, and above all, providing a stronger remedy for oral agreements.[74] In developing the theory of contract the chancellors (mostly ecclesiastic persons) drew impetus from the canon law, in which the requirement to keep one's word and to threaten sanctions for breach of good faith had been a long-established maxim.[75]

It is more than interesting that the decisive moments of development in the common law of contract – the general sanctioning of breach of contract and then the emergence of the consideration theory – were forthcoming after all, not in the realm of equity, but in the narrowly understood body of common law which was of course largely influenced by the substance of equity and even stimulated somewhat by the pressure of the widening jurisdiction of the courts of chancery.[76]

(d) Assumpsit

Of course, common law would not have been common law had it been developing its own law of contract through reliance on already established means. We can take it for granted that this was not the course taken but a new path, the performance of a spectacular trick so striking even in the development of English law: drawing on the delictual writ of trespass by developing it in an ingenious way. Instead of removing the formal shackles of covenant or relaxing the rigidities of debt (principle of *guid pro quo*, fixed sum of money) the common law sought and found a new point of departure by a sudden turnabout. "The life of the law has not been in logic; it has been in experience!"

The writ of trespass was originally applied in cases where the defendant used force and broke the king's peace (*"vi et armis et contra pacem domini regis"*) in attacking a thing held by another person or on the physical integrity of that person. Later (beginning around the second part of the 14th century) its uses in delictual cases were greatly extended to cover direct attacks on things or persons, the damage suffered being merely an indirect consequence of the action or omission of the defendant. In such event the plaintiff was granted a remedy in the form of "action of trespass on the case".[77]

[74] Cf. Fifoot: op. cit., pp. 302 et seq., 330.

[75] Cf. Fifoot: op. cit., p. 304 et seq.; Holdsworth: op. cit., I, p. 455 et seq., V, p. 294 et seq. For the considerable role played by the practice of ecclesiastical courts in elaborating the concept of contract, see Pollock–Maitland: op. cit., II, pp. 189, 197 et seq.; Holdsworth: op. cit., II, p. 86.

[76] Cf. Holdsworth: op. cit., I, p. 455 et seq., III, p. 453 et seq., VI, London, 1937, p. 658 et seq.; Fifoot: op. cit., p. 330.

[77] For the widening use of trespass, see Fifoot: op. cit., pp. 44 et seq., 66 et seq.

According to Fifoot, the threads of assumpsit, a peculiar variant of this "action on the case", can be traced back to the last decades of the 14th century.[78] First in a narrow but later a widening range of cases, assumpsit provided a remedy for breach of contract, and, in its final shape, even considered penalty for non-performance of an obligation assumed. The process of more than a century, in which assumpsit developed from delictual roots ("deceit" the tort of fraud, constituted another source of the new contractual institution beside "trespass on the case") into the most adequate general remedy for contract is very interesting, though difficult to unravel.[79] (Unlike covenant, the term itself – assumpsit = assumed – proved true to the promise it held out.)

The fact is that by the middle of the 16th century the modern concept of contract had in essence been formulated in related cases,[80] with the action of assumpsit resting on the idea of contractual promise or assumption of obligation. Assumpsit came into wider use half a century later. In the famous Slade's Case[81] of 1602, in which the position of the plaintiff was represented by Coke and the defendant's by Bacon, the court held the following: "Very contract executory imports in itself an assumpsit, for when one agrees to pay money or to deliver anything, thereby he assumes or promises to pay or to deliver it, and therefore when one sells any goods to another and agrees to deliver them at a day to come, and the other in consideration thereof agrees to pay so much money at such a day, both parties may have an action of debt, or an action on the case on assumpsit, for the mutual executory agreement of both parties imports in itself actions upon the case as well as actions of debt."[82] Thereby recognition was accorded to the principle that procedural consequences are also involved by a pledge not expressed but written into an agreement (based on debt = *in debitatus assumpsit*). Short of spelling out in explicit terms this principle also implied with unconscious prudery, that any breach of contract was subject to legal sanction. Thus by abandoning its delictual traits, the action of assumpsit became a general common law sanction for breach of contract by the early 17th century and enabled English law to keep ahead of the Continent, and practical means came to the general sanctioning of contract.[83]

78 Fifoot: op. cit., p. 331. The roots of assumpsit are traced back to a case in the middle of the 14th century by Holdsworth: op. cit., I, p. 456, III, p. 429; Plucknett, T. F. T.: *A Concise History of the Common Law,* London, 1948, p. 441 et seq.; and, without mention of the dispute, by Zweigert – Kötz: op. cit., I, p. 233 et seq. Compare also Weber: op. cit., pp. 120, 214.

79 Holdsworth: op. cit., III, p. 428 et seq. and, in particular, Fifoot: op. cit., p. 331 et seq.

80 Fifoot: op. cit., p. 339.

81 4 Co. Rep. 91a, 92b, quoted by Holdsworth: op. cit., III, p. 444 et seq.; Fifoot: op. cit., p. 371 et seq.

82 Cf. Pollock – Maitland: op. cit., II, p. 196; Holdsworth: op. cit., III, p. 451 et seq.; Fifoot: op. cit., p. 358 et seq.

83 Cf. Eörsi: op. cit., p. 130.

It was no wonder that the action of assumpsit, associated with informal contracts and free from technical rigidities, became more and more commonly used in practice. In the Slade's Case the Queen's Bench (the report itself saying King's Bench, although the case was adjudicated in the reign of Queen Elizabeth) ruled that "both parties may have an action of debt, or an action on the case on assumpsit, for the mutual executory agreement of both parties imports in itself actions upon the case as well as actions of debt". This amounted to the recognition of assumpsit as a general alternative to debt.

The English courts resorted at other times to assumpsit in admitting the actionability of unfixed sums of money. In the first quarter of the 17th century they broadened the scope of the action of assumpsit to include claims for sums of money deriving from contract (assumed under agreement) which were not minutely specified in every detail, but were nevertheless deemed reasonable. Such problems presented themselves mainly with the providing of services in the nature of undertaking (shipping, safekeeping of things, etc.) and owing to the unforeseeable magnitude of costs. As has been mentioned formerly, in connection with debt, the common law courts granted a remedy only for claims for fixed sums of money.[84]

In addition to problems encountered in execution, the delictual origins may also have been a factor, in that assumpsit was available only for claims of damages for breach of contract and could not be used to enforce performance in kind, much like the other contractual institutions of the common law which were also little understood.[85] Recourse to it in the latter case was by way of exception, and was used by equity through the institution of specific performance.[86]

Down to about the 18th century it was a discretionary right of the Court of Chancery to decide whether or not the defendant should effect performance in kind; where so required by the precepts of justice and equity, such claims were also admissible in cases concerning transfer of chattels or obligation to carry out some activity. This gave rise to the rule that specific performance may only be ordered in the event that payment of damages is unlikely to give an appropriate remedy. In practice, this restrictive provision limited the possibility of enforcing performance in

[84] Fifoot: op. cit., p. 360 et seq. For other uses and benefits of the action of assumpsit, see ibid.

[85] It is nevertheless worth mentioning that during the 13th and 14th centuries action for specific performance was discretionarily but in good conscience practiced by the common law courts, in proceedings based on covenant. Difficulties in execution and other factors might have also played a part in that this recourse fell into disuse in the 15th century, and that enforcement of specific performance was brought within the "exclusive jurisdiction" of the court of equity. See Fifoot: op. cit., pp. 259, 262.

[86] Cf. Holdsworth: op. cit., I, p. 456 et seq., VI, p. 658 et seq. For the present status of specific performance, see Salmond – Williams: op. cit., p. 593 et seq. and, in particular, Chitty: *On Contracts,* 1968, I, p. 709 et seq.

kind largely to contracts involving landed property. The exceptional nature of this recourse is further accentuated by rules which, for different reasons, refuse to permit the enforcement of performance in kind despite the fact that payment of damages is avowedly an inadequate remedy. It is worth citing in this regard the view of Max Weber, who holds that the difficulty with which execution in kind was received into English law can be attributed to the sociological features and its lesser bureaucratic nature. Additionally, as the consequential continuity in the administration of justice confronted it with the development of continental law, this form of adverse judgement owing to the rapid growth of sovereign power, had been accepted relatively early, at the beginning of the middle ages.[87] This assertion would deserve a more thorough examination from the point of view for instance, of whether the common law practice in the 13th and 14th centuries with respect to covenant[88] is to be viewed as an exception standing beside the rule or as implying something more (let alone again, the possible factors behind the continuous development of law!). What seems certainly plausible is that at least in the initial period, until the 17th century approximately, the adverse judgement to pay money is not a concomitant of advanced marked conditions. It is not a product of social development at a level at which the society has learned to measure everything in terms of money.[89] Later, during the full-scale period of capitalist development, the contribution of the sociological factor cannot be called into question either. This is also evidenced by the confines in which specific performance came to be practised.

(e) Consideration

A presentation, however brief, of the evolutionary history of the English law of contract cannot be concluded without discussing, if only in outlines, the theory of consideration which is perhaps the most famous – one might say most notorious – constituent element of this line of legal development abounds which in oddities, logical puzzles, and ingenious solutions. Next we shall attempt to confine our discussion to what appears to be absolutely necessary, focusing attention on the core and substance of this phenomenon.

Since the historical roots of the consideration theory are based in a wide variety of institutions as English lawyers themselves seem to feel, we can safely do without a presentation of the doctrines or origin.[90] Not

[87] Weber: op. cit., p. 94.
[88] See fn. 85.
[89] Weber: ibid.
[90] For a critical appraisal of major theories, see Fifoot: op. cit., p. 395 et seq. For the appearance of the doctrine in judicial practice, see: ibid., p. 399 et seq. Cf. Holdsworth: op. cit., VIII, London, 1937, p. 2 et seq.

questioning but accepting the probability of the theoretical and historical antecedents of consideration, we find Fifoot's to be the most realistic summary account of the subject: "But neither in origin nor in nature is it occult." Contract in any legal system may be based upon the principle either of promise or of bargain, and the one has no innate superiority over the other. Though the choice was not consciously present in the minds of the Elizabethan judges, they were impelled by every tradition of the common law to prefer the principle of bargain. Gratuitous promises were associated with the writ of Covenant and were excluded from the province of Debt *sur* contract. During the early experiments with Assumpsit the idea of reciprocity was constantly asserted and because of this idea, St. Germain made his student reject the suggestion that a past benefit might support an obligation. The large commercial interests of the new age sought a general sanction not for charitable gifts but for business enterprise. In such an environment it is not surprising that the judges should have required some material inducement to the defendant's undertaking. This was a requirement the plaintiff might meet in one way or another. He might discharge the burden of proving that he had conferred a benefit upon the defendant a fact to which the proceedings in Debt had long accustomed litigants; or he might show that he had bought the defendant's promise by the tender of his own. Act or promise was the price to be paid for success in the new consensual action of Assumpsit. Thus the doctrine is neither an exotic idea imported from a more luxurious jurisprudence, nor need its source be pursued with care and cunning through the labyrinth of the past though it was a domestic invention of the common law. The 'mystery of consideration' which the Victorian lawyers found so fascinating becomes no more than "the practical answer to an urgent problem."[91] We think that the essence of the "fascinating doctrine" is especially incomprehensible to the "continental minds", except in such a real-life approach.

By the early 17th century this doctrine had been fully absorbed into judicial practice and consideration became a prerequisite for successful action in any matter involving breach of contract, except for contracts written into a sealed deed.[92] It was virtually by this process that the English law of contract rose to its full stature, taking independent and roundabout paths and developing just in time to be able to meet the needs created by the rapid advance of capitalism.

Numerous attempts have been made to define the essence of consideration from various angles. Fifoot presents one approach as early as 1857,[93]

[91] Ibid., p. 398 et seq.

[92] Ibid., p. 406. Cf. Holdsworth: op. cit., I, p. 456, V, p. 321 et seq.; Chitty: op. cit., p. 15 et seq.

[93] Fifoot: op. cit., p. 401.

while Holdsworth cites a 1875 case as giving the "classical definition" of consideration, which "may consist either in some right, interest, profit, or benefit accruing to the one party, or some forbearance, detriment, loss or responsibility given, suffered or undertaken by other."[94] The substance of the whole doctrine may be reduced to the fact that a contract can only have the sanction of the law "upon sufficient consideration (compensation)".

No doubt that this fundamental precept of the Anglo-Saxon law of contract has been largely eroded by the demands of the 20th century. An equally certain fact is that the problematic nature of the whole doctrine was further accentuated by the Victorian mystification and theorization of history as criticized by Fifoot. It is by no chance that even Holdsworth concludes his 50-page essay on the history of the doctrine by saying: "In fact, the doctrine of consideration in its present form is something of an anachronism", and considering earlier proposals of a similar orientation, he arrives at the conclusion that this doctrine should be abandoned and recognition of the legal effect of contracts should not be subject to any particular condition (apart from the formal requirements of law).[95] While judicial practice, especially in the United States, has been moving rapidly towards the relaxation and breaking down of consideration since the 1920's and the 1930's, it would be too early to speak of the disappearance of its doctrine.[96]

(f) Reform of procedural law – Traditionalism in substantive law

Thus with the widespread use of assumpsit and the crystallization of consideration theory and its practical application, the English law culminated in general concept of contract. As we have seen, practice opened the way to the actionability of all contractual agreements, and usually in the form of damages, laid down sanctions of any breach of contract by the beginning of the 17th century. Theoretical elaboration, owing to the specific state of English theory,[97] was slow in coming, but the 17th and

[94] *Currie v. Misa*, 1875, L.R. 10. Ex. at p. 162, quoted by Holdsworth: op. cit., III, p. 413.

[95] Holdsworth: op. cit., VIII, p. 47.

[96] Cf. Anson, Sir William R.: *Law of Contract*, ed. by A. G. Guest, Oxford, 1969. p. 16 et seq. Atiyah, P. S.: *An Introduction to the Law of Contract*, Oxford, 1971, p. 23 et seq.; and, in particular, Chloros, A. G.: *The Doctrine of Consideration and the Reform of the Law of Contract*, Int. and Comp. Law Q., 17 of 1968, p. 137 et seq.; Chitty: op. cit., I, p. 50 et seq., particularly p. 56 et seq.

[97] As Max Weber writes, jurisprudence of a standard to be called science in the continental meaning of the term was virtually absent in England until quite recently, but in any case at least down to Austin's day. Op. cit., p. 285.

18th centuries bore fruit to the process of theoretical clarification as well. In his famous commentary published at the end of the 18th century, Blackstone had already given a clear and concise definition of contract. "A contract. . . is . . . an agreement, upon sufficient consideration, to do or not to do a particular thing."[98]

The general concept of contract, with consideration at its centre, covered the whole array of facts which were open to legal redress to be sought by "contractual" actions evolved by common law throughout centuries. It is extremely important to note, however, that this concept was at the time formulated with regard to the make-up of claim only. Whereas with regard to substance, the consequences of breach of contract in the law of procedure the system of *actiones* prevailed. This was true until the reform of the administration of justice and of procedural law in the second part of the last century[99] as has been mentioned in another context above. This is well illustrated by Blackstone's system among others; in his work he includes contract among the instances of acquisition of property (2nd book), limiting their discussion to the making of contract, chiefly agreement and consideration and giving a classification of contracts by subject-matter. The problems relating to breach of contract are given a separate treatment under the heading of private wrongs (3rd book). This not only shows that the law of contract "even in the scheme of Blackstone. . . appears as a mere supplement to the law of property",[100] but also that even in his approach the concept of contract was unable to break through the magnetic field of traditional *actiones.*

As noted earlier, these *actiones* retained their hold even after the reform of procedural law, namely the abolition of *actiones* and the introduction of a uniform civil procedure. This is so much the case that even the Anglo-Saxon lawyer of this century is compelled to distinguish between three classes of contractual obligations different in content: 1) in a form derived from assumpsit, instead of an obligation to effect some performance, a contract under the law of obligations still creates an obligation to pay damages for performance contrary to contract and for non-performance; 2) contracts originating from an action of debt (still commonly called debt) create an absolute claim for a fixed sum of money, or agreements written into a deed, or real contracts; and 3) there exists a class of contracts allowing for performance in kind (specific performance). The reforms of the administration of justice and of procedural law unified the different systems of courts and procedures of the common law of equity, but did not consolidate the rules of substantive law accordingly

[98] Blackstone: op. cit., II, 1774, p. 442.
[99] Cf. Rheinstein: op. cit., p. 129.
[100] Pollock – Maitland: op. cit., II, p. 184. Cf. Schwarz, A. B.: *Einflüsse deutscher Zivilistik im Auslande.* In: Rechtsgeschichte und Gegenwart, Karlsruhe, 1960, p. 61.

laid down by them. Therefore with respect to structure and content, the English-American law of contract is still lacking in uniformity, bearing the increasingly outdated and uncomfortable marks of its singular evolution.[101]

(g) No full-scale codification

Neither was the tradition-bound character of the English law of contract changed to any significant degree by the fact that from the last century onwards the effect of legislation was increasingly felt in the field of substantive law as well. This was due to the fact that most legislative enactments were confined to removing the ill-effects of the rules that had emerged from case law. It was not until the turn of the century approximately that more comprehensive legislations affecting at least some specific areas, were passed at a time when Bentham's earlier calls for codification[102] insisting on the rationalization and simplification of law, as well as on increased legal certainty, had encountered certain trading interests. This period saw the birth of highly important commercial legislations: the Bill of Exchange Act (1882), the Partnership Act (1890), the Sale of Good Act (1897) and the Marine Insurance Act (1906). Legislative concern with different sections of contract law has continued in our century and has even received fresh impetus in recent decades. Rather than discuss legislative activity relating to general questions of contract (e.g. the Misrepresentation Act of 1967) we shall only exemplify with a few relevant statutory enactments: Road Traffic Act (1960), Resale Prices Act (1964), Monopolies and Mergers Act (1965), Hire-Purchase Act (1965), etc., as well as some international conventions (concerning international sale of goods, carriage of goods by road and air, and so on). Apart from the fact that most of these legislative acts ("codifying statutes") were likewise aimed at consolidating the rules which had been formulated mainly in the practice of common law courts, the whole body of legal material cannot be overshadowed even by details as important as these: the English law of contract is still an uncodified field of law embedded in traditions.[103]

The necessity for the systematization and rationalization of law is a traditional and long-existing vulnerable spot of English law.[104] This statement of Wieacker is not in the least exaggerated: "*So blieb auch die theoretische Wirkung des Vernunftrecths auf die Jurisprudenz bei der*

[101] Rheinstein: op. cit., p. 233 et seq. Cf. ibid., p. 129 et seq.; Salmond – Williams: op. cit., p. 576 et seq.; Chitty: op. cit., Vol. I, p. 659 et seq.

[102] Bentham, Jeremy: *A General View of a Complete Code of Law,* 1802, in: The Works of Jeremy Bentham, III, London, 1843.

[103] Cf. Zweigert – Kötz: op. cit., I, p. 250 et seq.

[104] Cf. Weber: op. cit., pp. 101, 215.

eingewurzelten Abneigung des englischen Rechtsgeistes gegen System und allgemeine Begriffe im ganzen gering. Jeremy Benthams . . . Kampf gegen die historische und traditionelle Kasuistik des 'unsichtbaren' Common Law und für eine rationale Kodifikation hat zwar vielleicht die kontinentale Kodifikation mit angeregt, in seiner Heimat aber kennzeichnenderweise kein Echo gefunden."[105]

Different authors offer different explanations for non-codification. Weber for instance, sees the main motivating causes in the sociological complexion of the legal profession and in the absence of scientific pretentions;[106] while Vadon, in his search for the factors responsible for non-codification, refers to several factors such as the specifically practical nature of legal education; the English national pride being forged in the continuity of development; the integrity of common law, the non-acceptance of Roman law; the compulsory system of precedents; the complementarity of statute law; and the fragmentation of reforms.[107] It is hardly worth arguing about which of these – really existing – traits is the cause and which is merely an attendant circumstance or perhaps simply a symptom of the non-codification of English law.

The essence, the underlying cause is traced by Eörsi to the English compromise of classes and its specifics, which are found to be at the root of the other characteristic features of English legal development as well: "Landowners had no interest in the generalization of codification of bourgeois legal ideas. . . This position generated a strong aversion for any legal generalization, and saved the case approach of judge-made law and left its mark on English legal development. This aversion and case approach became submerged in tradition, the inertia of which incessantly reproduces its impact on legal development and secures this reproduction even after the original causes of the birth and consolidation of tradition had sunk into oblivion or had ceased to exist altogether."[108] No matter how appealing and real a core it may have this explanation does not seem convincing in every aspect. In our opinion, concentrated expression of essential points may result in oversimplification. In its present state the English law raises so many objective obstacles to codification that it would take several decades even for the most revolutionary legislator to overcome them. Forceful guidance by a Napoleon and contributions by three Pothiérs and three Cambracéres' would perhaps prove just

[105] Wieacker: op. cit., p. 279. Cf. ibid., p. 497 et seq.; Weber: op. cit., p. 285.

[106] Weber: op. cit., pp. 101, 215, 285.

[107] Vadon, Jean: *Le problème de la codification du droit anglais,* 1962, p. 55 et seq., quoted by Varga, Csaba: *Kodifikáció az angolszász rendszerekben* (Codification in the Anglo-Saxon Systems), Állam- és Jogtudomány, XVI, 1973, p. 627. Cf. Schwarz, A.B.: *Grundzüge der englischen Rechtsquellenlehre.* In: Zivilgesetze der Gegenwart, II, Berlin, 1931; Pound, Roscoe: *Codification in Anglo-American Law.* In: The Code Napoleon and the Common Law World, New York, 1956.

[108] Eörsi: op. cit., p. 134; cf. pp. 117, 524.

as insufficient for the venture of accomplishing a task greater than the codification of the English law of contract. Systematization and selective evaluation of elements of current law are in themselves an immense enterprise to undertake. The hold of traditions in this material presenting another objective difficulty, while modernization – elaboration of a law appropriate to a modern and constantly changing pattern of economic and social conditions – is a still more formidable challenge to meet, let alone "minor" problems like the separate development of Scottish law bearing the imprint of continental inspiration.

Thus the more than sceptical statement by Guest on the ongoing work of codification concerning the law of contract is corroborated not only by his personal prestige: ". . . the work of codification [is] both difficult and protracted. It therefore seems unlikely that the common law of contract will be banished from the courts for some considerable time to come."[109]

It appears (at least our continental mind is inclined to believe) that the systematization of contract law is further hindered by the lack of classification carried out at an appropriate level of abstraction and based on workable criteria of delimitation. Indeed, as we shall discuss in greater detail presently, the basic blocks and prefabricated elements of the codification of contract law are made up of the types of contract in the existing continental codes. It is equally true that more than one conceptual abstraction of the common law of contract is likely to generate overlaps tending to hamper codification. In the introduction to this chapter, we have referred to the institution of agency which comprises numerous kinds of representation, inclusive of commission involving *del credere* liability.[110] The conceptual range of bailment is still more "complex", if possible, as the common law includes here all forms of possession of an alien thing involving the obligation of safekeeping and return. This is the case whether such obligation arises out of a legal relationship, either gratuitous (deposit, agency, loan for use, etc.) or onerous (lease, safekeeping for good consideration, processing, carriage, lien, etc.); or whether the relationship is established in the interest of a bailor (deposit, agency, safekeeping for good consideration, processing, carriage, etc.) or of a bailee (lease, lien), who is perhaps the principal beneficiary (loan for use); and whether safekeeping of a thing is the sole or exclusive purpose of the legal relationship or exclusive purpose of the legal relationship or is a natural, indispensable, collateral (use, or collateral security for the satisfaction of bailee, administration, transportation, processing, etc. in the interest of bailor) and so on.[111] A code based on these and similar legal

[109] Guest, A.G., in: Chitty: op. cit., Vol. I, p. VIII.

[110] Cf. Chitty: op. cit., II, p. 2 et seq.

[111] Cf. ibid., p. 77 et seq. Chitty discusses the common law rules for all the mentioned types of contract, except for carriage, solely in the chapter on bailment, devoting a separate chapter to carriage by land and air only (ibid.).

notions can hardly be conceived of, at least in the continental way of thinking.

Yet in concluding our reflections, decency requires the practise of self-criticism of our timid criticism. We feel prompted to do so not only as a result of the success of the Uniform Commercial Code[112] but above all, by our lack of competence: the continental lawyer dipping into the common law must realize that the logic of his thoughts is too tied to the shackles of his legal education and he needs to further study to grasp the essence of a legal world so external to him, let alone forming a judgement on the future of this fascinatingly alien system of law. For that matter, the sole purpose the author has pursued in writing this chapter has been to make a control test in undertaking an appraisal of the continental concept of contract law, namely to see whether legal regulation of the exchange of commodities is possible (and if so how, by what means, and at what price) without categorization of contracts or more accurately without a cetegorization as we conceptualize it. The common law is able in the whole, to give a positive answer to this question. And if we have succeeded in giving a more or less authentic, but in any case a very sketchy portrait of the English law of contract in pursuit of our basic objective, the result of our work is little short of "preterintentional". In this endeavour however, it was by no means our intention to give the reader the impression that the two portrayals of contract law were to suggest that the continental law is the "ideal" and the common law the "deformed".

[112] Cf. Robinson, William G. – Catena, Arnold P.: *Business Law,* Boston, 1972, p. XI et seq., with the full text of the Code reproduced in the form of appendix (ibid.).

III. GENERAL CONCEPT OF CONTRACT AND CHANGING FUNCTIONS OF THE TYPES OF CONTRACT

"The movement of the progressive societies has hitherto been a movement *from Status to Contract.*"

1. Changes in functions of the types of contract

The fact that under the stress of socio-economic transformations and alterations in legal systems the millenary institutions and devices of civil law have undergone numerous changes in function, while retaining similar or largely similar legal forms, is hardly disputed by anyone in a theoretical context. Concrete inquiries into institutional history nevertheless reveal frequent instances in which changing functions are ignored in historical comparisons, not receiving any mention and attention when the forms of a given institution – whether of Roman law, the Middle Ages, classical capitalism, imperialism, or perhaps socialism – are viewed in juxtaposition. With the spread of the Marxian view of history, functional changes that result from the most profound transformations, namely those of social formations, usually have not escaped the attention of researchers. The latter have indeed been successful mostly in identifying various objectives and functions which they found determined by different socio-economic foundations and underlying identical or similar approaches by capitalist private law and socialist civil law. The achievement of results has been facilitated by mutual attempts[1] to clarify the conceptual bases of

[1] See, on the one hand, Eörsi, Gyula: *Jogösszehasonlítás és békés együttélés* (Comparison of Laws and Peaceful Coexistence), Állam- és Jogtudomány, VII, 1965. p. 380 et seq.; *Reflexions sur la Methode de la Comparaison des Droits dans le domaine du Droit Civil.* Rev. int. dr. Comp., 19 of 1967. p. 397 et seq.; Szabó, Imre: *Az összehasonlító jog elméleti kérdései* (Theoretical Questions of Comparative Law), Állam- és Jogtudomány, XV. 1972, p. 197 et seq.; *La comparaison des institutions juridiques,* Acta Juridica, XV, 1973. p. 131 et seq.; Eörsi, Gyula: *Comparative Civil (Private) Law,* Akadémiai Kiadó, Budapest, 1979, Chapter VIII on Convergence in Civil Law, p. 363; Mádl, Ferenc: *Az összehasonlító nemzetközi magánjog elmélete* (The Theory of Comparative Private International Law), Állam- és Jogtudomány, XV, 1972, p. 485 et seq.; Harmathy, Attila: *Összehasonlítás a „gazdasági szerződések" körében* (Comparison in the Realm of "Economic Contracts"), Állam- és Jogtudomány, XV, 1972, p. 597 et seq.; and on the other hand, Loeber, D. A.: *Rechtsvergleichung zwischen Ländern mit verschiedener Wirtschaftsordnung,* RabelsZ, 26, 1961, p. 201 et seq.; Zweigert, K.–Puttfarken, H. J.: *Possibilities of Comparing Analogous Institutions of Law in Different Social Systems,* Acta Juridica, XV, 1972, p. 107 et seq.; Cf. Harmathy, Attila: *Nemzetközi Kerekasztal Konferencia Budapesten az összehasonlító jog főbb kérdéseiről* (International Round Table Conference in Budapest on the Main Questions of Comparative Law), Állam- és Jogtudomány, XII, 1969, p. 715 et seq.

East-West comparisons of law, which have gained considerable momentum in recent decades. This is the case, since presentation of the different socio-economic functions, as transmitted by the rhyming institutional schemes of capitalist private law and socialist civil law is a concern of the comparative lawyer and the legal historian alike. On the other hand, the change in functions of some legal institutions which are not related to the thrust of development of socio-economic conditions, itself generated by shifts in the mode of production. However, they are "merely" induced by essential modifications in the legal system, as well as naturally provoked by the changing pattern of production relations and often remain in obscurity.

The evolutionary history of the types of contract offers good examples of change in both kinds of function. Changes in function precipitated by the transformations of social systems and arising from modifications in the system of economic management will be discussed in connection with the contractual system of socialist law. Modern developments in contract law will similarly receive separate treatment. This chapter is concerned with how the significance of types of contract as inherited from Roman law was altered by the recognition of the general binding force of contract. It is also concerned with how and to what extent the law of contract, built as it is upon legal concepts that had been evolved on the plane of the specific, was affected by the general advance of the idea of contract.

As a beginning, the essence of change in functions may be summarized as follows: before the general binding force of contract was recognized, the only navigable routes of commodity and money relations had been the diverse channels through which the types of contract were developing without any legal remedies other than those provided by them as available to participants in business transactions. Whereas after the legal principle of sanctioning all contracts had evolved, the types of contract preserving their legal form assumed a role similar to that played by the recommended sea-lanes on the open boundless ocean, with the types of contract serving as models for an adequate legal regulation of commodity exchange. It was completely freed from the shackles of legal form.

In order to clarify the essence of change in functions it seems desirable to review the course of development in which the continental private law came to accept the general binding force of contract. The process embracing the period from Roman times to the 18th century offers lessons pointing far beyond the compass of our concrete subject, not the least as a comparison with the entirely different path of common law, which as discussed in the preceding chapter, led to similar results none the less.

2. *Nudum pactum*

The closed and formal system of types and the lack of informal agreements of legally binding force, are just as the different types of contract, a legacy of Roman law underlying the evolution of the continental law of contract. In the first chapter we have briefly indicated that the classical Roman law of contract was based on compulsory types and did not recognize the general binding force of contract. The making of agreements rested on freedom of contract, as we now understand the term, but the forms of transaction – more specifically of action – were dominated by rigidity; the contracting parties were free from the pressure of law in deciding to enter or not to enter into an agreement, but the legally binding character of their relationship was conditional on the use of such forms of contract as were recognized by law. Reason being that there were not any new forms of contract available for the parties to have their free agreement enforced by legal means.[2]

(a) The classical Roman law was thus a long way from recognizing any general concept of contract:[3] economic demands – the needs of commodity exchange – did not bring enough pressure to bear on legal thinking (which rose to the level of the specific but got stymied there) to reach that stage. The arsenal of the classical Roman law of contract – the closed system of types – provided a sufficient measure of protection for all economic goals.[4] About 90% of contractual relationships is estimated to have been handled through the four classical consensual contracts alone,[5] with four real contracts also available for business dealings. On the other hand, the *stipulatio* opened up practically boundless possibilities for the law of contract to enforce all agreements by invoking the clause of *stipulatio* to that effect. Kaser saw the principal role of *stipulatio* in extending the scope of the system of actions,[6] while Levy, too, finds that the form of *stipulatio* which was simple in structure but able to cover any contractual obligation; this was accounted for by the fact that the classical Roman law could do with a few types of contract.[7]

Indeed, the law of the classical age had a lacuna only in cases where one of the parties effected performance outside the recognized types of

[2] Cf. Kaser, Max: *Das römische Privatrecht,* I, 1955, p. 398 et seq.; Betti, Emilio: *Der Typenzwang bei den römischen Rechtsgeschäften und die sogenannte Typenfreiheit des heutigen Rechts,* in: Festschrift Wenger, I, München, 1944, p. 249 et seq.; Marton Géza: *A római magánjog elemeinek tankönyve. Institúciók.* Textbook on the Elements of Roman Private Law. Institutes), Budapest, 1963, p. 196 et seq.; Brósz, Róbert – Pólay, Elemér: *Római jog* (Roman Law), Budapest, 1974, p. 386 et seq.; Diósdi, György: *Atipikus szerződések a bírósági gyakorlatban* (Atypical Contracts in Judicial Practice), Jogtudományi Közlöny, XXVI, 1971, p. 89 et seq.

[3] Cf. Betti: op. cit., pp. 256, 265.

[4] Kaser: op. cit., p. 400.

[5] Seuffert, Lothar: *Zur Geschichte der obligatorischen Verträge,* Nördlingen, 1881, p. 1.

[6] For abundant instances of application, see Kaser: op. cit., p. 450; cf. ibid.: p. 400.

[7] Levy, Ernst: *Weströmisches Vulgarrecht. Das Obligationenrecht,* Weimar, 1956, p. 34.

contract and on the basis of an informal agreement, e.g. under a barter agreement. Although the failure of the performing party to secure counter-performance by way of a separate *stipulatio* was a daily occurrence, there was no means by which to claim outstanding performance, a remedy (*conditio*) being available only for reclaiming the performance effected.[8] For instance, the number of contracts for work, labour and materials, in which counter-performance was something else than money was growing. Thus the *actio locati* or *conducti* was not available. It is strongly disputed whether the classical law had already developed – and if so, in what form – some sorts of a legal remedy for such and similar agreements. Kaser offers convincing arguments in support of the possibility that the classical law had devised some redress for such transactions.[9] (As far back as the classical age, legal recognition might have been indispensable in cases where a contract had indisputably been entered into between the parties but there was uncertainty as to whether it covered sale or *locatio conductio,* lease or *locatio conductio operis,* etc., as well as in the cases of commision and barter.)[10] There is evidence to show that this area too had already been covered by the actions *praescriptis verbis* of postclassical law.[11]

If the actionable pacts (*pacta practoria, pacta legitima* and *pacta adiecta*) are also included among the said remedies, we can hardly think of any agreement for which the Romans had not devised some practical legal remedy. It is no wonder that Diósdi questions the existence of practical difference, which is generally emphasized by the modern science of civil law between the Roman law of contract and the legal systems based on the general binding force of contract.[12]

Yet it would be wrong to blur the theoretical difference. (Not even practical differences must be disregarded. *Stipulatio* for instance, is a truly admirable invention of Roman law but – for all its simplicity, practicability and broad applicability – it was a formal transaction, and had it not been for the difficulties this involved for business dealings the said problems would not have arisen in connection with the innominate real contracts.)[13] The classical Roman law was guided all along by the idea

[8] Kaser: op. cit., pp. 400, 484 et seq.

[9] Kaser: op. cit., p. 484 er seq. For possible Hellenic influence, see ibid., p. 400.

[10] Ibid., 485.

[11] Kaser: op. cit., II, p. 302 et seq.; Levy: op. cit., pp. 23 et seq., 32; Marton: op. cit., p. 198.

[12] Diósdi: op. cit. On the other hand, for doubts expressed about the theoretical nature of divergence, with a skeptical look at the freedom of types in modern laws, see Betti: op. cit., pp. 256, 264 et seq., 269 seq.

[13] Interesting and enlightening as it may be this presentation of the ingenious expedients which the limits of the closed system of types caused the Roman lawyers to contrive would take us far from our subject. Similar "trick"' were also incorporated in other more primitive laws (Greek, German, etc.), but were practised at a near-equal level perhaps by none except the common law. For amazing inventions by *iuris consulti* (e.g. types of transactions used for purposes extraneous to them), see Ihering, Rudolf: *Geist des römischen Rechts,* 1923, 2,2, p. 528 et seq.; 3,1, p. 281 et

that legal obligation is created by nothing but specific types of contract ("*re, verbis, litteris, consensu*"[14]) and that pacts were not enforceable except those with a *causa.*[15] The closed system of types of contract did not leave any room, not even exceptionally, for the contracting parties to broaden the legal channels of commodity relations by including individual or perhaps even random dispositions with the sanction of the law.[16] We stress again that, practical differences notwithstanding, all these features draw a theoretical line of distinction between the classical Roman law of contract and the modern laws lending general sanction to all contractual agreements. This theoretical distinction, which we shall try to amplify later in this chapter, is not manifested least in the changed function and role filled by the types of contract.

It would be amiss to single out some particular factors for explaining this break in the spate of the still rightly admired achievements of the classical Roman law of contract. It stopped short of taking the last step.[17] There is no doubt – and this is the first aspect to mention – that the development of law, even if coping with difficulties and taking roundabout ways, was always able to satisfy the basic socio-economic needs and the demands of an expanding commodity exchange.[18] It is equally true that the Roman lawyers' way of thinking was a contributory factor to the "avoidance" of general categories at the level of contract.[19] In addition, it is extremely important to refer to considerations of justice and legal certainty. Even the Roman administration of law, highly developed as it was, had ground to feel that it could not afford to provide a remedy for all informal agreements without raising serious threats to the postulates of legal certainty. (The consensual contracts, and in some respect the *stipulatio,* had already opened rather wide avenues for obtaining the sanction of the law.) This aspect is also underlined by Nizsalovszky: "In my view, the small number of recognized types of contract in the classical Roman law. . ., the lack of a general rule giving binding force to meetings of minds in the way of contracts is accounted for by the fact that the law enforcement machinery was initially unable to keep pace with the growth of incipient commodity production and turnover. This is why the availability of remedy was subjected to the requirement that a transaction

seq. (Scheingeschäfte); Rabel, Ernst: *Nachgeformte Rechtsgeschäfte,* Sav. Z. rom. Abt. 27, 1906, p. 290 et seq., 28 of 1907, p. 311 et seq. Compare also Knüttel: *Typenkombinationen von Kauf und Pacht bei Abzahlungsgeschäften,* in: Studien im Römischen Recht, Max Kaser zum 65. Geburtstag, Berlin, 1973, p. 33 et seq., Rez.: A.c.P. 175, 1975, p. 253.

[14] Gai. 3,89.; cf. Betti: op. cit., p. 255 et seq.

[15] Cf. Levy: op. cit., p. 16 et seq.

[16] Cf. Betti: op. cit., pp. 257, 260 et seq.

[17] For addenda to the economic and social causes of the use of compulsory types under Roman law, see Betti: op. cit., p. 262 et seq.

[18] Cf. Kaser: op. cit., Vol. I, p. 400; Seuffert: op. cit., pp. 13 et seq., 31.

[19] Cf. Levy: op. cit., p. 16 et seq.; Kaser: op. cit., I, p. 201; but compare Ulp. D.2.14. pr.-2.

should be effected in an appropriate form, in which case its purpose was indifferent, or that the performance stipulated should fit into any of the established types."[20]

(b) The post-classical law of the late imperial period, particularly in the western part of the Empire, went far to relax the closed system of types of the classical age. The doctrine of *cause* faded into the background and the dominant part in the qualification of contracts was played by the economic goal. Two mutually complementary tendencies can be observed. On the one hand, there are traces of neglect to differentiate elaborately between types of contract, with their boundaries roughly drawn and blurred, and the distinction by *causa* fading. Also the dividing line between gratuitous and onerous contracts eroded (e.g. in the case of *commodatum, depositum,* lease), while qualified contracts were often used to conceal changed economic goals or contents.[21] On the other hand, there were more and more signs of the concept of contract developing, of a larger role being played by agreement: the scope of enforceable contractual promises widened (the most significant moment being the recognition of gift-giving as a contract),[22] and consensus as a fact creative of obligation assumed greater importance, especially in the East.[23] Thus, the growth of economic and military troubles in the Empire, and the decline of contract and legal life in the classical age, entailed rifts in the type structure of contracts. The concept of contract then began to spread, under the influence of Greek and Christian philosophies as well.

The changing fate of *stipulatio* was part of the developments in post-classical law: this ancient and most common transaction in Roman law gradually lost its original formal character, and under Hellenic influence developed into a general written agreement, into a written document.[24] This process was advancing more swiftly and more spontaneously in the western part of the Empire: in the 5th century the agreements committed to writing without the clause of *stipulatio* were largely regarded as actionable, and the *stipulatio* itself, without a role to play any longer,

[20] Nizsalovszky, Endre, *Az állami vállalatok forgalmi viszonyainak új alakulásához* (New Pattern of Economic Relationships between State Enterprises), Állam- és Jogtudomány, XI, 1968, p. 526.

[21] Levy: op. cit., pp. 14, 18 and, in respect to individual types of contract, 163 et seq., 169 et seq., 173 et seq., 249 et seq. For a general treatment of *"Simplifizierungstendenz"* as a feature of legal life in this period, see Schulz, Fritz: *Geschichte der römischen Rechtswissenschaft,* Weimar, 1961. p. 366 et seq. All this is a splendid example bearing out the statement of Marx: *"Das Recht kann nie höher sein als die ökonomische Gestaltung und dadurch bedingte Kulturentwicklung der Gesellschaft."* See *Kritik des Gothaer Programms,* Marx–Engels Werke, Dietz Verlag, Berlin, 1962, p. 21.

[22] Levy: op. cit., p. 236 et seq.; Kaser: op. cit., II, p. 288 et seq.

[23] Levy: op. cit., pp. 14 et seq., 24, 28, 37 et seq.

[24] Levy: op. cit., p. 35 et seq.; cf. Seuffert: op. cit., p. 23 et seq.; Pólay, Elemér: *A dáciai viaszostáblák szerződései* (Contracts of the Dacian Wax Tablets), Közgazdasági és Jogi Könyvkiadó, Budapest, 1972, pp. 80 et seq., 261.

slowly died away.[25] The *stipulatio* hardly received any mention in the western statutes and law books. It vanished without leaving a trace in the terminology of the *Lex Burgundiorum*, the *Codex Eurici* and the other *Leges Visigothorum.*[26] A similar trend of development, though slower and centrally oriented, forced its way respect to *stipulatio* in the Eastern Roman Empire, as it became increasingly difficult to distinguish agreements by *stipulatio,* which turned into written documents, from pacts that were put into writing but were not actionable.[27] Finally a decree of Emperor Leo at the end of the 5th century practically recognized all kinds of contracts as being a *stipulatio* or an actionable transaction.[28]

As demonstrated, developments in the post-classical period were an indication that delineation between legally binding transactions and mere pacts was losing ground and that the theoretical recognition of the generally binding force of contract was not long in coming. While the conceptual clarification of differences between pact and contract, and while a general theory of contract was still far from evolving;[29] there was hardly anything further left, than for the practical changes that had taken place during the period from the 4th to the 6th centuries, particularly in the vulgar laws of the western part of the Roman Empire, but to receive a scientific generalization in the law of contract. It was a paradoxical game of history that jurisprudence in that period was non-existent in the West. That being the area where the decline of the classical Roman law of contract was far more pronounced and practice moved closer to the concept of generally binding contract. On the other hand in the East, the ambitious plan of Justinian set the scientific community working on the codification of classical law. Justinian, the great Emperor-Codifier, *"fasziniert von der Mission, als Restaurator der goldenen Zeit des römischen Rechtes in die Geschichte einzugehen, . . . versucht durch weite Strecken die klassische Analyse zu retten. Auf breiter Basis präsentiert er die Förmlichkeiten der Stipulation und die Klaglosigkeit des pactum."*[30] And although Justinian also was unable to fully ignore the changes of

[25] Levy: op. cit., p. 39 et seq.

[26] Ibid., p. 43.

[27] *"Der Übergang der stipulatio in eine Schuldurkunde* ließ *sie jedoch dem pactum näherkommen, so nahe, daß es problematisch wurde, die beiden Geschäfte auseinanderzuhalten. Denn auch ein pactum mochte schriftlich abgefaßt werden und wurde es ohne Zweifel in allen bedäuteren Fällen. . . . Der Unterschied zwischen einer verbindlichen stipulatio und einem unverbindlichen pactum lag dann also nur darin, daß eine Dokument die Klausel interrogatus spondidi in diesen oder jenen Worten enthielt und das andere nicht. Eine solche Haarspalterei kann sich indessen in der Praxis unmöglich behauptet haben."* Ibid., p. 37.

[28] Ibid., p. 39 and fn; Seuffert: op. cit., p. 27 et seq.

[29] Levy: op. cit., p. 17; cf. p. 21 et seq.

[30] Op. cit., p. 53.

preceding centuries, he was also unable to reestablish the differences between written *stipulatio* and *pactum,*[31] yet posterity must nevertheless proceed from the maxim of Roman law that *"nuda pactio obligationem non parit, sed parit exceptionem"*.[32]

It followed from the principles of Justinian's codification that the use of compulsory types was also maintained, although without any insignificant concessions: the contracting parties were allowed a wide scope of action to modify the types of contract, using new ones and neglecting others, while the *actiones praescriptis verbis* left the door wide open to obtaining legal remedies for transactions.[33]

In summary it may therefore be stated that Justinian's codification has preserved for us incalculable values by systematizing the classical law of contract, but at the same time, it has blocked a straight line of developmental process towards recognition of the general binding force of contract. The permanence of the principle of *nudum pactum* made its effect felt for centuries, presenting a challenge to the continental lawyers of posterity. The divergences between the classical and the vulgar, and between what was dead and living were bound to confuse posterity. In this as in many other aspects, the codification was an expression of two souls, the result being a combination of unprincipled compromises and sharp contradictions. The judicious vulgar law, which was of an incomparably lower standard in juristic refinement and expressiveness, had devised more practicable solutions in this field.[34]

3. *Summa Theologica – Curia Mercatorum*

Over periods of centuries, spanned by the successive waves of the great migrations and then by the emergence and predominance of the feudal mode of production, there was not any economic demand for the Roman law, either in its classical formulations (with the principle of *nudum pactum*) or in the vulgar law approach (without differentiation between contract and pact).

On the other hand the glossators – the first learned commentators in medieval times on the masterpiece of the ancient law which itself was

[31] Cf. Levy: op. cit., p. 55 et seq.

[32] D.2,14,7,4. According to Diósdi, this maxim applied not to atypical contracts, but to supplementary agreements made *a posteriori* to modify contracts. See op. cit., p. 89, fn2.

[33] Cf. Betti: op. cit., p. 266; Levy: op. cit., p. 32.

[34] *"Das Klassische und das Vulgare, das Abgestorbene und das Lebendige. . .: diese Widersprüche konnten und mußten die Folgezeit verwirren. Die Kodifikation war hier wie an unzähligen anderen Stellen ein Ausdruck der zwei Seelen. . .; unbefriedigende Kompromisse und scharfe Gegensätze waren das Resultat. Das nüchtern eingestellte Vulgarrecht, das an juristischer Bildung und Ausdrucksfähigkeit auf einer ungleich tieferen Stufe stand, hatte hier handlichere Lösungen zur Verfügung gestellt."* Op. cit., p. 59.

revived by the needs of rapidly expanding trade in northern Italy during the 12th and 13th centuries – immediately found themselves confronted with the problem of Roman law. Roman law conserved by Justinian, as to whether or not obligations undertaken by informal agreement, deriving from contract not conforming to a given type, were enforceable by action. This question was clearly answered in the negative by Irnerius, Accursius and others. It is noteworthy however, that in arguing for the actionability of contracts they attached great importance to agreement between the parties, e.g. in their treatment of innominate contracts.[36]

In the period of glossators the canon law had already drifted away from the approach of Roman law on the basis of principles of moral theology. The writings of the Fathers of the Church and later Thomas de Aquino's deeply penetrating *Summa Theologica* clearly reflected the view that while simple informal promise does not create legal obligation, it is morally binding on promisor. This approach was soon adopted by the criminal courts of the church, so that breacher of an informal agreement became liable to indictment under a procedure of *denuntiatio.* This legal concept exercised some influence on the civil jurisdiction of the church as well, but it was unable even after the long controversy it had stirred, to become a predominant, and still less a generally accepted approach. It was not until the 15th century nearly two hundred years later, that the general binding force of agreements was adopted in the civil jurisdiction of the church courts. Whereas at the end of that century some writers sought without success to extend this principle to legal disputes between civilians outside the Pontifical State (*in foro saeculari*).[37]

While the canon law gradually recognized the legally binding nature of all contracts within the framework of church jurisdiction, the renowned commentators of Roman law[38] virtually upheld the maxim of *nuda pactio obligationem non parit.* Thus the emergent contrary approach of canon law was unable to displace the doctrine of Roman law from both theory and civil jurisdiction.[39] Bartolus[40] refers to canon law practice in his treatise's section entitled "*De differentia inter ius canonicum et civile*"

[35] Savigny, Friedrich Karl von: *Geschichte des römischen Rechts im Mittelalter,* Heidelberg, 1850, IV, p. 9 et seq., V, p. 262 et seq.

[36] Cf. Seuffert: op. cit., p. 39 et seq., but compare Ulpian: D.2.14.1.pr.-2. See also Dilcher, Hermann: *Der Typenzwang im mittelalterlichen Vertragsrecht,* Sav. Z. rom. Abt. 77, 1960, p. 270 et seq.

[37] Seuffert: op. cit., pp. 45 et seq., 79 et seq., 84 et seq. Cf. Wieacker, Franz: *Die Privatrechtsgeschichte der Neuzeit,* Göttingen, 1967, p. 238. Thomas de Aquino writes this: '*...secundum honestatem, ex qualibet promissione homo homini obligatur, et hoec est obligatio iuris naturalis. Sed ad hoc quod aliquis obligatur ex aliqua promissione obligatione civili, quaedam alia requiruntur.*" *Summa Theologica,* Pars 2^{a} 2^{ae} qu LXXXVIII. Art. Ad primum. Torino–Roma, 1940, p. 502.

[38] Savigny: op. cit., VI, particularly p. 137 et seq.

[39] Seuffert: op. cit., p. 52 et seq.

[40] Savigny: op. cit., VI, p. 140 et seq.

(Nr. 70) in his very arrangement of the subject emphasizing the different approaches of Roman law and canon law. He discusses Roman law as an applicable law and challenges the views, that practically speaking, *nudum pactum* ceased to exist in Justinian's law as a consequence of the fact that the informal contracts of gift had been recognized and the availability of other actions had been extended.[41] Baldus,[42] another famous post-glossator (*Tractus de pactis,* Nr. 15),[43] as well as the Italian jurisconsults of the 15th century similarly adopted the distinction made by Roman law (*contractus vs. nudum pactum*).[44] Yet that century already saw an increasing number of question marks and exceptions; the controversy was renewed about whether *nudum pactum* really existed. Many of those who accepted the maxim of Roman law viewed it as contrary to *naturalis ratio,* and finally a claim for damages was recognized (by *actio ex dolo*) for non-fulfilment of agreement.[45] The lability of the Roman law approach was also signalled by the growing attention Italian lawyers paid to the justification of *nudum pactum* in that century. One of their explanations concerned the need for the protection of laymen, of people unexperienced in business dealings. The appearance of the *pactum geminatum* theory was related to this argument; the double or repeated contractual agreement was gradually recognized as legally relevant and enforceable because that class of transactions was less exposed to the risk of careless action. (The theory was of course covered with the cloak of Justinian's dogma: the first agreement was conceived as a *pactum* creating *naturalis obligatio,* and the second as a *constitutum.*[46] It is very characteristic that in fighting the burdensome elements of Roman law, the Italian lawyers could not but rely on the devices thereof. Their own arsenal was much too poor while Roman law was much too authoritative!)

The more and more pressing demands of expanding trade could hardly wait for the outcome of the battle between contemporary jurisprudence and the shackles of Roman law. The fact that the legally binding force of informal agreements was first recognized in commercial transaction should be considered to have been a logical rather than an accidental development. The view was already prevalent in the 14th century that the plea that an agreement between merchants had been made informaliy and hence it had not created legal obligation did not stand a chance of success before the separate commercial courts (*curia mercatorum*). Bartolus, Baldus and several other commentators held the view that the enforceability of claims arising from informal agreements followed from the

[41] Seuffert: op. cit., p. 58 et seq.
[42] Savigny: op. cit., VI, p. 208 et seq.
[43] Seuffert: op. cit., p. 60 et seq.
[44] Ibid., p. 67 et seq.
[45] Ibid., pp. 69, 71, 78, 80, 85.
[46] Ibid., pp. 75 et seq.

principle of equity (*aequitas*) before the commercial courts. Though not without controversy, this concept was adopted by Italian theory and judicial practice in the 15th century.[47] This is another proof eloquent that sooner or later, the requirements of economy and trade virtually break through the legal principles and rules that are out of tune with them. Failing other solutions, the flow of economic transactions rolls over the obstinate precepts of old on the rubber ball of equity. In addition, the "battle" of *nudum pactum* gave occasion to an interesting intellectual encounter: Thomas de Aquino's *Summa Theologica* found its "echo" in the practice of the *curia mercatorum.*

4. Hesitation of German law in the 15th and 16th centuries

The Roman law was received on German soil together with its refined system of categories of contract and its differentiation between contract and *pactum.* As Wieacker writes objectively, the whole body of the law of obligations as found in Roman sources was received, together with the highly refined casuistry of classical jurisprudence with its immeasurable reserves of timeless rationality. Since however, Roman law did not leave any room for a systematic and conceptual generalization of the theory of the law of obligations in conformity with classical jurisprudence and the form of literary presentation, the general theory of obligations and the system of the general rules of obligations remained totally unknown to ordinary law (Gemeines Recht) as they did to its medieval predecessors.[48] This is clearly shown, in connection with the absence of a general concept of contract by the devices of *Klagspiegel*, a 15th century law-book, which is of paramount importance from an acceptance viewpoint.[49]

The urban law of Freiburg (codified by Ulrich Zasius, a friend of Erasmus from Rotterdam) form 1520 is seen as the first to have spelled out the general binding force of contract on German soil: a considered promise must be kept because it is so required by *naturalis ratio.* In justifying this maxim of theoretical significance and in appealing to human nature and common

[47] Ibid., pp. 53, 59 et seq., 65, 67, 83 et seq. For a detailed account of the development of commercial law in this period, see Engellmann, Woldemar: *Die Wiedergeburt der Rechtskultur in Italien durch die wissenschaftliche Lehre,* Leipzig, 1938.

[48] *"Rezipiert wurde . . . ausnahmslos das gesamte Obligationenrecht der römischen Quellen und damit die aufs höchste verfeinerte schuldrechtliche Kasuistik der klassischen Jurisprudenz mit ihren unermeßlichen Reserven an zeitloser Rechtsvernunft. Da aber für eine systematische und begriffliche Verallgemeinerung der Theorie des Schuldrechts nach der Eigenart der klassischen Jurisprudenz und ihrer literarischen Dartstellungsform kein Raum gewesen war, so blieb auch dem Gemeinen Recht wie seinen mittelalterlichen Vorgängern eine allgemeine Theorie der obligatio und ein System des allgemeinen Schuldrechts . . . so gut wie unbekannt."* Wieacker: op. cit., p. 238.

[49] Seuffert: op. cit., p. 87 et seq., with a convincing refutation of Stintzing's authoritative opposite view.

sense, the framer of the urban law of Freiburg clearly followed the reasoning of Italian lawyers of the 15th century. He also maintained the inconsistency around the innominate contracts by recognizing the actionability of agreements only if one of the performances has been effected.[50] By so doing he practically stumbled upon the first step of theoretical significance which he had just made towards incorporation of the general actionability of agreements.

The urban law of Freiburg was far from making a breakthrough in recognizing the general binding force of contract, although its effect can undoubtedly be chiefly detected in the South German territories. Legal literature throughout the 16th century remained strongly divided between the Roman law approach and the new trend: the stubborn advocates of *nudum pactum* were contradicted with writings narrowly interpreting and even definitely attacking that principle on the basis of canon law or natural law, as well as by works expounding the general actionability of agreements on a theoretical plane.[51] The turn of the 16th and 17th centuries saw a growing number of the latter writings, but the arguments in support of Roman law did not totally disappear. Those advocating the general recognition of the legally binding force of contract based their reasoning upon canon law or natural equity or both.[52]

A similar picture presented itself in the local German law-books. The various provincial and urban laws, insofar as they contained provisions and general rules of contracts, were moving by stages and very slowly towards an awareness of the general legal relevance of contracts. It is worth noting that the acceptance of the new principle advanced southwardly, with several local laws adopting almost literally the formulations of the Freiburgian law, inclusive of the said inconsistency concerning innominate contracts. It is no less characteristic that the umbilical cord tying local laws to Roman law was not entirely cut even after the general actionability had been fully accepted in theory: the Bavarian *Landrecht* issued in 1756 was the first local law to fully and consistently adopt the principle that enforceable obligations are created by any contractual agreements.[53]

5. Triumph of Natural Law

The general spread of the idea of contract was undoubtedly fostered by the demands of time as well as the increasingly rapid expansion of trade. There was however a pervasive intellectual trend still needed, which

[50] Ibid., p. 99 et seq. About Zasius: Wolf, Erik: *Große Rechtsdenker der deutschen Geistesgeschichte,* Tübingen, 1963, p. 59 et seq. and Liebs, Detlef: *Römisches Recht,* Göttingen, 1975, p. 218 et seq.

[51] Ibid., p. 102 et seq.

[52] Ibid., p. 118 et seq.

[53] Ibid., p. 144 et seq.

equipped with sufficient scientific armour and prestige would be able to counterweight the near-mythical status of Roman law. It was a necessity in order for it to espouse and carry to triumph the idea of contract which had been in throes for long centuries by evolving an ideology to undergird it. A theory of that kind emerged in the 17th century: such influential thinkers of natural law as Grotius of Holland or Pufendorf and Thomasius of Germany clearly stated their case for the general binding force of contract.[54]

We can pay tribute to Grotius as the father of contract law in the modern era. He was the first to recognize the theoretical significance of a free and reasonable declaration of will as a fact generative of rights by itself, irrespective of form and type.[55] Thereby he laid the modern foundation for one of the basic institutions of bourgeois private law. Relying on Ulpian he stated: *". . . nihil esse tam congruum fidei humanae, quam ea quae inter eos placuerunt servare".*[56] In connection with the distinction made by Roman law between contract and pact, nominate and innominate contracts, he was still more assertive in writing this: *"At jus naturae ignorat haec discrimina: neque vero qui innominati ab illis dicuntur contractus aut minus sunt naturales aut minus antiqui: imo permutatio, quae innominatis accensetur, emtione et simplicior est et antiquior. . . Nos ergo naturam sequentes, contractus omnes diremtorios, nullo nominatorum aut innominatorum discrimine, ad tria quae diximus genera revocabimus."*[57]

Grotius and the other natural lawyers of the 17th century thus exposed and were notorious in their view which had been professed centuries before. Namely that the inactionability of informal agreements was an approach peculiar to Roman law and opposed to natural human rationality.[58] Some of the German natural lawyers including Thomasius, supported their position with arguments borrowed from canon law and German customary law. Others like Pufendorf regarded the arguments of natural law to be conclusive for substantiating the case for the general binding force of contract.[59]

It may be stated that in the end, natural law carried to fruition the general concept of contract, the idea of extending general legal recognition to agreements. This view can be regarded as having been prevalent in the 18th century.[60] The codes framed at the turn of the next century on

[54] Ibid., p. 130 et seq.

[55] Cf. Wieacker: op. cit., p. 293 et seq.; Diesselhorst, Malte: *Die Lehre des Hugo Grotius vom Versprechen,* Köln, 1959; Jörgensen, Stig: *Vertrag und Recht,* København, 1968. p. 141 et seq.: Die Lehre des Grotius vom Vertrag.

[56] Grotius, Hugo: *De iure belli ac pacis,* Liber 2, Caput XI, §I.4.

[57] Grotius: op. cit., Liber 2, Caput XII, §III.3.

[58] Cf. Seuffert: op. cit., pp. 69, 130.

[59] Cf. ibid., pp. 134, 137.

[60] Cf. Wieacker: op. cit., pp. 237 et seq., 373 et seq.; Seuffert: op. cit., p. 138 et seq.

the basis of natural law (the Prussian *Landrecht*, the *Code Civile* and the Austrian Civil Code) could already build their laws of contract on this principle although somewhat different in other aspects.[61]

Thus the idea of agreements having inherent legal effect, the first brilliant sprouts of which sprang from the consensual contracts of Roman law generally accepted on the continent, after long centuries of debate, with the aid of the theory of natural law.[62] This is the case even though their generalization was advocated by the practice of both canon law and the *curia mercatorum*, although on different theoretical grounds. Afterwards mere rearguard action followed. In France, where in the 16th century a great deal of controversy was still going on between famous jurists – those adhering to Roman law (Cujacius, Donellus and others), and those arguing on the basis of canon law for the legal recognition of informal agreements[63] –, the proposition that discrimination between contract and pact be maintained was rejected as an outmoded approach, and the theory of free use of categories came to prevail in the course of framing the *Code civil* (Art. 1134).[64] In Germany, debates continued for a considerable length of time. In 1881 it was still possible for Seuffert to write: *"Das gegenwärtige gemeine Recht ist in diesem Punkte verschieden vom römischen Recht. Es besteht allgemeine Übereinstimmung darüber, daß heutzutage jeder formlose Vertrag ein vollwirksames, klagbares Forderungsrecht zu erzeugen im Stande ist. Es ist noch nicht sehr lange her, daß dies unbestritten ist. . . . Schloßmann ("Der Vertrag") bestreitet nicht, daß im heutigen Recht das durch einen formlosen Vertrag ingegangene Versprechen erfüllt werden muß. Allerdings findet Schloßmann den Grund dieses oportet nicht in der bindenden Kraft des Willens, sondern in dem Verschulden des dem Versprechen zuwiderhandelnden, den Vertrag nicht erfüllenden Promittenten."*[65] We stress once again that the debates in the 19th century were no more than peripheric in Germany as well. The theoretical breakthrough of natural law in the 17th century had also dogmatically been elaborated by the law of obligations of *usus modernus*, cutting through both the compulsory types of contract in Justinian's law and the

[61] Cf. Charmatz, Hans: *Zur Geschichte und Konstruktion der Vertragstypen im Schuldrecht*, Brünn – Wien, 1937; reprint edition: Frankfurt/M, 1968, pp. 32 et seq., 36 et seq., 88 et seq., 149, 156.

[62] Cf. Wieacker: op. cit., pp. 229, fn12, 238; Seuffert: op. cit., p. 166 et seq.; Jörgensen: op. cit., p. 61. For the process leading to the recognition of the general binding force of contract in the German vulgar law, and for other theories concerning the origin of this principle, see Seuffert; op. cit., pp. 4 et seq., 130, 133 et seq. According to Jörgensen, the principle concerning the legally binding force of contract was generally accepted by the Scandinavian law around 1700, in the course of codification. See op. cit., p. 15.

[63] Seuffert: op. cit., p. 110 et seq.

[64] Charmatz: op. cit., p. 151. Cf. Gaudment, E. – Desbors, H. – Gaudment, J.: *Théorie générale des obligations*, Paris, 1965, p. 200 et seq.; Ripert, G. – Boulanger, J.: *Traité de droit civil*, Paris, 1958, III, p. 1285; Marty, G. – Raynaud, P.: *Droit civil*, Paris, 1962, II, p. 35.

[65] Seuffert: op. cit., p. 2, fns 2 and 3. Cf. Világhy, Miklós – Eörsi, Gyula: *Magyar polgári jog* (Hungarian Civil Law), II, 1965, p. 7; Eörsi: op. cit., pp. 130, 166.

contractual formalism of earlier German law by extending recognition to the general consentual contract.[66]

Thus although at a later period than in common law and even though with greater difficulty, the principle of the general binding force of contract was adopted on the continent as well. Where by the best legal device to ensure orderly arrangements for economic relationships had likewise been evolved in response to the demands of capitalist development. This fact reduced to its essential point, is commonly expressed along these lines: "Economic development, which turned everything into a commodity, inevitably led to the rise of the principle which gave recognition to the general binding force of contract as an abstract form. From that moment on contracts were binding not only in the various types, but all contracts, and nearly all agreements irrespective of content, became binding within the limits recognized by law."[67]

An attempt to disclose the process which "of necessity" led to the legal sanctioning of contract has been made by reviewing the evolutionary history of common law in the preceding chapter and the development of continental law in this section of our study. Our inquiry has led us down two different paths, two approaches totally different in aspects of detail, two strongly conflicting forms of legal thinking: the common law with its original "self-luminous" oddities and peculiar curiosities, and the continental private law with its unequal skirmishes with the outmoded devices produced by Roman ingenuity. And yet the final result – as regards substance, even though with notable discrepancies – was the same: general recognition of the legal relevance of economic agreements.

[66] *"Im Schuldrecht des Usus modernus wurde die Vertragstypik des justinianischen Rechts wie der Vertragsformalismus des älteren deutschen Rechts durch die Anerkennung des allgemeinen Konsensualvertrags überwunden."* Wieacker: op. cit., p. 242. Viewed differently by Eörsi: op. cit., p. 130.

[67] Világhy – Eörsi: op. cit., I, p. 210. Cf. Eörsi: op. cit., p. 40. The following assertion of Max Weber is also worth quoting: *"Das Maß der Vertragsfreiheit. . .ist natürlich Funktion in erster Linie der Marktverbreiterung. Bei vorherrschender tauschloser Eigenwirtschaft hat das Recht naturgemäß weit stärker die Funktion, durch gebietende und verbietende Sätze. . .die Rechtsverhältnisse nach aussen abzugrenzen. . . . Mit jeder Erweiterung des Markts vermehren und vervielfältigen sich die Rechtsgeschäfte. . . . Die heutige Bedeutung des Kontrakts auf dem Gebiet des wirtschaftlichen Gütererwerbs ist in erster Linie Produkt der intensiven Steigerung der Marktvergesellschaftung und der Geldverwendung."* Rechtssoziologie, Neuwied, 1960, pp. 107, 110. Weber's discussion of the substance, economic background, historical evolution, limitations and practical significance of the freedom of contract (ibid., p. 106 et seq.) lends support to András Sajó's general statement on Weber's legal sociology: "The contentions that Weber wanted to give priority to the spiritual over the economic sphere stem from the same misconception as the economism of vulgar Marxism does, against which it is really necessary to underscore the significance of the non-economic sphere. While on the priority of spheres, what we must point out is precisely the absence of any such priority in Weber's approach." See Állam- és Jogtudomány, XVII, 1974, p. 743 et seq., but compare Lukács, György: *Az ész trónfosztása* (Dethronization of Reason), Akadémiai Kiadó, Budapest, 1974, p. 467 et seq. For a full-length presentation, in a Marxist approach, of Max Weber' concept of the relationship between the economy and law, see Peschka, Vilmos: *Max Weber jogszociológiája* (The Legal Sociology of Max Weber), Akadémiai Kiadó, Budapest, 1975, p. 115 et seq.

6. The types of contract in a new role

This also entailed a change in the classical role initially played by the types of contract. The long-drawn-out period during which the law did not sanction any contracts other than those fitted into specified schemes or types (apart from *stipulatio* and later from the group of written agreements that transceded significant boundaries of types) had come to a close. Following the recognition of the general binding force of contract, when the law allowed for remedies to enforce all agreements in theory, the various types of contract assumed the basic function of orienting the parties and assisting the courts in the administration of justice. Henceforth the law simply provided models for the commonest types of economic transactions, while the rules on categories of contract served primarily to law down norms intended to make allowance for the interests of contracting parties and to ensure a proportional sharing of risks involved in transactions.[68] The rules of law serve as a guide to consideration of eventual disputes but in no way represent the only salutary avenues of legal protection. The dispositive nature of the overwhelming majority of rules on types of contract is another indication of the change in function.

That period, the turn of the 18th and 19th centuries, is the heyday of the bourgeois freedom of contract, with private initiative enjoying the widest possible recognition and support of the law. Under such circumstances, legal regulation must not inject rigidity into economic transactions by insisting on the *numerus clausus* of the types of contract recognized by the law of obligations.[69]

The predominance of commodity production brought with at a fundamental change in legal approach to private law contracts. While the legal systems of simple commodity production strictly determine and delineated the legally recognized channels of commodity and money relations, the private law of classical capitalism took economic relationships off the compulsory course marked by earlier law,[70] and in theory gave free rein to agreements in the private domain – even the Roman private law pointed far beyond its own economic conditions. Under conditions of simple commodity production, the protected spheres of commodity turnover were demarcated by legal regulation in a positive manner: the primitive laws provided protection only in a few actions, mainly of a delictual nature, available for transactions amid the strictest and even sacred formalities; the classical Roman law recognized commodity rela-

[68] Cf. Charmatz: op. cit., pp. 152 et seq.

[69] Leenen, Detlef: *Typus und Rechtsfindung*, Berlin, 1971, p. 126. Cf. Bekker, Ernst Immanuel: *System des heutigen Pandektenrechts*, II, Weimar, 1889, p. 118; Hedemann, Justus Wilhelm: *Schuldrecht des BGB*, Berlin–Leipzig, 1931, p. 214; and, in particular, Scherrer: *Die geschichtliche Entwicklung des Prinzips der Vertragsfreiheit*, 1948.

[70] Cf. Betti: op. cit., p. 275.

tions in a wide variety of types of contract and with the broad possibilities of *stipulatio.* It nevertheless squeezed them into prescribed stereotypes or subjected them to formal rigidities.[71] As against this and in its stage of free competition, the private law of capitalism, removed the excessive and burdensome barriers raised by formal rigidities and abandoned the use of compulsory types of contract. This was done in an attempt to keep commodity and money relations within bounds suited to bourgeois class interests by imposing negative bans although initially with the least possible restrictions. The rules on types of contract laid down by the private law of classical capitalism, were not yet intended to restrict private initiative and to safeguard "social interests" by complementing and specifying the general limits to the freedom of contract with respect to types. It was only some 100 years later, after the aggravation of the contradictions of capitalism, that this became a function of regulations concerning the categories of contract. A mark of that process was to be the invasion of peremptory norms into the body of rules governing contracts.

Thus the principle of freedom of contract came to prevail over the elaborate structure of the categories of contract: contracting partners were free to choose the types of contract, departing from them, mixing them, etc. as their economic purpose might require. This implied a significant change in function, even if the bulk of economic transaction continued to be handled by means of typical contracts or qualified transactions which were moulded in response to the real life[72] necessities.

The described change in the functions of types of contract is both a sign and a means of increasing the role, which becoming as it does of overriding importance in certain aspects, is allotted to the legal institution of contract in a capitalist society. Mostly in civil law, the capitalist system

[71] This basic approach of regulation is associated with the essential dogmatic specificity of precapitalist laws that "the emergence of contract and the rise of valid contract appear in the same context. By and large, the emergence of contract coincided with the rise of valid contract even in Roman law. the product of the most developed commodity-producing society previous to capitalism. Separation had been theoretically impossible until contract developed into a general fact creative of obligation. No contracts other than specified (compulsory types) had been known to any given society until commodity relations came to establish themselves. The use of compulsory types had always been coupled with the question of enforceability, even though in less rigid form, as in the post-classical Roman law. There were not any other contract than that which was legally enforceable was classified as contract. Non-detachment of valid and invalid contract from contract itself is likewise accounted for by its impress of *actio.*" See Asztalos, László: *A szerződés létrejötte és érvényessége* (Constitution and Validity of Contract), Acta Fac. XI, Budapest, 1969, p. 4. The negative, prohibitive rules of Roman law, primarily on transactions *contra bonos mores,* only lend colour to this general picture. Cf. Weiss, Emília: *A szerződés érvénytelensége a polgári jogban* (Invalidity of Contract in Civil Law), Közgazdasági és Jogi Könyvkiadó, Budapest, 1969, p. 11 et seq.

[72] A partially contrary view seems to emerge from Diósdi's article (op. cit., pp. 89 et seq., 94), as also from Betti's exposition (op. cit., pp. 256, 264 et seq., 269 et seq.). The shifts of emphasis are due, no less than to the fact that the Roman law is not compared with the private law of classical capitalism either by Betti or Diósdi.

abolishes class privileges in order to turn commodity exchange, and on the legal plane, contract into the main tools of exploitation. This accounts for what Maine calls progress from status to contract and what is formulated by Marx and Engels as substitution of privilege for law.[73]

7. As constituent elements of codified laws

The codes framed at the turn of the 18th and 19th centuries are a good reflection of the new situation and the changed function of the types of contract as they occurred with the recognition of the general binding force of contract. The fact that the Prussian *Landrecht* (1794),[74] the *Code civil* (1804)[75] and the Austrian Civil Code (1811)[76] all proceeded from the generally binding nature of agreements is perhaps due to the influence of natural law, which – with different features and to varying degrees – ultimately manifested itself as the spirit of the age acting in those works of codification. The three codes, differing so much in their underlying concepts as well as in their manners and methods of creation (as regards the total picture no less than the devices of contract law) use the same point of departure in this respect, namely abandon the distinction between *pactum* and *contractus,* generalize the actionability of innominate contracts and allot a greater role to consensuality. In one word, they opt for the general concept of contract as the benchmark. This concurrence appears strange and striking in one of the axioms of contract law at the code of enlightened patriarchal despotism,[77] the Austrian code likewise initiated from above, and the *Code civil* which is a consistently bourgeois act of legislation, keeping in content ahead of the former by a whole period of history[78] while having moved away from natural law in many aspects. If one considers that the three codes, as a whole or in part, bear the marks of different economic, social and other factors of their formulation, such concurrence can only be explained by the fact that

[73] Eörsi: op. cit., p. 64. For the motto of this chapter, a statement by H. S. Maine (perhaps the most famous words in all English juristic literature), Ancient Law, London–New York–Toronto, 1946, p. 141. Pollock offers an appropriate comment on this: ". . .that dictum should be limited to the law of property, taking that term in its widest sense as inclusive of whatever has a value measurable in exchange." Law Quarterly Review, XXI, p. 291 et seq. Max Weber's view is similar to that of Maine's; for his survey of development from "status contracts" (*Statuskontrakten)* to "special purpose contracts" (*Zweckkontrakte*"), see op. cit., p. 110 et seq.

[74] For a general appraisal, see Wieacker: op. cit., p. 333 et seq.; Eörsi: op. cit., p. 161.

[75] For a general appraisal, see Wieacker: op. cit., p. 337 et seq.; Zweigert, Konrad–Kötz, Hein: *Einführung in die Rechtsvergleichung auf dem Gebiete des Privatrechts,* I, Tübingen, 1971, p. 189 et seq.; Eörsi: op. cit., p. 161.

[76] For a general appraisal, see Wieacker: op. cit., pp. 342 et seq., 501; Zweigert – Kötz: op. cit., p. 92 et seq.; Eörsi: op. cit., p. 147. Compare also Weber: op. cit., p. 263 et seq.

[77] Engels: Anti-Dühring, Marx–Engels Werke, Band 20, Dietz Verlag, Berlin, 1962, p. 110.

[78] Eörsi: op. cit., p. 163.

without overlooking the differences in the natural law of Germany and France, the principle of the general binding force of contract had by that time come to prevalence, mostly with the help of the natural law approach. This essentially occurred in all the three countries at least as the will for codification was concerned. Of course, this in itself remains but a surface phenomenon, just as the similarity in systematization does in regard to the fact that obviously following the Justinian's institutes model, both the Prussian *Landrecht* (Part I, Titles XI, XIII and XI) and the *Code civil* (Part III, Title 2) discuss contracts as instances of acquisition of property. This does not approximate very much the two codes even in respect of their systems for the arrangement of contract law in the *Code civil,* which despite being a target of never-ending criticism from posterity,[79] is a far cry from the contractual "system" of ALR. The latter deals with partnership contract for instance under the heading of common ownership (Title XVII), regulating and systematizing contracts, even in their general aspects, primarily from the point of view of their consequences in the law of property (e.g. Titles XX and XXI).[80] Regarding to the essence, the expression of the content of the bourgeois freedom of contract, the Code of the French revolution expropriated by the bourgeoisie, towers high above the two other contemporary codes. If not for anything, the *Code civil* "is the code of the bourgeoisie which led the revolution of 1789, but confiscated its results for its own profit", while one of its guiding principles is "political and economic liberalism and individualism" – writes Julliot de la Moradiere.[81] This superiority in substance is also clearly expressed in the role assigned to the types of contract. Whereas the Austrian ABGB gives a rather detailed regulation of the categories of contract logically systematized and easy to review, the ALR injects its notorious casuistic approach even into the body of rules on contracts (Title XI consists of nearly 1200 articles, 362 dealing with sales alone), the *Code civil* covers only the major types of contract, the legal consequences of facts being governed by the most general principles only.[82] Such economy was practized by the framers of the French law as intentionally and deliberately as the casuists aimed for completeness in elaborating the Prussian monstre code.[83] The *Code civil* adopted just as the two other codes did, the major types of

[79] Charmatz: op. cit., pp. 129, fn3, 268, with French literature indicated. It is to be noted that Cambacérès' drafts did not yet include the rules on contract in the section dealing with acquisition of property (op. cit., pp. 131, 148).

[80] Eörsi's critical statement nevertheless appears to be exaggerated: "Essential progress was represented by the provision on the expansion of the free practice of trade or industry, but the contractual system – if a 'system' can be spoken of at all – was lagging far behind that of the common law." (op. cit., p. 163)

[81] Quoted by Eörsi: op. cit., p. 153.

[82] Charmatz: op. cit., p. 175, cf. p. 154 (on the basis of the preparatory material for A.C.c.).

[83] Cf. Charmatz: ibid.; Koschaker, Paul: *Europa und das römische Recht,* München – Berlin, 1953, p. 183 et seq.

contract of Roman law, but its framers – much more than those of ABGB, in particular the ALR – were aware of the fact that those types no longer served as exclusive tools for the legal enforcement of agreements as they did in Roman law, but were to be conceived merely as agents of model rules for the most common contracts which called for separate regulation in view of a particular class of interests.[84] As can be seen, the French law-makers were fully conscious of the change that had occurred in the function of the types of contract. While adopting the types at Roman law because its rules were accepted as the best and most fortunate means of expressing any given class of interests, and on the whole, respecting Roman law as a written rationality (*la raison écrite*),[85] they recognized the impossibility of squeezing rapidly expanding economic transactions a few types. By the same taken they also knew that the nominate contracts of Roman law which were almost the same as the types of contract assimilated by the *Code civil,* had been surpassed by the Roman law itself.[86] Awareness of the change in the functions of the types of contract is characterized by the fact that, once the revolutionary wave had come to a lull and the Roman law had been moulded into an acceptable shape, Cambaceres found it necessary to justify in particular the adoption of the types of contract evolved by Roman law. In his report on the third draft, he supported his arguments by the theory of *gemeines Recht* on the trichotomy[87] of *essentialia, naturalia* and *accidentalia negotii.*[88] Therefore here lies the importance of the fact that the contract rules of the *Code civil* rested mainly on Roman law as it survived in the *droit écrit* and the Digests, without any need for any significant departure from the prevailing law.[89]

The recognition of the general binding force of contract and the related change in the functions of the types of contract are reflected in the rules governing all contracts which, even in their systemic arrangements, are separated by the codes from the norms applicable to individual types of contract. The general rules on contract appear more or less consistently in all the three codes. They discuss them separately from the special provisions relating to individual contracts. This is a concomitant of the

[84] Charmatz: op. cit., p. 152 et seq., fn121.

[85] Ibid., p. 154 et seq.

[86] *"Die contractus nominati des römischen Rechts, die sich mit den Vertragstypen des Code civil fast vollständig decken, schon vom römischen Recht weit überholt waren."* Ibid., p. 153.

[87] Charmatz: op. cit., p. 151. It should be noted that classification in Roman law came in for a share criticism during the preparatory work for the *Code civil,* the argument being that it "is entirely based on external criteria". Ibid., p. 157.

[88] On the doctrine, see Dernburg, Heinrich: *Pandekten,* II, Berlin, 1888, p. 214 et seq.; Bekker: op. cit., pp. 120, 131 et seq.; Windscheid–Kipp: *Lehrbuch des Pandektenrechts,* I, p. 383. Cf. Betti: op. cit., p. 267 et seq.; Leenen: op. cit., p. 122 et seq.

[89] Cf. Charmatz: op. cit., pp. 131, 144 et seq. See also Wieacker: op. cit., p. 343. For the pervasive influence of Roman law on the rules of ALR and ABGB concerning contracts, see Charmatz: op. cit., pp. 80 et seq., 183.

surface phenomenon of systematization, a formal mirror of the change in the substance of contract law as described above.

The general concept of contract unknown to Roman law was unable to establish some sort of a separate body of general rules on contracts. This did not mean however, that the Romans had not evolved principles and rules pertaining to the general part and being applicable to all contracts as we now understand the terms. Given the nature of the contract law in which they evolved and the use of compulsory types, these generally applicable maxims of law were also spelled out in connection with the contractual disputes, mostly in rather concrete form and reflecting the case-law approach. That most of the more general rules were connected with *stipulatio,* a device of contract law which, overarching all types of contract, virtually played the general role of contract cannot be seen as having been a freak of chance. Setting of conditions and time-limits, impossibility of performance, immoral deal, error, interpretation of transactions, penalty, etc. are but a few examples mentioned at random among the questions covered by the general provisions laid down in the Digests and Institutes concerning *stipulatio*.[90] Another main source of "general part" problems in Roman law arises by sales involving incidents like agreement on essential points, setting of conditions, illicit deals, fraud, earnest, surety, transfer of risk, default in performance, warranty, consequences of subsequent impossibility, etc.[91]

Generalization; abstract thinking advanced parallel to the recognition of the general binding force of contract and received its main impulse as well from natural law. The elaboration of the general questions of contract was then completed by the science of the Pandects in Germany,[92] whereas in France the general rules on contracts were sharply separated by Domat from the provisions governing individual contracts. This dichotomy was also followed by the *Code civil* although its system was modelled on Justinian's Institutes.[93]

An attempt to give prominence to the general rules on contracts and consistently separating them from the special provisions was even made by the Prussian *Landrecht.* That attempt and in particular the dispute surrounding the question during the work of codification, deserve attention even if the final solution leaves much to be desired. What we have to point out first is that several drafters of the Code were decidedly against the casuistic approach. They wanted general provisions and were opposed to an exhaustive catalogue of rules.[94] At the same time, these codifiers favoured a comprehensive general part on contracts, aware of the im-

[90] See, in Hungarian translation, Diósdi, György (ed.): *A római jog világa* (The World of Roman Law), Budapest, 1973, p. 160 et seq.

[91] Ibid., p. 167 et seq.

[92] Wieacker: op. cit., p. 238; cf. ibid., p. 373 et seq.

[93] Charmatz: op. cit., p. 156, with relevant literature indicated. Cf. ibid., p. 149.

[94] Ibid., p. 78.

possibility to provide a normative regulation for all channels of economic relationships. They wanted to base the special provisions for individual contracts on a full-scale compilation of the general rules on contracts, and to solve the problems of mixed contracts by relying on the rules included in the general part.[95] On this point we refer to the position of two authorities. During the preparatory work of ALR (1783) von Tevenar, Prime Minister of the Province of Magdeburg and head of one of the committees for codification, wrote: "He who is unable to find the individual rule among the general principles by which to decide any particular case should not deal with legal transactions. In my view, a code cannot be expected to offer verbatim solutions for all contracts and transactions; but praise goes to a code in which the general principles necessary for decision are clearly defined with allowance for all interrelationships. Such an approach lends itself to easy solution of most problems which the exponents of casuistry are using up their minds and pens discussing about it."[96] No less interesting is the opinion of Kircheisen, another leading lawmaker, who wrote this in connection with a draft of *Landrecht:* "By working hard I have made my general title on contracts so complete and exhaustive as to avoid overlaps in the successive titles on individual contracts, and to dispense with repeating those rules that are common to all contracts".[97] (Thus it was not necessarily the competence of experts involved in the codification that determined what finally came of the Prussian *Landrecht.* It was an antipublicity work of codification for all times, a startling memorial to the casuistic approach.[98]) In the final text, a separate title (Part I, Title 5, Art. 453) following the title on declarations of will is devoted to the general aspects of contract (concept of contract, capacity to make contract, admissible objects of contract, declaration of acceptance; form, confirmation, interpretation, fulfilment, termination of contract; warranty of quality and title, involvement of third persons, etc.), not free from repetitions and overlaps. In spite of the fact that the view of those favouring a separate general part prevailed during the work of codification, and that this resulted in much shorter

[95] Ibid., p. 83 et seq.

[96] *"Wer in jedem vorkommenden besonderen Fall aus den allgemeinen Grundsätzen die individuelle Regel zur Entscheidung nicht finden kann, der muß sich mit Rechtsgeschäften nicht befassen. Man kann und muß es nach meiner Einsicht von einem Gesetzbuche nicht erwarten, daß darin alle durch mancherley Zusätze implicierte und durch einseitige Handlungen auch Verträge unendlich modifizierte Geschäfte und Verbindlichkeiten wörtlich entschieden seien; sondern ein jedes Gesetzbuch verdient Beyfall, wenn darin die allgemeinen Grundsätze zur Entscheidung deutlich bestimmt, auch vollständig vorgetragen werden. . . .Wenn die Sachenrechte in das rechte Licht gestellt werden, so erledigen sich die meisten Fragen, worüber sich die Casuisten den Kopf und Feder abnützen, von selbst."* Quoted by Charmatz: op. cit., p. 78.

[97] *"Ich habe meinen ersten Generaltitel von den Verträgen mit Fleiß so vollständig und ausführlich ausgearbeitet, damit ich bei allen künftigen Titeln über einzelne Verträge diejenigen Sätze vermeiden könnte, welche alle Verträge untereinander gemein haben."* Quoted by Charmatz: op. cit., p. 93.

[98] Eörsi: op. cit., p. 163.

rules chiefly on sale,[99] the code is often repetitive of most of the general rules on contract, mainly of those governing the contract of sale (making, formation, validity and termination of contract, causes of invalidity, etc.). It also goes so far as to create "separate general parts" (*Grundsätze*, etc.) with respect to some classes of contract. That a special provision "extends" the general rules on contract to the contract of sale (I.T., XI. T., I. Ab., § 2) is of no avail, for the rules on this contract alone contain nearly as many provisions as are the norms of the general part. Thus the general binding force of contract and the changed functions of types are expressed by the Prussian code merely *à la Landrecht* in its systematic arrangement as well.

The Austrian ABGB was more consistent in separating the general rules of contract from the provisions relating to the types of contract. (The draft code decreed by Maria Theresa (*Codex Theresianus*), although it arranged some of the general provisions under a separate chapter, did not yet develop a clear arrangement of material and included a number of norms applicable to all onerous contracts mainly among the rules governing the contract of sale.)[100] Martini's original draft of ABGB represented cosiderable progress in this direction.[101] The general chapter on contracts (*"Von Verträgen überhaupt"*) formally proclaimed the principle of freedom of contract, gave a definition of contract, and contained general provisions regulating questions like invalidity of contract, disposing capacity, setting of conditions, joint liability, etc. On the other hand, it made the arrangement of subjects more complicated by inserting a separate "general part" covering certain norms common to onerous contracts (e.g. warranty, *laesio enormis*) for the purpose of making a (somewhat overdrawn) distinction between onerous and gratuitous contracts and even by summarizing the governing principles common to contracts of use.[102] This notwithstanding, Martini's draft led to highly important results in the search for ways and means of codifying the rules on contract and marking out the planes of the general and the specific in the code. The final text of ABGB omitted the "inserted general parts"[103] and placed all of the most important common rules (including the norms for warranty and the prohibition of *laesio enormis*) among the general provisions on contract. The changed function of types of contract after the general recognition of contract and the new role allotted under these circumstances to the rules on types are candidly reflected in the opinion of Zeiller, the framer of the Austrian Civil Code: The rights and obligations generated by the different classes of contract may be easily defined on the basis of the general

[99] Cf. Charmatz: op.cit., p. 93 et seq. On the dispositive nature of contract law in the Prussian *Landrecht*, see ibid.

[100] Charmatz: op. cit., p. 55; cf. ibid., pp. 45 et seq., 70, 73.

[101] Cf. ibid., p. 183.

[102] Cf. ibid., p. 186 et seq., 189. It is to be noted that innominate onerous transactions were to have been governed by the general rules on onerous contracts.

[103] Cf. Ibid., pp. 203, 210 et seq.

principles of contract law. Still, in order to facilitate beginners' application of the rules and to strengthen their judgement, it is necessary for some nominate contracts to receive treatment in the code.[104] This statement makes it clear that the father of ABGB, similar to Tevenar whom we have quoted above, argued for a separate regulation of the types of contract practically if not for any other reason than that of making himself clear and that what he held essential was the formulation of the general principles and common rules of contract law. This is an eloquent testimony to the change which occurred in the functions of types of contract after agreements had been put under general sanction and the compulsory types of contract had been abandoned. By and large, this change in functions is expressed by the Austrian Civil Code in contrast to the Prussian *Landrecht,* which was bent on giant mania. The former only gives model dispositive rules and guidelines for the administration of law in respect to the commonest types of contract, thus fulfilling the abiding idea of Zeiller: Here, too, the great but naturally difficult art of the lawmaker consists in giving neither too little nor too much.[105]

The relationship between the general rules on contract and the norms for the typ of contract as well as the functions to be fulfilled by the two classes of rules were seen in the same way by the framers of both the *Code civil* and the Austrian Civil Code. They made conscious efforts to draw a sharp line between the general part and the rules on the types of contract, assigning to the latter a complementary role as model rules.[106] They regarded the general rules of contract as expressing nature-rightly principles and saw advantage in including a general part by contrast to the deficient system of Justinian's *Corpus iuris.*[107] They viewed the general rules (Art. 1107) on all contracts (nominate as well as innominate) as forming the basis of the whole of contract law and as being a set of provisions from which to depart was warranted in a few cases only. They invoked partly such departures, partly the special significance attached to the different types in explaining the need for the elaboration of rules on the types of contract.[108] All this goes to show that the framers of the *Code civil* wanted to have both the freedom and the restriction of economic relationship covered by the general rules of contract, and to reserve a role for the types of contract in fundamentally facilitating orientation and legal practice in the field of contractual obligations. They thus hoped to

[104] "*Auch lassen sich die bei den einzelnen Arten der Verträge vorkommenden Rechte und Verbindlichkeiten, wenn nur erst der ausdrückliche Inhalt eines geschlossenen Vertrags gegeben ist, vermittelt der allgemeinen Grundsätze des Vertragsrechts von selbst bestimmen. Um jedoch den Anfängern die Anwendung zu erleichtern und ihre Beurteilungskraft zu schärfen, sollen einige der benannten Verträge erörtert werden.*"Quoted by Charmatz: op. cit., p. 197.

[105] "*Die große, aber freilich schwere Kunst des Gesetzgebers sei auch hier, nicht zu wenig und nicht zu viel zu thun.*" Ibid., p. 199.

[106] Cf. ibid., pp. 149, 156 et seq., and the preparatory materials for codification as indicated.

[107] Ibid.

[108] Ibid

give adequate expression to the change in functions which the types of contract had undergone owing to the recognition of the general binding force of contracts. From this it follows that the rules on the types of contract are of a dispositive nature as well in the *Code civil,* and moreover, a large part of them have their role confined to interpretation of transactions or are clearly intended to provide model transactions by describing the attributes of the commonest types.[109] The framers of the Code wanted to leave the widest possible scope of freedom for the parties in the field of contracts, but relied on dispositive rules to prevent judicial arbitrariness. They indicated the line along which legal disputes are amenable to adjudication in the absence of an agreement between the parties or in cases where the content of contractual stipulations cannot be established. By laying down rules on the types of contract, the French code following the path of Roman law, sought to provide a guide to consideration of the commonest situations involving typical contractual interests in case of disputes when the agreement of the parties do not give any orientation to the judge.[110] This is a classical example of the dispositive law of contract,[111] just as it is in the Austrian ABGB. The goal of a systemic separation of the general from the special rules was not fully accomplished by the *Code civil* either. It's rules on sale for the most part covered questions (e.g. warranty) which were of more general relevance and affecting several types of contract.[112] (True, this uncertainty of systematization can also be observed in subsequent codes, the framers of which could helpfully draw upon a larger body of experience accumulated in codification.[113])

Despite the controversial issues and inconsistencies, the general part on contracts has proven to be of lasting value in both content and structure. Savigny lays special emphasis on the role of general rules on contracts with regard to the future development of the types of contract the

[109] Cf. ibid.; Villányi, László: *Kötelmi típusok. Vegyes szerződések* (Types of Contract. Mixed Contracts), in: Szladits, Károly (ed.): *Magyar Magánjog* (Hungarian Civil Law), IV, Budapest, 1942, p. 1, fn2; Nizsalovszky, op. cit., p. 525 et seq.

[110] Cf. ibid., p. 153 et seq., with preparatory materials indicated

[111] Cf. Weber: op. cit., p. 123 et seq.; Sundberg, Jacob: *The Law of Contracts,* Jurisprudential Writing in Search of Principles, Scandinavian Studies in Law, 7, 1963, p. 128.

[112] Cf. Charmatz: op. cit., p. 162, with relevant literature indicated; Ferid, Murad: *Das französische Zivilrecht,* I, Frankfurt/M–Berlin, 1971, p. 584 et seq.

[113] It will perhaps suffice to refer by an example, to the arrangement of the rules on warranty of title in BGB (cf. Charmatz: op. cit., pp. 227, 260; Leenen: op. cit., p. 163). Similarly, pertaining to the problems of separation of the general and special rules on contract but with deeper roots, are the cases in which the rule is included among the general provisions. In regard to substance, it is nevertheless a norm oriented toward the group of special provisions and formulated mostly with sale in view. This is pointed out by Emília Weiss in connection with the rules for invalidity (op. cit., p. 159), but neither is the regulation of warranty of quality free from problems in respect of contracting (Art. 311 of the Hungarian Civil Code). Dieter Medicus tries to describe, also on a general plane, how the law-maker was influenced in formulating the general rules on contract by a "subconscious" awareness of the specifics of the individual types of contract. See *Modellvorstellungen im Schuldrecht,* in: Festschrift Felgentraeger, Göttingen, 1969, p. 309 et seq.

general tenets being likely to provide an example for the regulation of newly emergent types.[114] However, there were also views in later times which insisted that an array of rules now included in the general part of the so-called law of obligations should regain their due place in the set of rules on the major and most elaborate types of contract.[115] At any rate the subsequent codes, such as the Hungarian Civil Code, followed the systemic arrangements of the *Code civil* and the Austrian ABGB in the field of contract law, setting out the general rules on contract and the special provisions on the types of contract under separate sections.

To sum up, we may state that the codes adopted at the turn of the 18th and 19th centuries were decisive to the fate of contract categories. They transplanted, as it were, the types of contract from the ordinary law, which was based on Roman law, to the capitalist private law. The types of contract which had lost their old functions in consequence of the recognition of the general binding force of contract, came to assume a new role as constitutive elements of the systems of codes. With the compulsory types abandoned, a part of the rules on the types of contract adopted from the Roman law became the core of the general norms governing contracts, and the types which thus fell into disuse and changed function were geared to carry the fabric of contract law in the system of codes. Primarily the *Code civil,* but also the Austrian ABGB are clear reflections of this change in function: the types of contract are building stones of these codes, which – with their dispositive rules and provisions concerning the interpretation of transactions and the definition of terms – were destined to serve as an orientation, in the form of assistance to the settlement of legal disputes, for the handling of economic relations streaming through the broad channels of the bourgeois freedom of contract.

The classical types of contract, which were slowly breaking up and losing their contours when removed from the husk of *actiones* in the late imperial period, had once been saved by Justinian codification, thus reaching the medieval law of the continent and surviving it. The works of codification in modern times – the first codes in the modern meaning of the term[116] – did something similar: cast the types of contract in a modern mold and give them codified sanction in the role which they assumed in the wake of the general recognition of agreements.

[114] Savigny, Friedrich Karl von: *System des heutigen römischen Rechts,* II, Berlin, 1840, p. 2; Puchta: *Pandekten,* Berlin, 1856, §218.

[115] *"Eine Reihe von Materien, die jetzt ihre Stelle im s.g. allgemeinen Theil des Obligationenrechts haben; soll der ihnen gebührende Platz im Gebiete des wichtigsten und ausgebildetesten Einzelvertrags wieder angewiesen werden."* Bechmann, August: *Der Kauf nach gemeinem Recht,* I, Erlangen, 1876, p. V.

[116] On the modern meaning of codification, see Schwarz, Andreas B.: *Rechtsgeschichte und Gegenwart,* Karlsruhe, 1960, p. 68; Eörsi: op. cit., p. 523; Varga, Csaba: *A kódex mint rendszer* (The Code as a System), Állam- és Jogtudomány, XVI, 1973, p. 277.

IV. CRISIS PHENOMENA IN THE TYPIFICATION OF CONTRACTS

"Die Funktion des Vertragsrechts ist die Vertragsgerechtigkeit, nicht mehr die Vertragsfreiheit."

1. Development toward monopoly capitalism and the classicism of the German BGB

The early 19th century codes – the *Code civil* and the Austrian ABGB – had a valid claim in assigning to the rules of contract types an auxiliary role in facilitating business transactions. Having come to life as they did at the height of classical capitalism, these codes had a social background and substance to their underlying nature-rightly concept of the freedom of contract. This is fully applicable to Napoleon's Code which was a summation of private law of a consistent bourgeois revolution, and although to a much smaller degree also holds true for the Austrian Code, which had emerged from a checkered process of capitalist development. Free competition, holding out unlimited prospects for individual and social advancement, was still forging ahead triumphantly and its other aspect with its incipient serious social conflicts was not a preoccupation of the lawmaker. It is understandable that as highlighted in the preceding chapter, the compilers of the *Code civil* and the Austrian Civil Code should have been very careful to ensure that the rules of contract categories did not impose any limitations on the freedom of contract and thus should have framed their contractual systems, which were designed to modernize the Roman law types of contract, as collections of dispositive models intended for interpretation of transactions in order to facilitate the conclusion of contracts and the settlement of contractual disputes.[1]

The 19th century witnessed the rapid growth of capitalism throughout Europe and engendered fundamental changes even in the economic and social environment of the German territories which were undergoing a

[1] Charmatz, Hans: *Zur Geschichte und Konstruktion der Vertragstypen im Schuldrecht*, Brünn – Wien, 1937; reprint: Frankfurt/M, 1968, pp. 149, 156 et seq., 203, 347 et seq.; Villányi, László: *Kötelmi típusok. Vegyes szerződések* (Types of Contract. Mixed Contracts),, in: Szladits, Károly (ed.): *Magyar Magánjog* (Hungarian Private Law), IV, Budapest, 1942, p. 1, fn2; Nizsalovszky, Endre: *Az állami vállalatok forgalmi viszonyainak új alakulásához* (New Pattern of Economic Relationships between State Enterprises), Állam- és Jogtudomány, XI, 1968, p. 525 et seq.

retarded process of bourgeois revolution. The prevailing pattern of economic activity based on the feudal system of land tenure, was being increasingly displaced by the economic superiority of industrial and commercial ventures as well as the banking business. Despite the incomplete bourgeois revolution, there emerged a national market with its legal needs. A distinctive feature of German development was that Germany like other nations of Central and Eastern Europe, arrived at the monopoly stage of capitalism after a bourgeois revolution that had not been carried to completion. Consequently, in the last part of the previous century, the law not only had to meet the requirements of capitalist growth, but also the challenges of the economic and social development of monopolistic capitalism. New class conflicts were growing with the increasing pressure of the fourth Estate, the proletariat, which came to be serious social factor instead of the contradictions reconciled by compromises between the feudal nobility and the bourgeoisie.[2] While at that time the *Code civil* was framed and the bourgeoisie had expropriated for its own benefit all the gains of the victorious revolution and had every reason to rely on the economic and social omnipotence of free competition. Additionally, due to the belated process of bourgeois development, the idea of freedom of contract was little short of premature in the Austrian ABGB and the growth of monopoly capitalism no less than the social distress of the working class in late-nineteenth-century Germany, at the time the BGB was elaborated, placed a doubt upon the law of contract. The latter derived from Roman law and permeated with nature-rightly principles which was geared to capitalism of free competition.

These social question marks were largely dismissed in the course of German codification, most conspicuously in the law of contract. The regulation of contracts, above all the system of categories followed the Pandectist scheme which was based on Roman law. This is understandable since "Pandectists of good reputation and great respect, in the first place Windscheid and then Gottlieb Planck, were the main architects of the draft legislation. These jurists carried in their baggage precious antiquities of which they could not rid themselves to the extent they ought to have done under the new conditions."[3] The result was that the contract law of the BGB, devoid of the significant changes that had taken place over nearly a century, bore a marked resemblance to the contractual system of the capitalist codes of the early part of the century, and combined the principle of freedom of contract with the auxiliary role of categorization. Though the principle of freedom of contract is not spelled out in the code itself, as it is, for instance, in the Swiss OR (Art. 19), the preamble clearly

[2] Cf. Engels, Friedrich: *Zur Wohnungsfrage,* Marx–Engels Werke, Band 18, Dietz Verlag, Berlin, 1962, p. 647.

[3] Eörsi, Gyula: *Összehasonlító polgári jog* (Comparative Civil [Private] Law), Akadémiai Kiadó, Budapest, 1979, p. 167.

states that the whole of contract law is governed by this principle, and that within the bounds of the general and special provisions of the code, the parties may be free agreement give legal force to their economic relationships.[4] The overriding emphasis on the principle of freedom of contract came under sharp criticism already in those days, with Menger criticizing it plainly from a class standpoint.[5] The conservative, outmoded categorization system drew criticism from a greater number of scholars.[6] German jurisprudence is still of the viewpoint that the BGB with its contract categories which derived mostly from Roman law, would have been inadequate to meet the needs of a modern economy. The antique origin of its solutions had less drawbacks in the field of contract law because important areas of commercial law including numerous types of contract, had been codified and thoroughly elaborated in the German General Commercial Code of 1861 and its regulations had been brought into force as all-German commercial law in most of the German states.[7] This was sufficient to accommodate the basic requirements of the capitalist economy, and the elementary interests of the capitalist class. In 1895 a new German commercial act was adopted to promote bourgeois undertakings. In that situation the dominant class could "afford", without any particular prejudice to its fundamental interests, the luxury of classicism in the codification of types of contract in private law, with a resultant memorial to Pandectism rather than a code in accord with the demands of the time. Radbruch's general value judgement on the code holds true for BGB law contract as well which is more an end-product of the 19th century than a herald of the start of the 20th.[8] Whereas, in effect, "the pandectists' views became outworn after the German national unity had been forged and capitalism had entered its monopoly stage".[9] This is why the BGB which had placed the freedom of contract concept in the centre

[4] Cf. Charmatz: op. cit., pp. 224, 226, fn13.

[5] Menger, Anton: *Das bürgerliche Recht und die besitzlosen Volksklassen,* Berlin, 1904, p. 150 et seq.

[6] Chiefly Gierke, Otto: *Der Entwurf eines bürgerlichen Gesetzbuchs und das deutsche Recht,* 1889.

[7] Esser, Josef: *Schuldrecht,* I, Karlsruhe, 1970, p. 2. The separate codification of commercial law resulted in a duplication of some contract types, in addition to that of other legal material, in all those countries where, owing to the retarded process of bourgeois revolutions, it was impossible to satisfy primarily bourgeois requirements otherwise than by way of a separete bourgeois code, as, for instance, in Austria (1863) and in Hungary (1875), beside Germany. (A different kind of pluralism took shape in France.) For a general appreciation of commercial law, see Eörsi: op. cit., p. 184. Compare also: Nizsalovszky: op. cit., p. 536 et seq.; Grosschmid, Béni: *A kereskedelmi jognak különválásáról* (On the Separation of Commercial Law), in: Zsögöd, Benő: *Magánjogi tanulmányok* (Studies in Private Law), I, Budapest, 1901, p. 721 et seq.

[8] Quoted by Zweigert, Konrad – Kötz, Hein: *Einführung in die Rechtsvergleichung auf dem Gebiete des Zivilrechts,* I, Tübingen, 1971, p. 180. For a general appreciation of the BGB, see ibid., p. 173 et seq.; Wieacker, Franz: *Privatrechtsgeschichte der Neuzeit,* Göttingen, 1967, pp. 474 et seq., 503 et seq.; Eörsi: op. cit., p. 168.

[9] Eörsi: op. cit., p. 167.

of contract law, could not become a code meeting the requirements of its time. Its nature is basically individualist and liberal capitalist, which economic growth had already rendered obsolete; and it was only exceptionally that is satisfied the typical demands of monopoly capitalism.[10]

In the BGB as well, the roots of the very types of contract reach back to the Roman law in transformation of the science of the Pandects. Just as in the Austrian code of earlier 100 years, their codification received its formulations and systematic arrangements, as expressed in the theory of *essentialia negotii,* from the *usus modernus pandectarum.*[11] Furthermore, the BGB still was "more classical" and more closely akin in many respects to Roman law. A known example of this is the contract of agency, which is defined by the German code (Art. 662) in the early 20th century in the same manner it was by the private law of the Roman society based on classical slave labour, as a gratuitous transaction. Of course, under the pressure of the requirements of modern capitalism, this would have been an absolute impossibility which the framers of the BGB also had to bear in mind. The contradiction between longing for classicism and the pressure of modern demands was therefore thought to be reconciled by extending most of the rules on gratuitous agency to the contract of service in the conduct of business (*Dienstvertrag*) and to the contract of *locatio conductio operis* (Art. 675); namely to the "non-existent" instances of onerous agency. This "hoodmanblind" is rightly called by Csanádi a "wonderful capriole" by which German jurisprudence created a gratuitous kind of agency non-existent in practice, in order to apply its rules to real agency which in turn was christened contract of *locatio conductio* operis or of service.[12]

There is, however, one essential difference between the rules of BGB on the types of contract and those of the codes framed in the early part of the 19th century: the German code was the first to lay down peremptory rules for contract categorization. This was an unmistakable manifestation of monopoly capitalist tendencies, a response to symptoms of social crisis and strain: the state and the law could no longer remain content with a general prohibition of morally offensive or usurious transactions (Art. 138), but were compelled to interfere with traditional aspects of the private sphere and to restrict the freedom of contract by formulating concrete limitative and prohibitive rules. The constrained acceptance of social change is indicated by the fact that the first draft of the BGB, similar to the codes of the turn of the 18th and 19th centuries, did not

[10] Ibid., p. 168.; cf. Zweigert – Kötz: op. cit., p. 174 et seq.

[11] Cf. Bekker, Ernst Immanuel: *System des heutigen Pandektenrechts,* II, Weimar, 1889, p. 121 et seq.; Charmatz: op. cit., pp. 10, 22, 30; Leenen, Detlef: *Typus und Rechtsfindung,* Berlin, 1971, p. 124; Wieacker: op. cit., p. 237 et seq.

[12] Csanádi, György: *A megbízási jogviszony* (The Contract of Agency), Közgazdasági és Jogi Könyvkiadó, Budapest, 1959, pp. 18, 41 et seq.

contain a single peremptory rule among the provisions relating to the types of contract.[13] By contrast, the rules for *Dienstvertrag* in the final text (Articles 617, 618, 629, 630) included peremptory norms which were later followed by others regarding leases (Art. 552/a).[14] These were the first signs of the change, which the rules of bourgeois law on the types of contract had undergone in this century, under pressure of economic and social transformations. At the end of the last century, legislation and jurisprudence were still tenaciously clinging to the omnipotence of the freedom of contract, attributing with abiding faith to the social leverage of unlimited free competition despite the appearance of monopoly capitalist tendencies and the social strains. Part of the truth is the fact that the continuance of these principles was sought not only by the BGB and not only by German jurisprudence. The statement "*qui dit contractuel dit juste*" was made by a French scholar of that same period.[15] It was the radical socio-economic development of this century that enforced considerable limitations on the freedom of contract in both public and private law and awakened the bourgeois jurisprudence to the need of taking today a more realistic approach to the strain between ideal equality before the law and economic inequality,[16] quoting Esser.

At any rate, the very appearance of peremptory rules among the provisions of BGB on the categories of contract, imparted a new character to this area of law. What had come about was firstly pointed out in Charmatz's book even though the consequences entailed by the inclusion of peremptory norms are slightly overstated in his discussion of certain aspects.[17] By explicitly stating the value judgement of the legislator the dispositive rules had added to the significance attached to the qualification of contracts as somewhat often, the essentially different legal consequences depend on the classification of a given contract into one type or another. By simply so doing, the BGB assigned different roles to, and placed greater emphasis upon the classification of contracts, than did the earlier codes in which the facts pertaining to the types of contract and the models for the interpretation of transaction entailed comparatively few and rather general consequences.[18] The application of peremptory norms gave still greater significance to the classification of contracts into cate-

[13] Cf. Charmatz: op. cit., pp. 226, 260. See also Ehrlich, Eugen: *Das zwingende und nichtzwingende Recht im Bürgerlichen Gesetzbuch für das deutsche Reich,* Jena, 1899. On the general aspects of the contractual system in the first draft, see Bekker: op. cit., p. 127 et seq.

[14] Cf. Charmatz: op. cit., p. 348 et seq.; Esser: op. cit., p. 83; Raiser, Ludwig: *Vertragsfunktion und Vertragsfreiheit,* in: Hundert Jahre Deutsches Rechtslebens, I, Karlsruhe, 1960, p. 102; Wieacker: op. cit., pp. 238, 430 et seq.

[15] Foulée: *La science sociale contemporaine,* 1880, p. 410; quoted by Esser: op. cit., p. 82.

[16] Esser: ibid.

[17] Charmatz: op. cit., VIII, pp. 226 et seq., 245, 260, 348 et seq.; cf. Villányi: idem; Nizsalovszky: idem.

[18] Cf. Charmatz: op. cit., VIII, XIV, p. 348 et seq.; Villányi: ibid.; Nizsalovszky: ibid.

gories, because the parties could no longer sidestep the intention of the legislator by a meeting of minds. The legal consequences of their transaction came to be determined by the qualification of their legal relationship instead of by their agreement. As a result of partially peremptory rules laid down for *Dienstvertrag,* the delineation of the *locatio conductio operis* contract and the labour contract for instance, became a watershed from the point of view of fundamental interests.[19] This set in motion the process which led to a reduction of the sharpening contradictions of capitalist society and led up to the restriction of the freedom of contract through a peremptory regulation of the types of contract.[20] It forced it to resort to other, more effective means of legislative intervention.[21]

Rabel and Charmatz see merit in that this change was not present to the minds of the framers of the BGB.[22] The legislators were compelled by the social forces working behind the labour contract to restrict the freedom of contract in this area by the formulation of peremptory rules. However, they failed to percieve all the implications which the play of forces conveyed for the code as a whole. Charmatz complains even on the general plane that the German code deals with the types of contract in the same way as the earlier codes did. This in spite of the BGB having created a closer relationship between the facts of types and the corresponding legal consequences, whereby the qualification of a concrete contract assumed an incomparably greater importance.[23] While there is a real substance to his criticism, he apparently gives an exaggerated evaluation of the change in the statutory definition of types of contract; a change in nature is, in our view, out of question. Leenen's position is more convincing: in spite of a closer connection between facts and legal consequences and of the appearance of peremptory rules, the BGB-rules on the types of contract should be viewed as definitions of types, and not of terms as was the case with earlier codes. His argument is supported by numerous examples taken from legal practice and illustrating analogous applications of peremptory rules with his final conclusion being that the categories of contract in the BGB are from the technical aspect of legislation real types that allow for concretization by the judge.[24]

We must agree with Charmatz, however, in that the law of obligations would have required reshaping at the time the BGB was adopted. Even

[19] Cf. Charmatz: op. cit., p. 245.

[20] Cf. Tuhr, Andreas von: *Der allgemeine Teil des deutschen bürgerlichen Rechts,* II/1, München – Leipzig, 1914, p. 177 et seq., particularly p. 181 et seq., and II/2, München – Leipzig, 1918, p. 1 et seq. Shortly after the BGB's entry into force, economic and social transformations led to similar results in the supplementary articles to the Austrian Civil Code: Dritte Teilnovelle zum ABGB, 1916; cf. Charmatz: op. cit., p. 350 et seq.

[21] Cf. Esser: op. cit., p. 82 et seq.

[22] Charmatz: op. cit., VIII, fn16.

[23] Charmatz: op. cit., p. 260. The nature of contract types in the BGB is treated somewhat differently: ibid., p. 258.

[24] Leenen: op. cit., p. 131 et seq.

though he is short on saying in which direction and for what reason chiefly.[25] Despite the disturbing ring of his social demagogy Betti's study is clearer on this point.[26] In his view, the rules on types of contract in the modern (meaning: modern bourgeois) law, should be assigned a role in supplementing the general limitations and prohibitions by contract law. He considers excessive freedom of contract to be socially damaging, and for its restriction he wishes to rely on the types of contract as media of canalization.[27] While realizing that modern business relations are hard to imagine with compulsory types of contract and that the closed system of types as it existed in Roman law is unknown to the bourgeois law,[28] he holds that legal recognition of atypical contracts is only possible with strong limitations.[29] He condemns, and indeed reproves, the individualist brand of legal liberalism[30] which had originated from the abstract ideology of the French revolution, recognized such an unlimited scope for individual will, and a blind and limitless freedom of contract.[31] If we disregard the (occasionaly fascistoid) phraseology of Betti's argumentation, we can make out a correct diagnosis from his contentions. He lucidly exposes the crisis-ridden economy and society of monopoly capitalism and states that it cannot any longer tolerate the freedom of contract in its classical form, and that statutory restrictions should be imposed on the outgrowths of this principle which are a threat to bourgeois society. The efficiency of his curative devices is a different matter (needless to say, not from the point of view of remedying the fundamental social contradictions, as even the means of law in their entirety, let alone the rules regarding the types of contract, are insufficient to meet this task), but he appears to be overestimating the role of provisions on individual contracts even in the regulation of contractual relationships. At any rate, the Italian *Codice civile* (Art. 1322) tries to bring economic relationships under its control by also restricting the scope of legal protection for innominate contracts: these are admissible only if they embody interests deserving of protection by the legal system. Thus the Italian code relied on the doctrine of *causa,* as revived by a special, objective interpretetion,[32] and on the restriction of the freedom of categorization to meet the obvious contradictions and social strains generated by the monopolistic capitalist stage of bourgeois economy and society.

[25] Charmatz: op. cit., p. 225 et seq., but compare ibid., p. 353 et seq.

[26] Betti, Emilio: *Der Typenzwang bei den römischen Rechtsgeschäften und die sogennante Typenfreiheit des heutigen Rechts,* Festschrift Wenger, I, München, 1944.

[27] Betti: op. cit., p. 273.

[28] Ibid., pp. 270 et seq. 281.

[29] Ibid., pp. 273 et seq., 280 et seq.

[30] Ibid., p. 274.

[31] Ibid., p. 280 et seq.

[32] Cf. Betti: op. cit., p. 275 et seq.

As we have seen, the BGB turned a blind eye to most of the contradictions which had undeniably come to the open by that time. The code of the 20th century became the crowning and epitome of the past century.[33] As Esser writes with apt but perhaps indulgent understanding, the framers of the BGB, having a fully liberal attitude towards the freedom of contract, found a solution to the problem of labour safety, by taking the traditional patriarchal approach rather than bearing in mind the more and more evident need to protect the social interests of the so-called Fourth Estate.[34] The mark of new times on the classical Babel tower of the types of contract, was signalled first of all by the appearance of peremptory rules, and by a more exact coordination of facts and legal consequences. On the other hand however, these changes gave rise to what may be called an entangled maze of 20th-century litigations; the problem of mixed contracts under the continental law of contract, mainly in Germany.

2. On the theory of mixed contracts

The questions of qualification and classification of contracts mingling up elements of various types did not arise, needless to say, in the practice of the BGB for the first time. It will suffice to go back to Grotius to find examples. In his famous work he makes special mention of mixed contracts, referring, amongst others, to specific cases of sale-*cum*-gift and sale-*cum*-undertaking.[35] The Prussian ALR contains concrete provisions on contracts, including mixed contracts which are not covered by special rules (1. Teil, 11. Titel, Art. 875), but the minor importance of this question is shown by the fact that it does not even receive mention in the commentaries on the code, including Dernburg's textbook.[36] It is given a somewhat more complete treatment in the Austrian ABGB and its literature. Zeiller's commentary already deals with mixed contracts, and in general terms, he finds Art. 7 to be the clue to the difficulties of legal practice in connection with them, but he refers to the problem in relation to other provisions (e.g. Art. 1159) as well. The later Austrian legal literature takes a similar view, without attaching any particular importance to the question.[37] Mixed contracts are a totally neglected area in French law. By formulating the legal consequences of the types of contract in a more general way, the *Code civil* in which casuistry is deliberately eschewed.

[33] Eörsi: op. cit., p. 162.
[34] Esser: op. cit., II, Karlsruhe, 1969, p. 140.
[35] Grotius, Hugo: *De iure belli ac pacis,* Liber 1, Caput 11, Art. 875. Cf. Charmatz: op. cit., p. 339 et seq.
[36] Cf. Charmatz: op. cit., pp. 83 et seq., 127 et seq., 263 et seq. The problem is later discussed by Dernburg: *Das bürgerliche Recht des Deutschen Reichs und Preussens,* II/2, 1899, pp. 251, 521.
[37] Cf. ibid., pp. 219 et seq., 284 et seq.

automatically allows less room for difficulties in litigation. Therefore this problem is discussed only superficially even in jurisprudence (Planiol, Gaudmet), while legal practice did not hesitate much to adopt the theory of absorption firstly and then to move increasingly towards a loose concept of combination.[38]

We can safely say, then, that the problem of mixed contracts was caused by the BGB, and the great debate that followed its forceful entry to becoming a central concern of legal practice and of theories on contract law. As previously noted there is no doubt that the qualification and delineation of contracts acquired much greater importance under the BGB approach, yet it is difficult to indicate the measure of contribution which the famously precise German jurisprudence made to this objective groundwork. The legislator specifically left the task of tackling this problem to jurisprudence (and drew criticism from Rabel and then Charmatz for that option). Indeed with its legendary thoroughness, German jurisprudence did fashion in a short time several theories on the complex of mixed contracts, and its achievements wielded considerable influence on scientific thinking and judicial practice in Hungary as well.[40] Understandably, the debates were prompted by the delineation of *Dienstvertrag* and the contract of *locatio conductio operis,* and by the regulation of their mixtures.

A full account of this complex issue would change the character and outgrow the limits of our study, yet we cannot pass over silently even if in outline. Twentieth-century contract history is not entirely without foundation. The studies on general questions of the typification of contracts are likewise, in their majority with the legal consequences, involved in the mixtures of various types as they occur in real life. Therefore as far as details are concerned, we shall confine ourselves to indicating the abundant literature available on the subject, but deem it necessary to provide a survey of the principal theoretical approaches.[41]

The debates start with the concept itself or with the conceptual framework of the problem. Nearly all authors draw a dividing line between mixed contracts by sketching different contours although the differences

[38] Cf. ibid., pp. 21, 159 et seq., 169, 175 et seq., 278 et seq. The first and still the most authoritative study on the scientific classification of contract types in the French legal literature is from the pen of Planiol: *Classification synthétique des contrats,* Revue critique de Legislation et de Jurisprudence, 1904, p. 470 et seq. In the more recent French literature, see Overstake, Jean-Francis: *Essai de classification des contrats spéciaux,* Paris, 1969, with an extensive list of sources.

[39] Ibid., pp. 227, 229 et seq.

[40] Villányi: op. cit.

[41] The main purpose of Charmatz's quoted book is to provide a survey of the problems of mixed contracts. For a full and exhaustive account of some theoretical approaches, see p. 261 et seq. (German, Austrian and French literature), Among more recent works, see Larenz, Karl: *Methodenlehre der Rechtswissenschaft,* Berlin, 1969, p. 443; *Lehrbuch des Schuldrechts,* II, München, 1968, pp. 5, 129 et seq.; Esser: op. cit., I, p. 100 et seq.; Leenen: op. cit., pp. 133 et seq., 166 et seq.; De Nova, Giorgio: *Il tipo contrattuale,* Padova, 1974, pp. 59 et seq.

are not of great moment. The mixture of collateral services that do not fit one type of contract or another is not included by Larenz,[42] for instance in the class of facts to be treated as mixed contracts, whereas others (Enneccerus and Lehmann,[43] Esser[44]) speak of *contractus mixtus* in that case as well. Again, there are a number of more or less diverging views concerning the subtypes of mixed contracts.[45] Yet there is the almost generally held view according to which all transactions which are not regulated by law in their concrete forms, but their ingredients or at least some of them are legislatively covered in connection with the different types of contract are to be classified as mixed contracts.[46]

Each of the innumerable theories on the legal classification of mixed contracts sprang from the German *Begriffsjurisprudenz* which prevailed in the early part of this century; what happened at the most was that the trend of interest-minded research (Heck,[47] Hedemann[48]) also imprinted itself on the essentially repetitious theories during the incessant debates. In terms of thrust, the proposed solutions may be bracketed in three classes, in which each concept is a variation or combination of three basic approaches.

The first concept is usually referred to as the theory of absorption. In the search for a solution to the problem of mixed contracts, judicial practice in Germany and particularly in France initially took the approach under which nothing but the performance stipulated in a single type of contract was regarded as of overriding relevance. Hence, they were subjected to the rules of the "principal type" only, with no consideration for the specifics of other types. This variation was theoretically elaborated in detail by Lotmar,[49] who without followers in science, is nevertheless held to be the last representative of the pure theory of absorption.[50]

The second approach is the theory of combination, according to which the mixed contracts carry the legal consequences statutorily established for the different types of contract. An allowance is to be made for the

[42] Larenz: *Schuldrecht*, II, p. 5.

[43] Enneccerus–Lehmann: *Recht der Schuldverhältnisse*, Tübingen, 1958, p. 395.

[44] Esser: op. cit., I, p. 102.

[45] See e.g. Hoeniger, Heinrich: *Untersuchungen zum Problem der gemischten Verträge*, I, *Die gemischten Verträge in ihren Grundformen*, Mannheim, Leipzig, 1910, p. 1 et seq.; Leonhard, Franz: *Allgemeines Schuldrecht des BGB*, München, Leipzig, 1929, p. 325 et seq.; cf. Enneccerus – Lehmann: op. cit., p. 395; Esser: op. cit., p. 102 et seq.

[46] Enneccerus – Lehmann: ibid.; Büren, Bruno von: *Schweizerisches Obligationenrecht, Besonderer Teil*, Zürich, 1972, p. 2 (mixed contracts are put in a class with atypical transactions).

[47] Heck, Philipp: *Grundriß des Schuldrechts*, Tübingen, 1929; new edition: 1959, p. 244 et seq.

[48] Hedemann, J.W.: *Schuldrecht des BGB*, Berlin – Leipzig, 1931, p. 215 et seq.; cf. *Die Flucht in die Generalklauseln. Eine Gefahr für Recht und Staat*, Tübingen, 1933, p. 66 et seq.

[49] Lotmar, Philipp: *Der Arbeitsvertrag nach dem Privatrecht des Deutschen Reiches*, I, 1902, p. 177 et seq., particularly p. 191 et seq., but compare II, 1908, pp. 671, 820 et seq. For earlier exponents of the absorption theory, see Charmatz: op. cit., p. 297 et seq.

[50] Charmatz: op. cit., p. 302.

elements of blended types. This theory was thoroughly elaborated by Hoeniger,[51] who, following the steps of Rümelin,[52] plainly rejected the theory of absorption[53] as a result of his broadly based analysis. He wanted to solve the mixture of types by a blending of their corresponding legal consequences.[54] He thought his proposition could be consistently implemented by separating the facts pertaining to different types of contract and applying the legal consequences statutorily attached to each of them. Such a catalogue of facts combined with their corresponding legal consequences, could in Hoeniger's view, be the clue to handling the problem of mixed contracts.[55] Carried to extremes and inapplicable in practice, his theory contrived in the way of thought typical of the *Begriffsjurisprudenz* was rightly criticized even by his contemporaries.

The sharpest critic of Hoeniger's ideas and the architect of the main theory on mixed contracts is Schreiber,[56] who, analyzing the applicable German law of obligations, is led to the conclusion that the essence of types of contract cannot be understood from the BGB rules on the definition of terms but only from the totality of rules on a given type. Moreover, his definitions of contracts and their concrete rules are not always in accord. Therefore the facts pertaining to types of contract are to be seen as units and should not be split into constituent elements.[57] Consequently, the application of the rules on one type of contract to another type can never be conceived of in a direct way except in the form of analogous application of law, which is to say that only the general rules on contracts may be taken into consideration. Heck terms this concept as the theory of creation.[58]

For their excesses, none of these theories met with unanimous approval either in jurisprudence or in judicial practice. Of this problem, which was treated with German overzeal, Meerscheidt-Hüllesem wrote while the debates were still going on: We have labelled mixed contracts as a problem. They will cease to have a problematical nature when we rid our-

[51] See op. cit (Fn45); *Vorstudien zum Problem der gemischten Verträge,* Freiburg, 1906; *Das Problem der gemischten Verträge,* DJZ, 1913, p. 263 et seq. For earlier exponents of the combination theory, see Charmatz: op. cit., p. 298.

[52] Rümelin, Gustav: *Dienstvertrag und Werkvertrag,* Tübingen, 1905. Not too happily, he is trying to establish the main criterion for distinguishing the two transactions from the angle of legal consequences and finds it to be in the different function of risk-taking. Cf. Leenen: op. cit., p. 151, fn12. On the other hand, he demonstrates persuasively that there is not necessarily, and in each case, a Chinese wall between types of contract and that therefore, a combination of the legal consequences attached to them cannot be ruled out where appropriate.

[53] Hoeniger: *Untersuchungen. . .,* pp. 56 et seq., 360 et seq.

[54] Ibid., p. 382 et seq.

[55] Ibid.

[56] Schreiber: *Gemischte Verträge im Reichsschuldrecht,* Jherings Jahrbücher 60, 1912, p. 106 et seq. On the critique of Hoeniger's theory, see in particular p. 203 et seq., and on its practical inapplicability p. 208.

[57] Ibid., pp. 153 et seq., 160.

[58] Schreiber: op. cit., pp. 210, 216; Heck: op. cit., p. 244.

selves of the idea that we should have a legal stereotype readily applicable to every phenomenon.[59]

It should nevertheless be acknowledged, that the debates conducted with a high degree of legal expertise, did produce significant results. This is true not only in solving problems of legal practice with respect to mixed contracts, the litter which served as a take-off point, but also in defining the nature and role of the types of contract and giving them a general appreciation.

The concept of mixed contracts was crystallized and the subtypes in this category were also clarified. The different theories proved useful benchmarks both for legal classification and for judicial qualification in formulating approaches which, if looked at flexibly rather than rigidly and viewed as a complex, judicial practice could helpfully rely upon. The common view today is that none of the theories can offer solutions for all the problems but each of them provides some fruitful ideas concerning matters of detail. It is perhaps for this reason that the various approaches have moved much closer together.[60]

Furthermore, the debate which surrounded the problem of mixed contracts may be helpful in appraising the legal regulation of types of contract in a more thorough manner. The studies on the said polemics may claim credit for having established the view, now held of the legal nature of categories, that the statutory solutions can only be viewed as legal expressions of real-life types of contract rather than legal terms that are coupled with, and entail nothing but, specified consequences.[61]

In-depth analyses made it also possible to have a fuller grasp of the contradictions which had been working between the BGB's regulation of the law of contract resting on the classical idea of freedom of contract, and on types of contract derived from Roman law, and the conflict-ridden reality of the contemporary capitalist economy and society which are impressed with monopolistic features. This was an achievement even if they perceived the controversies mostly superficially, in the domain of law, and paid little attention to, or did not even reach the point of detecting the real economic and social antagonisms.[62] The proposals drawn up for a reform of the types of contract mainly from the angle of systematization are likewise of little value.[63] On the other hand, the debates on mixed contracts and on the general aspects of types related to them are highly important because they were the first signals of social upheavals beneath the classical edifice of the bourgeois law of contract as a

[59] Meerscheidt–Hüllesem, Eduard Fr. von: *Gemischte Verträge und Verträge eigener Art,* DJZ, 1910, p. 854 et seq. For an evaluation of theories, see Charmatz: op. cit., p. 341 et seq.
[60] Cf. Leenen: op. cit., p. 169 et seq.; Charmatz: op. cit., p. 348 et seq.
[61] Ibid., cf. fn33.
[62] Cf. Schreiber: op. cit., p. 130 et seq.; Charmatz: op. cit., particularly p. 353 et seq.
[63] E.g. Planiol: op. cit.; Charmatz: op. cit., p. 355 et seq.

whole, as well as of the rifts brought about by the contradictions of monopoly capitalism in the legal structure which had been geared to the requirements of capitalism at its phase of free competition. Further they constitute the first testimony to the process of "constrained adaptation" which the bourgeois law of contract has undergone in this century.[64]

3. Elements of the classical bourgeois law of contract reappraised

This process of peculiar adaptation – a kind of readjustment of the classical contractual maxims and institutions upheld while, abandoned to the requirements raised by the social and scientific-technical revolutions – is a general feature of post-BGB developments. Our study will discuss this process of adaptation solely from the viewpoint of change occasioned by it in the function and significance of contract types. With this central purpose in mind, we shall consider only the decline of the classical concept of contract, and shall not cover numerous salient aspects of detail[65] (such as changes in the bipartite approach to contractual relationships[66] or questions of so-called factual contracts[67]).

The changes which had begun to evolve in the capitalist economy and society during the second half of the past century continued and gained rapid momentum in the present century. The tremendous growth of productive forces pried open the traditional private law approach, including the frame of the classical bourgeois law of contract. The aggravated contradictions between the forces and relations of production were working in the same direction. These processes gathered speed particularly after World War II, when the law was barely able to keep pace in some areas with socio-economic developments which were accelerated still further by the scientific-technical explosion. In both production relationships and business operations, the relentless advance of concentration in the capitalist economy weakened the foothold of the basic institutions of the classical bourgeois law of contract, were geared to the transactions of one-time

[64] Eörsi: op. cit., pp. 230, 423.

[65] For a full-length assessment of changes in the bourgeois law of contract, see Eörsi: op. cit., p. 250.

[66] Harmathy, Attila: *Felelősség a közreműködőért* (Liability for the Contributory), Közgazdasági és Jogi Könyvkiadó, Budapest, 1974, p. 109, with an abundance of pertinent literature indicated.

[67] From the voluminous literature, see in particular Haupt, G.: *Über faktische Vertragsverhältnisse,* 1941; Simitis, Spiros: *Die faktischen Vertragsverhältnisse als Ausdruck der gewandelten sozialen Funktion der Rechtsinstitute des Privatrechts,* Frankfurt/M, 1957; Larenz, Karl: *Die Begründung von Schuldverhältnissen durch sozialtypisches Verhalten*, NJW, 1956, p. 1897 et seq.; *Lehrbuch,* I, First Edition, p. 33 et seq.; Esser: op. cit., I, p. 97 et seq. Among the opponents of the doctrine, see Flume, *Werner: Rechtsgeschäft und Privatautonomie,* in: Hundert Jahre Deutsches Rechtsleben, I, Karlsruhe, 1960, p. 183 et seq.

small contractors, and caused the bells of crisis to toll.[68] All this is a sectional phenomenon of the general crisis of society which Engels described a hundred years ago in these classically concise terms: the forces of production have risen against the outgrown mode of production.[69]

There are two phenomena which deserve special mention for their relevance to the role played by the types of contract. As Eörsi writes, in the field of contracts the growth of productive forces had two results: first it led to mass production and standard contractual terms; second, and in the opposite direction, it resulted in new individual contracts involving excessive legal and technical complexities and requiring a high degree of often diverse skills.[70] Both developments often eliminate the need for the types of contract, displacing them as categories of systematization and leading not rarely to a disregard for the dispositive law of contract as a whole.

In the case of complicated individual contracts "self-regulation" is usually so complete as to cause the role of dispositive statute law to fade entirely into the background and to be confined practically to the observance or prohibitive rules that are in the nature of *jus cogens.* The classification of contracts virtually loses its relevance in this respect because the contracting partners determine most of the possible consequences of their legal relationship, and hence the classification of their agreement into one or another type has no function to fulfill in an eventual litigation. This does not, of course, mean that "self-regulation" constitutes a kind of "new law" in each case. On the contrary, in the majority of cases the parties make a contract according to the dispositive rules of applicable law, and determine the rights and obligations just as the consequences of breach of contract, by having regard to the elements of prevailing law. Yet, given the material complexity and individuality of their legal relationship, they must perforce transcend the statutory boundaries of the types of contract, to make light of the limitations of types, even if their contract is essentially a typical one. Moreover, a comprehensive or exhaustive regulation is rather often warranted by the fact that legal relationships of this kind, given the complex nature of performances and the ramification of rights and obligations, do not fit into statutory types but are mixed or are atypical in character. The consequence is the same in all cases: the types of contract – the traditional ingredients of the classical law of contract – appear to be an outdated criterion for the classification of these contracts, and are therefore not used in practice, for the develop-

[68] E.g. Batiffol, Henri: *La "crise du contrat" et sa portée,* Archives de philosophie du droit, XIII, 1968, p. 13. Scepticism about the whole of bourgeois private law is expressed by Wieacker: *Das bürgerliche Recht im Wandel der Gesellschaftsordnungen,* in: Hundert Jahre Deutsches Rechtsleben, II. Karlsruhe, 1960, p. 1 et seq., particularly p. 18.

[69] Engels: *Anti-Dühring,* Marx–Engels Werke, Band 20, Dietz Verlag, Berlin, 1962, p. 108.

[70] Eörsi: op. cit., p. 250.

ment of productive forces has outreached the bounds of legal concept and applicability signified by the categories of contract.

The second phenomenon – the standardization of contractual terms called into life by mass production – involves problems of a similar origin and legal consequences. Whereas "self-regulating" agreements have in most cases partners who in theory are in a balanced – identical or similar – position with respect to both economic strength and legal expertise, standardized contracts which carry the risk of advantage being taken of the position of the contracting partner who is economically weaker or unfamiliar with the intricacies of law. The subjects of "self-regulating" agreements are typically large enterprise, while one of the partners to a standardized contract is normally an enterprise having superior economic strength and expertise, or even a monopoly position vis-à-vis a number of isolated small consumers being in a weaker position. This peculiar situation of "legal usury" gave rise to one of the greatest problems in the modern bourgeois law of contract: standardized contracts have grown in importance so much as to become an increasingly independent field of law beside the traditional law of contract. A vast body of contract control law modifying the law of contract from without comes to overlie the law of contract in broad and important areas such as consumer protection, insurance, and anti-trust legislation.[71] This is a very typical solution devised by the modern bourgeois law of contract: enmeshing the old from the outside, upholding rather than abandoning or eliminating it, or more accurately, displacing the traditional by reducing its incidents to the category of less important contracts.

4. Standardized contracts and the types of contract ignored

The transactions covered by the generic term of standardized contracts[72] show certain slight differences between the so-called blanket contracts, and the agreements subject to general terms and conditions of

[71] Eörsi: op. cit., pp. 251, 260.

[72] From the voluminous literature, see in particular Raiser, Ludwig: *Das Recht der Allgemeinen Geschäftsbedingungen,* 1935, new edition: 1961; Weber, Wilhelm: *Die Allgemeinen Geschäftsbedingungen,* Offprint of the 11th Edition of the Staudinger Commentary, 2/1, Berlin, 1968, p. 205 et seq.; Schmidt-Salzer, Joachim: *Das Recht der Allgemeinen Geschäfts- und Versicherungsbedingungen,* 1967; Rehbinder, Manfred: *Allgemeine Geschäftsbedingungen und die Kontrolle ihres Inhalts,* Berlin, 1972; Prausnitz, O.: *The Standardization of Commercial Contracts in English and Continental Law,* London, 1937; Kessler, F.: *Contracts of Adhesion – Some Thoughts about Freedom of Contract,* Colum. L. Rev. 43, 1943, p. 629 et seq.; Hippel, Eike von: *Die Kontrolle der Vertragsfreiheit nach amerikanischem Recht,* 1963; Keller, Heinz: *Allgemeine Geschäftsbedingungen,* Eine Rechtstatsachenuntersuchung in einigen Zweigen der schweizerischen Wirtschaft, Bern, 1970; Berlioz, George: *Le contract d'adhésion,* Paris, 1973. Cf. Harmathy, Attila: *Adhesion Contracts, Model Contracts,* in: Droit Hongrois – Droit Comparé, Akadémiai Kiadó, Budapest, 1970, p. 129 et seq.; Eörsi: op. cit., p. 254.

business. In the former case the conditions are specified by a concrete agreement itself, while the general terms and conditions of business are only referred to in the contract or are otherwise built into it (are annexed thereto or the contracting party is informed of them perhaps by means of notices posted somewhere, etc.).[73] Although this is not an entirely formal difference, it may acquire legal relevance (e.g. for ascertainment of consensus), but does not affect the substance: both kinds of standardized contracts imply the possibility for the economically stronger party to impose unfavourable conditions on his contracting partner.

This is what lies at the heart of legal problems; the *raison d'être* of standardized contracts, their function under conditions of mass production, and even their significant advantages are recognized by everyone. Standardized contracts do not but provide an opportunity, a means for the economically stronger partner or one in a monopoly position to do what he could do anyway. The root of the problem is in economic superiority or preponderance in the market (expertise, etc.), with standardized contracts serving only as an aid to possible abuse of such a situation. Owing to an imbalance in economic positions, the legally recognized full freedom of choice of the weaker partner is limited to the modest alternative, if that, of "take it or leave it", which is acting as a compelling factor for compromise, or often for acceptance of a humiliating situation should the partner dictating the conditions have monopolistic power in the given area. As they are built upon economic superiority standardized contracts themselves tend to increase secondarily, the disadvantageous position of the other contracting partner by adding legal superiority, advantages of substantive law (transfer of risk, clauses limiting and excluding liability, etc.) and benefits of procedural law (stipulation of arbitration) to economic supremacy.[74]

All these phenomena provide a typical example of the contradictions emerging between the level of development of the productive forces and the social conditions of private ownership. The bourgeois private and public law are unable to meet the resultant anomalies except by their own means. (The "socialist version" of this problem will be discussed below in Section 5 of Chapter V.) The principal means of law include peremptory rules on contracts, antitrust law, and preliminary administrative control, and chiefly, judicial review of blankets and terms of business.[75]

[73] A similar distinction is established by, e.g., Esser: op. cit., I, p. 92. No differentiation is made by, e.g., Eörsi: op. cit., p. 254. For the terms used in literature, see ibid.; Stoll, Hans: *Die Gültigkeit haftungsausschließender oder haftungsbeschränkender Klauseln nach deutschem Recht,* Deutsche Landesberichte zum IX. Internationalen Kongreß für Rechtsvergleichung, Ed.: Zweigert, Konrad, Tübingen, 1974, p. 16.

[74] Weber: op. cit., p. 222 et seq., with relevant literature indicated.

[75] In addition to the works listed in fn72, see *Richterliche Kontrolle von Allgemeinen Geschäftsbedingungen,* Volume of Essays and Studies, Arbeiten zur Rechtsvergleichung, Nr. 41. Frankfurt/M – Berlin, 1968; Raiser, G.: *Die gerichtliche Kontrolle von Formularbedingungen im*

Western theories would express the effect of misuse of standardized contracts by way of twofold prejudice to the traditional law of contract: by restriction or total exclusion of the freedom of contract and by massive evasion or global dismissal of the dispositive rules of law. The two approaches are closely interrelated: restriction of the freedom of contract of the economically weaker party involves setting aside the dispositive rules of law applicable to the transaction (weighting of interests and distribution of risks); seen from the other angle, the economically superior partner excludes the application of dispositive statute law by invoking his freedom of contract, in fact by relying on his economic strength. Already Kessler wrote on this that the freedom of contract was becoming a one-sided privilege.[76] This is the case in spite of the fact, that in the general view, the contractual blankets and the terms and conditions of business (delivery, payment, credit, insurance, etc.) do not have individually any legal effect whatever, becoming normative only upon inclusion in a contractual agreement.[77] The "freedom" of agreement being what it is, the actual situation is that the dispositive rules of law are displaced by unilaterally established conditions.

Jurisprudence has from the beginning taken a rather critical approach to this process. As Raiser pointed out 50 years ago, the function of dispositive law is not at all limited to a subsidiary regulation of contractual relationships, but is of great importance in a just and practicable accommodation of the adverse interests of contracting parties; therefore he went into battle against the advancing process of the dispositive law being generally superseded by the terms and conditions of business.[78] Raiser and the entire literature in his footsteps emphasize that the dispositive rules of law express the typical interests of contracting parties, and provide a legal basis for a just qualification of a typical case signified by the pertinent facts. Consequently, general disregard for dispositive rules in the unilaterally established terms and conditions of business does not in any way serve the purposes of dispositive regulation, and the "law" created by the general terms and conditions do not in the least express the legislator's will embodied in the different types of contract. Departure

amerikanischen und deutschen Recht, 1966; Stockar, Conrad H.: *Zur Frage der richterlichen Korrektur von Standardverträgen nach schweizerischem Recht,* Basel–Stuttgart, 1971. Compare also Zweigert – Kötz: I, Tübingen, 1969, p. 11 et seq.; Jörgensen, Stig: *Vertrag und Recht,* København, 1968, p. 25 et seq. The theoretical possibility of transforming dispositive provisions into peremptory rules as a legal means against unfair contractual stipulations was also raised during the German and Swedish Lawyers' Days of 1975. See von Hoffmann's und Siehr's account, RabelsZ, 39 of 1975, p. 525 et seq.

[76] Kessler: op. cit., p. 640. Cf. Eörsi: op. cit., pp. 254 with fn. 549, 486.

[77] In addition to the works listed in fn. 72, see Esser: op. cit., I, p. 92 et seq.; Sundberg, Jacob: *The Law of Contracts,* Jurisprudential Writing in Search of Principles, Scandinavian Law Review, 7, 1963, p. 133 et seq., particularly p. 143; Jörgensen: op. cit., p. 30 et seq.

[78] Raiser, L.: op. cit., p. 293 et seq.; Weber: op. cit., p. 226 et seq.

from legislative intend expressed in the dispositive rules on the types of contract is justified only in cases where the concrete facts are essentially different from the material situation, and interests underlying a given type of contract.[79]

The problems arising from standardized contracts have riveted science's attention on the general plane of rules governing the types of contract, and on the dispositive law of contract as a whole. The role of statutory types, most of which are still covered by dispositive rules, is emphasized time and again as a legal expedient for attainment of most important economic and business goals, weighting of interests and sharing of risks.[80] At the same time mainly in the Scandinavian legal literature there are to be found critical remarks which trace the emergence of standardized contracts, among other factors to the obsoleteness of statute law, the slowness of legislation, and the rigidity of types of contract. Moreover, they see some reason for such "extra-legal legislation". Jörgensen, for instance, illustrates this by referring to the obsoleteness of the Scandinavian Purchase Act of 1907, the latter which is largely a reflection of the pattern of technical and economic conditions at the turn of century. Indeed, the sluggish and cumbersome machinery of legislation leaves scope for standardized contracts (terms and conditions of business and blankets) to "legislatively cover" newer business relationships (credit operations, contracts of lease and delivery, etc.) that are not, or not adequately, regulated by law, hence being atypical in this context, but already crystallized into a type in economic life.[81]

The Act on General Terms and Conditions of Business (AGB – Gesetz), promulgated in the Federal Republic of Germany in 1976, is nevertheless clearly intended to uphold the dispositive rules on statutory types. Under the general clause (Art. 9), terms and conditions of business restricted the role or obligations of the parties emanating from the nature of the contract from the prevalent concept concerning economic relationships, to such an extent as to jeopardize thereby the attainment of the contractual goal which shall not have any effect. This regulation is going to great lengths to satisfy the demands of legal literature to reassert the role of the dispositive law of contract, and to prevent unilateral acts under the general terms and conditions of business from displacing legislative

[79] Cf. ibid.; Enneccerus–Nippersey: *Allgemeiner Teil des Bürgerlichen Rechts*, Tübingen, 1959/1960, pp. 301, 1011; Werp, Manfred: *Die Grenzen der Abdingbarkeit dispositiven Gesetzrechts, insbesondere beim Kauf- und Werkvertrag*, München, 1969.

[80] Cf. Leenen: op. cit., p. 127 et seq.; Larenz, Karl: *Allgemeiner Teil des deutschen bürgerlichen Rechts*, München, 1967, p. 26 Esser: op. cit., p. 96 et seq. The role of dispositive contract law is already discussed in similar depth by Weber, Max: *Rechtssoziologie*, Neuwied, 1960, p. 123 et seq.

[81] Jörgensen: op. cit., pp. 21 et seq., 45, 103. Supported by the example of the BGB-rules on *locatio conductio operis*, a similar view is taken by Leenen: op. cit., p. 164.

weighting of interests and value judgements from entire sectors of economic life.[82]

As can be seen, the battle is going on between the new "law" of standardized contracts and the traditional dispositive regulation of the types of contract. This with certain capitalist laws attempting with the West-German more vigorously and the Anglo-Saxon more cautiously, to arrest the tendency to supersede the applicable law, a process that can hardly be halted by legal means.

With the spread of standardized contracts, the role of types of contract is perforce diminishing. Therefore the trend is in its effect, similar to that indicated in connection with complicated "self-regulating" contracts concluded for individual performance. However, there are essential differences between the two phenomena. Without retreating here to what is not a negligible aspect, namely that "self-regulating" contracts leave less room for misuse of economic superiority, we state only that these differences are of a sociological character. In the case of "self-regulating" contracts. the problem is one of primary contradiction between the level of development of the productive forces, and the possibility for legal regulation, amounting to a kind of time lag between traditional legal stereotypes (types of contract in our case) and modern technology with an advanced pattern of business dealings. We might as well say that what we have is a modern version of an ancient problem – the traditional inertia of law, the limitations *an sich* of legal regulation – which in the age of the scientific-technical revolution manifests itself more frequently and more sharply than in earlier history.[83]

By contrast, the problems associated with standardized contracts are but reflected, at best expressed in a more accentuated way, in the law, for they are a manifestation of a contradiction between the forces and relations of production which in the domain of law reveals itself on the secondary plane. As has been noted, the legal problems involved in standardized contracts are rooted in the immense contradiction between the modern forces of production, and the private expropriation of the results of production. This is why they are being tackled so hopelessly, albeit with a high level of legal competence, and often with respectable courage by the bourgeois private law of private property. This dilemma is well illustrated by a statement in the commentary on the Uniform Commercial Code of the United States to the effect that legal protection from standardized contracts seeks to prevent oppression and unfair surprise, not to disturb transfer of risk resulting from the superior strength of business. As

[82] *Schweizerische Juristen Zeitung,* 70 of 1974, p. 216. On the search of Scandinavian law for ways of defence, see Jörgensen: op. cit., p. 27 et seq.

[83] The social "sensitivity" of law is discussed in general terms and in a different sense by Szabó, Imre: *A jogelmélet alapjai* (The Fundamentals of Legal Theory), Akadémiai Kiadó, Budapest, 1971, p. 168 et seq.

Eörsi aptly put it, superior force must be given way, with restrictions placed on extraordinary actions only.[84] The bourgeois private law is unable to break the mould in which it was cast by the social relations of private expropriation, so it cannot fully resolve the contradictions between the development of productive forces and the capitalist character of production relations. Nor can it eliminate by this same token, the possibility for misuse of economic superiority. Consequently, the problem of standardized contracts, being a secondary phenomenon in the sphere of law by reason of its origin, is not susceptible of complete solution by legal means. For a solution to be found to this problem, it is necessary to uproot the contradiction itself, to eliminate the conflict between productive forces and private expropriation, that is to abolish the private ownership of productive forces. (On the other hand, as socialist practice has also shown, socialism cannot offer an "automatic solution" either, but further efforts are called for.)

This does not of course mean that the bourgeois law has not achieved significant results in restricting or suppressing abuse of blanket contracts, and of the general terms and conditions of business. Bourgeois private law is seeking adaptation to the new pattern of conditions in this field as well. In Eörsi's terms, it is in the process of "forced adaptation".[85] Expression of the new requirements in the old law (e.g. restriction of the principle of freedom of contract by the general clause of *Treu und Glauben* in the West-German law)[86] or perhaps adoption of new restrictive regulations (e.g. the said West-German Act) is, however, but one method of such adaptation. A special form of legal adaptation to the development of the forces and relations of production is well exemplified, precisely in respect of standardized contracts, by a "relegation of the law to the peripheries", namely the said phenomenon of setting aside the dispositive rules on the types of contract, and this in a legal way, under the shield of the freedom of contract. "The third device of active adaptation is to exile the applicable law to the peripheries by means of commercial usages, contract forms and adhesion contracts which substitute the parties' contract law for statutory or case law."[87] Therefore it may be said, that rather often the role of types of contract ceases or at least slips far into the background in the field of standardized contracts, as it does in the case of complicated "self-regulating" contracts concluded for individual performance. Both cases imply inevitable loss of ground by the classical bourgeois law of contract owing to the accelerated development of productive forces, and to the contradictions between productive forces and the capitalist relations of production.

[84] Eörsi: op. cit., p. 256, with quotation from the commentary.
[85] Eörsi: op. cit., p. 423.
[86] Esser: op. cit., I, p. 95 et seq., with examples taken from the West-German judicial practice.
[87] Eörsi: op. cit., pp. 26, 486.

5. An alarm bell or a death knell?

It is small wonder that the economic and social transformations which in this century have radically undermined the classical bourgeois law of contract, depriving of substance its principles and institutions in broad areas, have caused the classification of contracts to be underrated in theory as well. The "off-season sale" of the classical armoury started with a reappraisal of the root idea, the principle of freedom of contract. This is why we have chosen the following statement to be the motto of the present chapter: "the function of contract law – as has been recognized by Ludwig Raiser – is . . . the contractual justice. This is a principle – no longer the freedom of contract – which today expresses the material function of contract law throughout the world. . . The modern task is to work out criteria and procedures for contractual justice, which it is necessary to develop precisely because the freedom of contract does not exist in reality."[88]

Attempts to bring new light to bear on the types of contract, and to define their functions can be discerned mainly in the Scandinavian jurisprudence. This is no accident if one considers that the Nordic laws, which once originated from continental (chiefly German) roots, have for quite a few decades now received impetus for further development and renewal from the Anglo-Saxon systems of law (mainly from the laws of the United States).[89] That is from laws which as presented at length in Chapter II, have evaded throughout their development, the continental categorization of contracts stemming from Roman law.

Naturally, criticisms have been levelled at the classical edifice of the contract types, shaken at times in its very fundamentals, in other countries and at earlier periods as well. In his monography on mixed contracts, Hoeniger termed the statutory categories as trammels, as fetters on the proper and adequate application of law, and therefore he made it a task of jurisprudence to split up the types and break them into their elements.[90] Rigid application of the types of contract was censured by Artur Meszlény in connection with the special status of the so-called independent agent: "From day to day life produces forms that fit no category other than agency, yet their very nature rules out the operation of its governing

[88] *"Die Funktion des Vertragsrechts ist. . . – wie Ludwig Raiser erkannt hat – die 'Vertragsgerechtigkeit'. Sie – nicht mehr die Vertragsfreiheit – ist heute in aller Welt das materiale Funktionsprinzip des Vertragsrechts. . . . Die moderne Aufgabe liegt darin, Kriterien und Verfahren für die Vertragsgerechtigkeit zu entwickeln, die herzustellen gerade deshalb nötig ist, weil es eine Vertragsfreiheit in Wahrheit nicht gibt."* Zweigert–Kötz: op. cit., II, pp. 7, 10, and (on the freedom of contract and its utopian nature) 8 et seq. Cf. Esser: op. cit., I, p. 82.

[89] Cf. Eörsi, Gyula: *A skandináv jogról és jogtudományról* (On Scandinavian Law and Jurisprudence), published by the Institute for Legal and Administrative Sciences of the Hungarian Academy of Sciences, Budapest, 1974, p. 9.

[90] Hoeniger: *Untersuchungen. . .* (see fn.45), p. 384 et seq.

principles."[91] In several parts of his book Charmatz points out that both German and French jurisprudence extensively disputes the existing system of categories questioning the earlier concept of its "perenniality", and calling for a law of obligations fitted to modern economic and social requirements.[92]

Nevertheless, overall criticisms of contract types are to be found chiefly in the Scandinavian literature of the past few decades. These differ from previous ones not only in questioning the modernity of classical categorization, and at times even its *raison d'être* under present-day circumstances, but also in outlining positive counter-proposals, theoretical approaches that are supported or perhaps even borne out by business practice. A higher degree of practicality is a general feature of the way they handle the problems discussed. Jörgensen says that in the most recent Scandinavian theory, the terms of legal transaction and declaration of will, are no longer used but are replaced by dispositive declaration. His emphasis is placed on legal consequences irrespective of whether there is a case of oral pronouncement, symbolic act, action or omission. When a conduct usually entailing a definite set of legal consequences is displayed, the typical legal consequences attached to it will normally ensue.[93] Olivercrona's view is similar in both substance and "theoretical inadequacy": the making of a contract may be likened to pushing a button and getting a box. This "box" contains not only the will of the parties but lots of other things; something that flows from type of contract, and something that the parties or one of them did not want (e.g. a term is construed by objective judicial interpretation to mean something else than the parties or one of them meant by it). Thus the reality of the contract is not in accord with the concordant declarations of will: what came out on pushing the button was not an entirely individual "box", but a standard box most fully in keeping with the intention of the parties. Therefore the court will also have primary consideration for the intention of the parties, and for the model corresponding to it with its foremost aim being to identify the contract with a known model, or if it fails, to establish a new model.[94] Eörsi adds that what is involved here is no mere pragmatism, for the "boxes" have a common material incident: the sharing of risk.[95]

[91] Meszlény, Artur: *Az önálló megbízott* (The Independent Agent), Jogtudományi Közlöny, No. 24 of 1920, No. 1 of 1921. Cf. Csanádi: op. cit., p. 102 et seq.

[92] Charmatz: op. cit., VIII, p. 22 et seq.

[93] *"In der neuesten skandinavischen Theorie spricht man auch nicht mehr von Rechtsgeschäften und Willenserklärungen, sondern von dispositiven Erklärungen. Man legt den Hauptwert auf die Rechtswirkungen der Erklärung ohne Rücksicht darauf, ob sie sprachliche Äusserungen, Symbole, Handlungen oder Unterlassen sind. . . . Wenn ein Verhalten, das gewöhnlich mit einem gewissen Komplex von Rechtswirkungen verbunden ist, beobachtet wird, so treten diese typischen Rechtswirkungen normal auch ein."* Jörgensen: op. cit., p. 40 et seq.

[94] On this argumentation, see Eörsi: *A skandináv jogról és jogtudományról* (On Scandinavian Law and Jurisprudence), p. 44 et seq.

[95] Eörsi: ibid., p. 46. Cf. Jörgensen: op. cit., p. 45.

No doubt that these concepts are more oriented towards real practice, than are concerned with, or for the time being, capable of furnishing a comprehensive theory based on an elaborated terminology. As is also indicated by Jörgensen's statements cited above, it is not easy to break away from the traditional, pandectist categories either. Olivecrona's model theory is more clearly illustrative of the direction in which judicial practice is going beyond the bounds of contract types: with the aid of categories smaller in dimension and closer to life.[96] In his clausal law approach, worked out as a supplement to the classical typification of contracts, Sundberg finds that the traditional types of contract are insufficient, primarily for giving a legal definition of the new pattern of economic relationships, as is the cumbersome and slow procedure of statutory categorization in general. The "clausal law", a term he practically uses to denote standardized contracts in the widest possible sense,[97] serves to help business dealings and legal practice over the "lacunas of law" which the rigidity of the classical types of contract, and the decades of delay in legislation have created for rapidly growing modern economic relationships and newly emergent kinds of transactions. It is in this sense that Sundberg terms his "clausal law" as being in the nature of *praeter legem* which will be an aid – perhaps temporarily, until a new legislation is adopted – to the law of the "classical school", namely the categorization of contracts, for "the classical school has little to offer. Only by pursuing conceptualistic methods, like subsuming the new phenomenon under a pre-existing contract type and thereby bringing all the legal consequences attached to that concept to apply, can the school lay down law in the classical sense.[98] Sundberg claims that the "clausal law" is a contribution to the traditional law, based on the categorization of contracts in dealing with certain transactions of international trade, in addition to a legal apprehension of new phenomena. This is facilitated by the identical formulation of certain stipulations in the business terms and conditions of numerous countries, e.g. in the ticket contracts of international air line companies.[99]

A striking feature common to Olivercrona's model theory, Sundberg's clausal law approach and the other Scandinavian attempts at surpassing the traditional rigid categorization of contracts, lies in emphatically asserted, conscious, and occasionally forceful efforts to avoid the continental method of systematization and definition of terms. The latter being burdened with the legacy of the science of the Pandects. Despite

[96] Cf. ibid.

[97] "Clausal law as a term is hereby adopted to signify those rules which are created by the contract and derive their force from the validity of the contract, and which set aside the law of the cases and the governmental legislation unless it is in cogens." Sundberg: op. cit., p. 129.

[98] Ibid., pp. 130 et seq., 149.

[99] Ibid., p. 131 et seq.

their exaggerations, these endeavours can be credited with a great deal of realistic elements adequate to meet modern requirements. They reveal in the first place the profound contradiction existing between the basically static nature of statutory typification, and the continual dynamism of the facts of life; a contradiction which had been recognized centuries before, but had not become aggravated until the economic, scientific, technical and social developments of the 20th century came into play.[100] Despite their valid criticism of the classical typification of contracts, and their flexible approach to the new social relations, the aforementioned concepts cannot be viewed as an alternative to the law of contract based on categories. Nor do their authors intend them to serve that purpose. It is markedly stressed by Sundberg that "the clausal law approach. . . is not meant to replace the Classical School. Its function is to supplement this school in the areas where the latter is unable to achieve results.[101] Jörgensen for his part deems it necessary to uphold the types of contract in order to ensure the stability and lucidity of law, although he believes this need can also be met by uniform contractual terms and by standard contracts. (He supports his position with a brief survey of the continental and Anglo-Saxon laws of contract.[102])

The foregoing shows that the category of contract types, along with other institutions of the traditional private law dogmatics, has eroded, and their functions and significance thrown into doubt by the economic and social transformations and the achievements of legal development during the past 100 years. This notwithstanding, it would seem unwise to be led by the said developments and critical remarks to the conclusion that the categorization of contracts is a fundamentally and totally outmoded approach to the legal expression of commodity relations. The said events marking the transformations of capitalist economic and social relations and the changes in the bourgeois private law, as well as a realistic evaluation of the theoretical criticisms incurred by the typification of contracts, should constrain us only from an overestimation of the role of contract types, not from the application of these categories. We can definitely agree with these criticisms in that the categories of contract must not be conceived of as means for the legal systematization of economic and social relations, which are in a state of constant development and flux, as a Procrustean bed of commodity relations. Neither must they be rejected as adequate elements of systematization, both in law (mainly codification) and in education, and as points of departure for legal certainty and for legal practice following continental traditions, as guides to the courts. In brief,

[100] Cf. ibid., p. 144. For a general analysis of the problem ("the adaptation of the necessarily rigid law to the socio-economic environment"), see Eörsi: op. cit., p. 413.

[101] Sundberg: op. cit., p. 149.

[102] Jörgensen: op. cit., p. 21, cf. pp. 15 et seq., 45 et seq. Compare also Betti: op. cit., p. 282.

there is a need to abandon outmoded schematism, together with rigidities tending to hamstring economic transactions as well as sound legal practice. These are attributes of all continental laws in the use of contract types. Their undue outgrowths and trammels should be thrown overboard without however discarding the idea of typification itself. Accordingly we think that the critical voices we have referred to, should be regarded not as a death knell of contract types, but as an alarm bell signalling real facts to be heeded by jurisprudence and legislation alike. Without taking a short cut to our inquiries in the next chapter, we feel we may on this score anticipate the statement that a realistic assessment of categorization as discussed above will offer fruitful lessons to act upon in undertaking a gradual reappraisal, *mutatis mutandis,* of the dogmatics and the system of the socialist law of contract as well.

V. PUBLIC PROPERTY AND THE CONTRACTUAL SYSTEM

"Our present-day conditions in Hungary have given rise to a contradiction – one between connective public property and separative commodity production."

---

1. Introduction

The contract laws of the first civil codes of the European socialist countries do not differ too widely, either in structure or in dogmatic approach, from the traditions of continental bourgeois laws: their point of departure is the general binding force of contract[1], and their structural pillars are the traditional types of contract[2] governed for the most part by dispositive rules. This structural affinity of the contractual systems is a striking feature of the bourgeois codes of private law and of the first socialist civil codes. Smaller differences can only be observed in the scope of regulated contract types, but most of them derive neither from the dissimilarity of social systems nor from the profound disparity in the property patterns. This is further proved by the fact that similar differences are also revealed by comparisons of both bourgeois and socialist codes.

Of course, the said structural similarities are merely formal in character, just as the considerable points of affinity or congruence found in the rules of bourgeois, and socialist contract laws are no more than superficial aspects. In his study on the comparability of the socialist and bourgeois laws of contract, Knapp is right in stressing that the contracts of both legal systems, wrapped though they are in similar cloaks, embody and serve to realize different economic goals, even in relationships between private persons.[3] The same is underscored by Ernő György: "The social function of legal institutions is thrown into sharp relief particularly by the changes taking place in the law of onerous contracts in the people's democratic

[1] E.g. the Soviet-Russian Civil Code of 1922, Art. 130; The Bulgarian Act of 1951 on the Law of Contract, Art. 9; The Hungarian Civil Code of 1959, Articles 198 and 200.

[2] E.g. The Soviet-Russian Civil Code of 1922, Art. 180 et seq.; the Bulgarian Act of 1951 on the Law of Contract, Art. 183 et seq.; the Hungarian Civil Code of 1959, Art. 365 et seq.

[3] Knapp, Viktor: *Verträge im Tschechoslowakischen Recht.* Ein Beitrag zur Rechtsvergleichung zwischen Ländern mit verschiedener Gesellschaftsordnung. RabelsZ. 27, 1961/62, p. 494 et seq. Cf. Graue, E. D.: *Vertragsschluß durch Konsens?* In: Rechtsgeltung und Konsens, Berlin, 1976, p. 120.

countries. . . The close relationship of contract types to the prevailing socio-economic conditions is brought out in strong relief by the deeply penetrating changes that have occurred in the character and content of legal institutions formally appearing to be identical. . .; old forms are filled with new contents."[4]

The formal or systemic affinity between the bourgeois and socialist laws of contract is nevertheless in need of some explanation. What are the underlying causes and factors of such superficial similarity? They are to seek on several planes.

In the first place, mention should be made of the existence of commodity relations as the root cause and of traditions as a surface phenomenon. The persistence of commodity relations as the ultimate determinant will be discussed at a later stage. Here we shall deal only with the other factors.

In spite of the tremendous revolutionary upheavals and epoch-making transformations, the hold of traditions was strongly felt both on the first socialist codes – the Soviet-Russian civil code of 1922 and those of the Soviet Republics assimilating it[5] – and on the early civil-law legislations of the people's democratic countries that had emerged after World War II. The action of other factors, varying somewhat by countries, was likewise noticeable.

The Soviet laws of 1923 were adopted under conditions of the New Economic Policy in the wake of war communism, when the system of a planned socialist economy was still in the making,[6] while market conditions and commodity relationships received renewed emphasis in commercial transactions with small-commodity producing peasant farms. Those factors provided an objective basis for the survival of the traditions of the contract law of bourgeois codes, and were coupled with a subjective one, namely the conception of Soviet legal theory which dominant in the late 1920's found its fullest reflection in the works of Pasukanis. At that time he explained the existence of law by the persistence of commodity relations, which in turn were in the accepted view of economic sciences survivals from the overthrown bourgeois order. This led him to the con

[4] György, Ernő: *A szerződések jogi szabályozásának átalakulása a népi demokráciában* (Transformation of the Legal Regulation of Contracts in the People' Democracy), Közgazdasági és Jogi Könyvkiadó, Budapest, 1958, p. 5; on a substantive discussion concerning the contracts of private persons and socialist organizations, see p. 153 et seq.; concerning transactions between citizens, see p. 189 et seq.; concerning problems with traditional dogmatics and terminology, see pp. 107, 133 et seq.

[5] For the text of the Soviet-Russian Civil Code of 1922 as well as the texts of the Ukrainian, Byelorussian, Uzbek, Grusian, Azerbaijan, Tadzhik, Armenian and Turkmenian codes, which follow the former almost word for word, see Novitsky, I.B. (ed.): *Grazhdanskoe zakonodatelstvo SSSR i soyuznykh respublik*, Moscow, 1957, p. 178 et seq.

[6] For similar arguments in another context, see Eörsi, Gyula: *A gazdaságirányítás új rendszerére áttérés jogáról* (On the Law of Transition to the New System of Economic Management), Közgazdasági és Jogi Könyvkiadó, Budapest, 1968, p. 124.

clusion that law as a whole is bourgeois in nature, and sharing the fate of commodity relations will not be too long in withering away, and giving way to fundamentally different rules to govern the socialist pattern of economic relations.[7] Given that general conception of legal theory, it is by no means surprising that the system of contract law at the civil law of the new Soviet republics stopped, similarly to the bourgeois codes of private law on the continent, at the principle of recognizing the general binding force of contract and at the function performed by the traditional qualified types of contract in facilitating economic transactions.[8]

When the early codified laws of the people's democratic countries (the Czechoslovak Civil Code of 1950 and the Bulgarian Act of 1951 on the Law of Obligations) were adopted, the small-commodity producing private farms were still playing a significant role. The contractual relatinoships of the national economies were in a state of flux, a factor which did not allow for lasting regulation by the law.[9]

The existence of small-commodity producing peasant farms was likewise of significance for the adoption of the Hungarian Civil Code (1959). As has subsequently been pointed out by many writers,[10] this accounted for the fact that the contract law of the code was geared basically to economic transactions between private persons, to economic relationships based on small-commodity producing private property and on personal property. The Hungarian code (in its original form from 1959) nevertheless made a great stride forward by laying down, after a thorough scientific preparation, a set of general rules (Chapter XXXV on Plan Contracts) to govern contractual relationships between socialist economic organizations under the system of direct economic management based on disaggregation

[7] Pasukanis, E.B.: *La théorie générale du droit et marxisme,* Paris, 1970, particularly p. 90 et seq.; German edition: Allgemeine Rechtslehre und Marxismus, Wien – Berlin, 1929, p. 34 et seq.; cf. Világhy, Miklós – Eörsi, Gyula: *Magyar polgári jog* (Hungarian Civil Law), I, Tankönyvkiadó, Budapest, 1962, p. 19; Szabó, Imre: *A jogelmélet alapjai* (The Fundamentals of Legal Theory), Akadémiai Kiadó, Budapest, 1971, p. 65.

[8] The Soviet-Russian Civil Code of 1922, Articles 130, 180 et seq.

[9] Cf. Eörsi: ibid.

[10] Csanádi, György: *A szerződési rendszer továbbfejlődésének problémái* (Problems of the Further Development of the Contractual System), in: Eörsi – Szilbereky (ed.): Jogi kérdések az új gazdaságirányítás köréből (Legal Questions of the New System of Economic Management), Közgazdasági és Jogi Könyvkiadó, Budapest, 1967, p. 26; Eörsi: op. cit., p. 129 et seq.; Harmathy, Attila: *A szerződéses rendszer típusproblémáiról* (On the Type-Problems of the Contractual System), in: *Jelentés a szerződések rendszerének vizsgálatáról* (Report on Research into the Contractual System), Manuscript, MTA Állam- és Jogtudományi Intézete, Budapest, 1970, p. 95. For the rules on civil society, see Világhy, Miklós: *Az egyesülésről* (On Association), Jogtudományi Közlöny, XXII of 1967, p. 512 et seq. On the dichotomy of contract laws after the consolidation of socialist power, cf. Eörsi, Gyula: *Comparative Civil (Private) Law,* Akadémiai Kiadó, Budapest, 1979, p. 481 et seq. For a summary account of contract law in the Hungarian code, see Kemenes, Béla: *A szerződések szabályozásának elvi kérdései a Polgári Törvénykönyvben* (Theoretical Questions concerning the Regulation of Contracts in the Civil Code), Acta Juridica et Politica Universitatis Szegediensis XIII, 1961, F.I.

of national plans.[11] That solution had some relevance beyond the actual needs of direct economic management in blocking a line of development toward an entirely different regulation of contracts between socialist organizations, in complete separation from transactions of private persons and without regard to the degree of justified differences in coverage. Such an approach made it possible for the applicability of some of the new, more up-to-date rules on national economic contracts to be extended to the entire contractual system of the civil code, or at least did not prevent the spread effect of certain modern principles to the rules governing contracts of private persons. In addition, this relative intra-code separation, with scope left for diffusion of regulative influence to other areas, largely facilitated the effort made after the indirect methods of economic management had come to prevalence, to bring into closer conformity the rules on contracts in the two areas of contract law: socialist organizations and private persons. This notwithstanding, if viewed in a "historical" retrospect of some 15 years, the contract law of the Hungarian Civil Code may be said to have reflected a transitory pattern of economic and social relations which characterized Hungary at the turn of the 1950's and the 1960's, in the period of the socialist reorganization of small-commodity producing peasant farms. The chapter on plan contracts established but a minimum linkage with national economic contracts that were governed by rules other than those of the Code. This was due largely to the prevailing system of economic management based on plan breakdowns: the use of compulsory types of contract, peremptory regulation, and the preponderance of administrative provisions all drew a dividing line between the substantive elements of the formally incorporated chapter on plan contracts and the other body of rules in the contract law of the Code. Eörsi rightly stated at the time of the reform of the economic mechanism: "The chapter on plan contracts is a separate body in the Civil Code. The compulsory use of types excluded socialist organizations from a whole range of contracts and did not allow them to rely on a series of other institutions (assignment, respite, set-off, etc.)."[12] As we see it today, the incorporation in the Code of the rules on contracts between socialist organizations has been borne out by subsequent developments, by the consequences of the change in the system of economic management, rather than by the pattern of conditions prevailing at the time the Civil Code was adopted. We shall come back to this point later.

The socialist civil codes of the 1960's, mainly those of the Soviet Union, were based on a different pattern of economic and social conditions and on a larger body of experience gained in codification. This was

[11] Eörsi, Gyula: *A tervszerződések* (Plan Contracts), Akadémiai Kiadó, Budapest, 1957, p. 672; on the transformation of the substance of traditional contract law, see p. 55 et seq.

[12] Eörsi: op. cit., p. 129, fn6.

true especially in the field of legal regulation regarding contractual relationships between socialist organizations. Among the codes of that period the Soviet Bases of Civil Legislation (1961) and the codes of the federated republics grafted onto them, as well as the Polish Civil Code (1964) covered the fundamental aspects of contractual relationships both in the socialist sector and between private persons, whereas Czechoslovakia adopted two separate codes: the Civil Code (1964) to govern contracts of citizens and the Economic Code (1964) to govern the so-called economic contracts in the sphere of the national economy. The legislation of the German Democratic Republic similarly follows the approach of separation under economic law: the Civil Code (ZGB), which took effect on 1 January 1976, and is applicable to the contractual relationships of citizens established with socialist economic organizations (*Betriebe*) and *inter se,* and is marked by noteworthy innovations in respect of systemic arrangement and of substance.

As regards the contractual system, the Soviet and Polish legislations which adopted the concept of a unified civil law and progressed mainly by a more complete integration of the general rules on national economic contracts, by a weighted regulation more in keeping with the economic significance of this field of law. Although both the Polish Civil Code and the Soviet civil codes of the 1960's were geared to a system of economic management based on compulsory plan instructions, and that their administrative elements concerning the strict breakdown of plans erected a wall between the sets of rules on the contractual relationships of private persons and socialist organizations, as the Hungarian solution did, they were more successful than the Hungarian code in achieving a systemic harmonization of the rules on contracts in the two spheres. This is mainly due to the difference in the structural arrangement of the general rules on contracts.

The Hungarian code gave practically no expression to the specific features of relationships between socialist organizations among the general rules on contracts. The transactions of private persons[13] being the predominant consideration in the formulation of all the rules concerning binding offer as well as conclusion, fulfilment and breach of contract, while most aspects of contractual relationships in the sphere of the national economy were covered by normative regulations of a lower level. The prohibition of credit[14] (the only specific of contractual relationships between socialist organizations, which deriving from the system of economic management based on compulsory plan instructions) was included by the Hungarian Civil Code among the general rules on contracts. This

[13] Cf. ibid. For a criticism of the obsolete general rules on contracts before the enactment of the Civil Code, see Eörsi: op. cit., p. 58, fn11.

[14] See the original wording of Art. 200, para. (3), of the Civil Code, which was repealed as of 1 January 1968 by Art. 27 of Law-Decree No. 39 of 1967.

same basic approach is shown by the provisions (for partial invalidity,[15] rights and time-limits of warranty,[16] etc.) which established the principal rule with mostly the simpler relationships of citizens in view and with exceptions allowed for the contracts of socialist organizations either in the code or in separate regulations. No other explanation can be offered for the fact that cooperation between parties is covered by the Code in connection with performance only (Art. 277, para. 2). The Code's silence on cooperation in the phase from conclusion to fulfilment of contract is not warranted by the subordinate function assigned to contracts under the system of economic management based on plan breakdowns, just as a provision for this obligation is not rendered needless by the normative regulation of cooperation at the level of a governing principle (Art. 4, para. 3). Here again, the legislator probably kept in mind the simpler legal relationships of citizens. Such unilateral citizen-orientation of the code's rules on contracts was undoubtedly a contributing factor in that the code did not play a guiding role in contractual disputes of socialist organizations even to the extent permitted by the system of direct plan instructions. From this it followed that, after the introduction of the new system of economic management and, in particular, the unification of the system of state administration, it was necessary to "reintroduce" sort of speak, the code's rules on contracts with regard to contractual disputes in the sphere of the national economy.[17] Thus there are two factors to be taken into account in seeking the causes which, despite the narrow bridge represented by plan contracts, led to a large degree of systemic separation between the sets of rules regarding national economic contracts and those of citizens under the system of direct economic management. Due mainly

[15] For a detailed discussion, see Weiss, Emília: *A szerződés érvénytelensége a polgári jogban* (Invalidity of Contract in Civil Law), Közgazdasági és Jogi Könyvkiadó, Budapest, 1969, p. 523 et seq.; cf. Eörsi: op. cit., fn6 at p. 129 et seq.

[16] Cf. Harmathy, Attila – Lontai, Endre: *Vita a minőségvédelem polgári jogi kérdéseiről* (Debate on Quality Protection under Civil Law), Állam- és Jogtudomány, XI, 1968, p. 474 et seq.; Zoltán, Ödön: *A szavatossági jogok új szabályozásáról* (New Regulation of Warranty Rights). Jogtudományi Közlöny, XXV, 1970, p. 69 et seq.; *A szavatossági jogok érvényesítésének új szabályozásáról* (New Regulation of the Enforcement of Warranty Rights), Jogtudományi Közlöny, XXV ot 2970, p. 341 et seq. Kemenes, Béla: *A fogyasztó érdekvédelmének egyes polgári jogi kérdései hibás teljesítés esetén* (Some Questions concerning the Protection of Consumer Interests under Civil Law), Jogtudományi Közlöny, XXIX of 1974, p. 614 et seq.

[17] The credit lies primarily with the Economic Tribunal of the Supreme Court for the "resuscitation" in economic disputes of the general rules of the Civil Code on contracts. Opinion No. 82/1973 of GKT, for instance, expressed: "Subject to Art. 241 of the Civil Code, contracts between socialist organizations may also be modified by the court in the absence of obligation to conclude a contract and if the parties have refused to submit to court action." Mention should also be made of opposite tendencies, however. According to Opinion No. 3/1973 of GKT, for instance, "the dispositive rules of law and the dispositive stipulations regarding the basic conditions of contract shall not be binding on the court in case of a contractual dispute". This position not only declares some sort of a special status conferred on economic disputes but also proclaims a concept that is unprincipled, unacceptable and even contrary to the generally recognized nature of dispositive rules (cf. Ministerial Motivation to the Draft Civil Code, Edition 1963, p. 219 et seq.).

to the direct methods of economic management, the offshoot was not only a tending away of contractual relationships between socialist organizations from those between citizens, although the underlying motive of differentiation was undoubtedly in the primary consideration for the latter, but also a virtual "foreclosure" by the Civil Code to regulate the contracts of the national economic sphere among the general rules on contracts, a phenomenon which served to reinforce the former.

By contrast to the approach of the Hungarian Civil Code, the Russian and Polish codes of 1964 kept in view the relationships of socialist organizations in laying down the general rules on contracts. It is natural, however, that this systemic unity, geared as it was to the system of direct economic management prevailing at the time of the adoption of these codes, should express in the first place substantive differences such as plan control, the obligation to make contracts, special rules on the settlement of disputes concerning the conclusion of contracts, or the prohibition of limitations on liability for breach of contract.[18] Especially the Polish Civil Code did more than honour the specifics deriving from the system of plan breakdowns. It did so by defining the legal character of general contractual terms, model contracts and business regulations, covering preliminary contracts, extending the obligation of socialist organizations to cooperate to the conclusion of contracts, having regard to the distinctive features of national economic contracts in the formulation of rules on fulfilment, etc.[19]

These preliminary remarks will perhaps suffice to bring the problem – namely the continuing quest of socialist civil law for an optimal regulation and systemization of contractual relationships between economic organizations – into sharp focus. When the first codified laws were drafted the dogmatic and systemic traditions of continental bourgeois laws were much too strong and came into play all the more easily since an important role was still being fulfilled by small-commodity producing private property relations, while the relationships between socialist organizations were not yet ripe for a more lasting legal regulation. The subsequent codes made significant steps forward in dealing with the problem, but did not get past the stage of experiments.

Today it is clearly seen that the nature and significance of contractual relationships between socialist organizations, and hence the mode of legal regulation, are closely related to the prevailing system of economic man-

[18] See Articles 159, 160, 165, 166 of the 1964 Civil Code of the RSFSR and Articles 397 to 404 of the Polish Civil Code.

[19] See Articles 384–85, 389–90, 386, 456 and 489 of the Polish Civil Code. The Polish code is forward-oriented also in respect of arranging the rules on types of contract, by incorporating the contract of delivery (Title XIII), establishing separate rules on contracting for building (Title XVI), and in general making more allowance for the special characteristics of contracts between socialist economic organizations.

agement. Though this linkage exerted an objective influence on the previous works of codification, it did not come to awareness in a measure to make for an optimal approach to codification. This is further indicated by the fact that the codes which were elaborated under the system of economic management based on plan breakdowns adopted various approaches to the arrangement of rules on the contracts of socialist organizations. The theoretical watershed is established between the codes proceeding from the unity of civil law, laying emphasis on the features common to contracts of citizens and of socialist organizations, and those opting for full separation under the economic law approach.

(a) The approach of full theoretical separation was adopted by legislation in Czechoslovakia and the German Democratic Republic.

(b) Basing themselves on the theoretical unity were the Hungarian Civil Code and those of the Russian Socialist Federal Soviet Republic and Poland, of which:

(i) the Hungarian Civil Code devised an intermediate level of abstraction in the institution of plan contracts between the general category of contract and the different types of contract: this as an expedient for incorporating the body of rules on contracts of a more permanent and general nature between socialist organizations. This approach resulted in an internal separation of rules comparable to a kind of differentiated integration;

(ii) the code of the RSFSR and chiefly the Polish code attained a perfect integration in respect of form and systemic arrangement by incorporating, in a breakdown by subject-matter, the principal rules on national economic contracts, as distinct from the transactions of citizens in the general rules on contracts. However, under the system of direct economic management, this implies a differentiation in terms of substance.

Before we embark on a fuller consideration of these approaches to codification, it appears necessary to explore the theoretical fundamentals of the economic background. We shall discuss two sets of problems: the principal aspects of socialist commodity relations and the linkage between economic management and the contractual system.

2. Public property and commodity relations

The historical linkage and close association between commodity relations and contracts has already been elucidated by Marx on the theoretical plane.[20] In previous chapters we have referred to this interrelationship at several places in an attempt to put the abstract interdependence between

[20] Marx, Karl: *Das Kapital,* Berlin, 1962 (Marx – Engels Werke, Dietz Verlag, Band 23), p. 99; *Grundrisse der Kritik der Politischen Ökonomie,* Berlin, 1953 (Dietz Verlag), p. 153.

commodity relations and contracts into the concrete context of the given economic and social conditions as well as to discuss it in conjunction with other factors of legal development. It is legitimate to inquire into the nature of this relationship under conditions of socialism in order to see how close it is, and how far it acts as a determining factor with regard to the different classes of contract. Moreover to find out whether contracts owe their function to the existence of commodity relations even after the socialization of the means of production. To answer these questions it is necessary to examine in greater depth a still more profound interrelationship: that which exists between public property and commodity relations.

Public property and commodity relations are, no doubt, contradictory terms, expressing perhaps the deepest antagonism which Marxist social science has been concerned with resolving since Marx. The introduction to the latest Soviet representative monography on the history of the political economy of socialism reasonably claims that "Perhaps nothing else than the problem of commodity and money relations has caused Soviet economists a greater difficulty, and at times a more serious feeling of despair. This is the only question where economic theory constructed more contradictory and often mutually excluding conceptions which sometimes captured the minds of economists, and at other times were rejected as not deserving serious attention. But regardless of whether one or another category and law of commodity production were acknowleged or refused, they pushed their way in real life and ultimately became *a fortiori* subject of scientific research. It is no exaggeration to say that the scientific standard of the political economy of socialism was dependent on the degree and depth of elaboration of the special mechanism through which the category and laws of commodity relations were operating under socialism. Needless to say that, given its scope, Soviet economic literature has accorded priority to the analysis and elucidation of commodity and money relations".[21] This is why the following statement by Eörsi has been chosen to be the motto of this chapter: ". . .our present-day conditions have given rise to a contradiction – one between connective social property and separative commodity production – which is acting as an optimal lever for development".[22]

For some 15 years now it has been the dominant, though not exclusive, view of socialist economic science, that commodity and money relations continue to persist after the socialization of the means of production,

[21] See *A szocializmus politikai gazdaságtanának története* (History of the Political Economy of Socialism), Kossuth Könyvkiadó, Budapest, 1975, p. 14. For a similar appraisal, see Ostrovityanov, K. V.: *Áru és pénzviszonyok a kommunizmus építésének időszakában* (Commodity and Money Relations in the Period of Building Communism), Kossuth Könyvkiadó, Budapest, 1963, p. 7. Cf. Valovoi, D. V.–Lapsina, G. Y.: *Szocializmus és áruviszonyok* (Socialism and Commodity Relations), Kossuth Könyvkiadó, Budapest, 1974, p. 174.

[22] Eörsi, Gyula: *A magyar civilisztika 30 éve* (Thirty Years of the Science of Hungarian Civil Law), Gazdaság- és Jogtudomány, IX of 1975, p. 303.

during the period of socialist construction, and in all sectors of the socialist economy.[23] The fact that this theoretical concept did not become a more or less hegemonic view except in the fifth decade of building socialism in practice can be traced to various sets of circumstances.

(a) The first cause to mention is no doubt the need for Marxist social science to have come to grips with the antagonism, which for long seemed unresolvable, between social property and commodity relations; not only was this without the assistance from, but was against the thesis of, Marx and Engels, who held that direct distribution of social labour would be realized under socialism, and therefore they ruled out the existence of commodity relations and the operation of the law of value in an economic system based on the social ownership of the means of production.[24] For a realistic appraisal of this thesis, however, at least two factors should be taken into account. First, Marx and Engels thought that the new social formation was to emerge from the worldwide victory of a socialist revolution, and therefore they based their theory on a set of economic and social conditions entirely different from those under which the socialist system actually emerged. Second, and this is a no less important aspect, Marx and Engels – applying as they did a strictly scientific method – always refrained from giving a kind of detailed prognosis on the future economic system of a socialist society. One of the most important differences which distinguished Marx and Engels from the Utopian socialists lies precisely in that they, unlike the latter, exercised a very great measure of restraint and caution in sketching the contours of a future socialist society – writes Brus, who continues his instructive criticism of the still fashionable trend of Marxianism. He states that some propositions of Marx and Engels in connection with the principles governing the operation of a future socialist economy serve only as a guidance of a very general nature. Marx and Engels formulated those propositions in two different contexts.

[23] Cf. – in addition to the works cited in fn21 – Vilmos, József: *Áruviszonyok a szocialista gazdaságban* (Commodity Relations in the Socialist Economy), Kossuth Könyvkiadó, Budapest, 1963, p. 138; Brus, Wlodzimierz: *A szocialista gazdaság működésének általános problémái* (General Problems relative to the Working of the Socialist Economy), Közgazdasági és Jogi Könyvkiadó, Budapest, 1966, p. 246, particularly p. 111 et seq.; Földes, Károly: *A szocialista tulajdon és az árutermelés* (Socialist Ownership and Commodity Production), Kossuth Könyvkiadó, Budapest, 1968, p. 424, particularly p. 124 et seq. It is to be noted that as late as 1950 books were still published in the Soviet Union (Malishev, I: *A munka társadalmi nyilvántartása és az ár a szocializmusban* [Social Accounting of Labour and Price in Socialism]; Sobolj, V.: *Népgazdasági mérlegtanulmányok* [Studies on National Economic Balance]) which considered commodity and money relations to be incompatible with socialism; for a criticism of them see Ostrovityanov: op. cit.

[24] The most frequently quoted statements of Marx on the disappearance of commodity relations in socialism are to be found in Marx: *Kritik des Gothaer Programms,* Berlin, 1962 (Marx –Engels Werke, Dietz Verlag, Band 19), p. 20 et seq. For Engels' arguments along similar lines, see Engels, Friedrich: *Anti-Dühring,* Berlin, 1962 (Marx – Engels Werke, Dietz Verlag, Band 20), p. 109 et seq. Cf. Brus: op. cit., p. 24 et seq.; Ostrovityanov: op. cit., p. 29; Vilmos: op. cit., p. 18 et seq.; Földes: op. cit., p. 127 et seq.; and – along similar lines but with shifts of emphasis – Valovoi –Lapsina: op. cit., p. 193 et seq.

First, only incidentally, in analyzing the laws of capitalism, mainly in emphasizing the historically transitory character of the capitalist mode of production. This applies in particular to the scattered observations made in *The Capital,* which may have played the same role in the analysis of capitalism as the references to the anatomy of man do in investigations into the anatomy of apes. Second, in dealing with the practical necessity for the ideological struggle, particularly in the period of analyzing the mistaken theses of programme.[25] One still cannot be surprised at the fact that the thesis of Marx and Engels on the disappearance of commodity relations has for a long period of time served as a point of departure for the socialist theory of commodity relations, establishing a principle which, although allowed for exceptions under the pressure of practical needs, remained a principle none the less. This is explained not only by the authority of the classics, but chiefly by the fact that Marx proved, precisely on the basis of a scientific analysis of capitalist commodity production, that the social formation of capitalism had outlived its day and that a socialist transformation of society were inevitable.[26]

Soon after the revolution, an analysis of the concrete conditions made Lenin realize the necessity of "maintaining" commodity and money relations.[27] This is indicated by the fact that he attached great importance to the reform of money circulation. He saw clearly that the abolition of price in war communism had been forced upon by the pressure of circumstances, as he was also aware of the special causes of that exceptional necessity, although he admitted the idea that this particular situation might imply more than a mere episode. The measures taken to mobilize all forces in defence of the achievements of the revolution may assume a

[25] Brus: op. cit., p. 23 et seq. A similar position is held by Ostrovityanov: op. cit., p. 25 et seq.; Földes: op. cit., p. 127 et seq.

[26] Cf. Világhy, Miklós: *Áruviszony és polgári jog* (Commodity Relations and Civil Law), Állam- és Jogtudomány, XI of 1968, p. 445 et seq. On the other hand, the "'scientific" experiments undertaken to verify or legalize the existence of commodity relations by invoking the classics are less undestandable. On such experiments in the Soviet Union, see Földes: op. cit., p. 127; Valovoi –Lapsina: op. cit., p. 194 et seq. In the Hungarian philosophical literature Attila Ágh argues that Marx held the exchange of commodities to be an inevitable phenomenon throughout the period of socialism (*Szocializmus és elidegenedés* [Socialism and Alienation], Magyar Filozófiai Szemle, No. 12. 1967, p. 478). This view is criticized by Friss, István: *Szocializmus és árutermelés* (Socialism and Commodity Production). Brus says on this score: 'For a long time we have tried to adapt Marxist economic ideas to the political necessity of the moment, either through specific interpretations of the texts, or by omitting from the history of science and discarding from the bookshelves or voluminous catalogues the names and works that were regarded as 'discredited'. After all, Marxist political economy, especially the economics of socialism, reminds us of the classic hero of Chamisso's short story, Peter Schlemihl, the man without a shadow: it was a science without history. . ." (op. cit., p. 21).

[27] The numerous statements made by Lenin under different sets of circumstances about the persistence of commodity relations are subjected to a detailed analysis by Valovoi–Lapsina: op. cit., p. 198 et seq. See also *A szocializmus politikai gazdaságtanának története* (History of the Political Economy of Socialism), quoted edition, p. 140 et seq. Cf. Brus: op. cit., p. 33 et seq.; Földes: op. cit., p. 135 et seq.

character which admits of no reversal, meaning that what seemed impossible by the light of a careful analysis of economic preconditions – a direct leap to a "strictly communistic" scheme of distribution of production and goods – may turn into a reality. Of course, with that conception prevailing, commodity and money relations were looked upon as a necessary evil to be rid of when the first opportunity arises. War communism appeared to be such an opportunity which people were eager to grasp.[28] This is evidenced by Lenin's oft-quoted appraisal made at the time the NEP was introduced: "We thought – or, perhaps more accurately, assumed with insufficient calculation – that by direct order of the proletarian state we would be able to organize state production and state distribution of products on communist principles in our country of small peasants. Life has shown that we were mistaken."[29] Later, Lenin also explained the necessity for the persistence of commodity relations by the circumstances of a transitory economy, and saw its source in factors external to socialism – in the existence of small peasant farms and particularly in the low level of industrialization.[30]

Down to the mid-1930's, the prevalent view in Soviet economic science was, as Lenin held, that the causes of the persistence of commodity relations were to seek in the conditions of a transitory economy. The majority of scholars were conviced that real commodity production would cease and the categories of value would wither away in a fully developed socialist society, with the commodity form of the exchange of activities to be replaced by the *forma naturalis.* Later, from the second part of the 1930's, there came to hold the field the so-called accounting-distributive concept which explained the existence of the categories of commodity and value. This was so because of the need for society to measure its labour and to distribute it among the sectors of the national economy and among the spheres of reproduction. In that period this virtually implied a formal recognition of commodity production and of the law of value.[31]

Without describing the variations[32] of these concepts it may be stated that, practically up to the 1960's, economic science was making renewed attempts to bring the theory on the withering away of commodity relations into line with the facts and the needs of practice. The last compre-

[28] Brus: op. cit., p. 33 et seq.

[29] Lenin, V. I.: *Művei* (Works), Vol. 33, Szikra, Budapest, 1953, p. 40.

[30] Brus: op. cit., p. 35 et seq. A somewhat different appraisal of Lenin's view is given by Ostrovityanov: op. cit., p. 29 et seq. According to Lisitchkin, Lenin admitted commodity relations even under full-scale socialism; see *Terv és piac* (Plan and Market), Közgazdasági és Jogi Könyvkiadó, Budapest, 1967, p. 62 et seq.

[31] Valovoi–Lapsina: op. cit., p. 174 et seq.; cf. p. 177 et seq. and Földes: op. cit., p. 151 et seq.; *A szocializmus politikai gazdaságtanának története* (History of the Political Economy of Socialism), quoted edition, p. 149 et seq.

[32] Ibid.

hensive theory is associated with Stalin, who except for economic relationships in the form of commodity still refused to acknowledge real commodity relations in the public sector, and attributed the existence of commodity and money relations in other spheres of the economy chiefly to the existence of cooperatives, the kolkhoz property, and the kolkhoz peasantry, along with other partial causes.[33] Then, at the turn of the 1950's and the 1960's the view was spreading and became predominant that the persistence of commodity relations was an inevitable concomitant of the socialist economic and social order.[34]

(b) In exploring the obstacles to a theoretical breakthrough attention should be called to at least three factors beside the said subjective considerations. An important fact is that the prolonged period of transitory economic conditions raised difficulties, in both the Soviet Union and the European people's democratic countries, in separating the truly transitory factors from the lasting economic elements and thereby increased the complexity of conditions for a theoretical clarification. Another set of factors may be said to be constituted by the long periods of war and reconstruction which, given the extraordinary circumstances then prevailing, called for makeshift solutions, literally pushing commodity and money relations to the peripheries, namely to the black market (war communism, the Great Patriotic War). The third factor can be discerned in the light of economic developments over the past decade, and of the advance of theory which set the stage for them. We have in mind the system of direct economic management based on the compulsory breakdown of strictly defined plan targets. This will be treated in the next section dealing with the relationships between economic management and contracts.

(c) For decades, the explanation and ideologization of the obstinately recurring onslaughts by "non-existent" commodity relations claimed the attention of socialist economic science virtually in a blind alley.[35] This

[33] It is noted that the concept of explaining commodity relations by the existence of the kolkhoz peasantry had been formulated before but was made predominant by Stalin. On this point see Földes: op. cit., p. 167; cf. Valovoi–Lapsina: op. cit., pp. 213, 226 et seq. and *A szocializmus politikai gazdaságtanának története* (History of the Political Economy of Socialism), quoted edition, p. 168 et seq. It is more than a paradox of specific historical conditions that at precisely the time when bisectoral ownership, the parallel existence of two forms of social ownership came to be the prevalent explanation for the subsistence of commodity relations under socialism, the use of commodity contracts in the production turnover of kolkhozes slipped entirely into the background and the compulsory delivery of agricultural products to state organs became the dominant practice. Cf. Genkin, D. M. (ed.): *A szovjet polgári jog* (Soviet Civil Law), Budapest, 1952, I, p. 301 et seq.

[34] See the works cited in fns21 and 23. For works advocating opposite views, see fn23.

[35] The said development of economic sciences concerning commodity relations under socialism had its reflection in jurisprudence as well. See Világhy, Miklós: *A magyar civiljogtudomány 25 éve* (Twenty-Five Years of the Science of Hungarian Civil Law), Jogtudományi Közlöny, XXV of 1970, p. 259; Sárközy, Tamás: *Indirekt gazdaságirányítás, vállalati árutermelés és a tulajdonjog* (Indirect Economic Management, Enterprisal Commodity Production, and Property Law), Akadémiai Kiadó, Budapest, 1973, p. 57 et seq.

entailed a long delay in fully clarifying the distinctive features of commodity relations under socialism, and we still suffer from a lack of clearly established results. Jurisprudence cannot dispense with such assistance from economics in laying the foundations for a socialist theory of contract, among others. A scientific exploration and a thorough analysis of the specifics of commodity relations is particularly indispensable for defining the real attributes of contractual relationships in the public sector.

Today there is more or less common ground in economic science concerning the statement that the existence of commodity and money relations is not, in the public sector either, a manifestation and still less a simple reflection of the effect of the law of value or of some other external factor.[36] There is less agreement among economists concerning the causes of commodity relations within the sphere of state property,[37] particularly the attachment of those relations to property (proprietary character of the separation of subjects)[38] and the operation of the law of value.[39]

However, some generalizations may also be made from the divergent views, some of which differ in terminology only, concerning the underlying causes. At the existing level of development of the forces of production and of the organization of production, work cannot be done except under conditions of an advanced division of labour, in economically isolated organizations, even on the basis of social ownership. Therefore labour is socialistic in nature, but is not also socially necessary in absolute terms and in all cases. While national economic planning based on the socialist ownership of the means of production is able, by setting the basic proportions between production and consumption, to ensure the directly socialist nature of the work of isolated organizations: not even the most

[36] Brus: op. cit., p. 112.

[37] For opposite views about the causes of socialist commodity production, see Ostrovityanov: op. cit., pp. 45 et seq., 53 et seq.; Vilmos: op. cit., p. 22 et seq. (within the public sector, p. 37 et seq.); Szabó, Kálmán: *A szocialista termelés alapvonásai* (Basic Features of Socialist Production), Kossuth Könyvkiadó, Budapest, 1964, pp. 324, 328 et seq.; Földes: op. cit., p. 170 et seq.; Valoëv –Lapsina: op. cit., p. 225 et seq.; cf. Brus: op. cit., pp. 95 et seq., 111 et seq.

[38] Vilmos argues that state enterprises are not owners vis-a-vis the state, but enjoy "a relative degree of independence" and, in relations *inter se*, "fact like owners isolated in a certain respect" (op. cit., p. 49 et seq.). In jurisprudence a similar view is held by Világhy, Miklós: *Az állam és vállalata* (The State and its Enterprise), Jogtudományi Közlöny, XXII, 1967, p. 577. In the debate conducted in *Közgazdasági Szemle* at the turn of the 1950's and the 1960's most authors stated their case against proprietary isolation within the public sector. Cf. Földes: op. cit., p. 178 et seq. The former view is more commonly held even today. Cf. Nemes, László: *Néhány gondolat a termelési viszonyokról folyó vitához* (Some Thoughts about the Debate on Production Relations), Közgazdasági Szemle, XXII, 1975, p. 1190 et seq. In jurisprudence Sárközy is of the view that "commodity relations. . .are necessarily and exclusively ones between material proprietors even under conditions of socialism" (op. cit., p. 61).

[39] Ostrovityanov: op. cit., p. 91 et seq.; Vilmos: op. cit., pp. 86 et seq., 115 et seq.; and in particular Brus: op. cit., Chap. 4, pp. 111 to157; as well as Földes: op. cit., Chapters VI to VIII, pp. 192 to 364. Compare also Valovoi – Lapsina: op. cit., pp. 221 et seq., 297 et seq.

advanced system of planification is able to guarantee, in a lasting way and in all cases, the socially necessary nature of the work (economic efficiency, quality and assortment of products, etc.) of isolated producing organizations which also embody separate interests. These are in effect the principal reasons for the existence of commodity relations, and for the necessity of relying on them, in the public sector.

As far as their benefit to jurisprudence is concerned, a great deficiency of the economic analyses made of the specifics of commodity relations in the sphere of state property lies in excessive generalizations. We refer not so much to assertions, which, taken by themselves, are downright meaningless, like "socialist commodity production is a peculiar commodity production", or "the pattern of socialist commodity and money relations is essentially different from that of commodity and money relations in all previous social formations", or "under socialism the categories of commodity and money are expressions of socialist relations of production" and so on.[40] They are meaningless because they are but slogans to be used in political pamphlets and in themselves offer nothing either for jurisprudence or for economics to go by. The theses that distinguish commodity relations based on state property only from commodity production based on capitalist private property are likewise of little value to jurisprudence in examining the contractual relationships of socialist organizations from a politico-economical point of view. Although being fundamental for economic science and indispensable for other social sciences including jurisprudence, they are too abstract to be applicable in concrete terms. In addition, such comparisons lose sight, not infrequently, of the fact that, owing to the various forms of intervention by the monopolies and the state, etc., the effects of commodity and money relations of classical capitalism, primarily the law of value itself, often make themselves felt in considerably changed forms even in the monopoly capitalist economy of today.[41]

As regards the distinctive features of socialist commodity relations, we find Kálmán Szabó's to be an appropriate point of departure: "The alterations in the substance of commodity, money and value. . .must never be construed to only mean that these categories now serve not the chase for profits but the interests of a socialist society. . . By alteration in substance we mean change induced by the effect of the specific conditions of socialism, in the nature of non-specific relationships that are expressed by the category of commodity.[42] In establishing the concrete specifics however, Kálmán Szabó also fails to distinguish the general socialist features of commodity relations which derive from the social ownership of the means

[40] E.g. Ostrovityanov: op. cit., p. 71.
[41] Brus: op. cit., p. 116 et seq.; cf. Földes: op. cit., p. 184.
[42] Szabó, Kálmán: op. cit., p. 324.

of production, from the attributes issuing from the system of direct economic management based on compulsory plan instructions. This is indicated by the following assertion, among others: "By planning, society anticipates recognition of the work done. . ., although to be made concrete recognition calls for additional, though not insignificant, devices subordinate to planned guidance (such as the system of delivery contracts, provision of credit on user's certificate)."[43]

We do not think in any way that the features of socialist commodity relations as disclosed by economic science can be relied upon directly for analyzing the contracts of socialist organizations. Still less do we believe that the elements of such categories as contract can be built directly on the categories of the political economy.[44] Yet we maintain that the specific features of socialist commodity relations as elaborated by economic science are instrumental in a more objective definition of the specific features of contractual relationships between socialist organizations. This is much more the case than attempting to disclose these features through the distorting-glass of legislative eventualities.

If, for the time being, we leave aside the specific features deriving from the direct and indirect systems of economic management (these will be treated in Section 3), the following features of socialist commodity relations may deserve attention from the point of view of relationships governed by the law of contract:

(i) Above all, commodity and money relationships between state economic organizations play no more than an auxiliary role in the social distribution of live and dead labour, in the synchronization of the structure of production with that of needs.[45]

(ii) Another important feature of the change in the character of socialist commodity and money relations is that "the contradiction between use-value and value, and hence between commodity and money, ceases to be antagonistic. The fetishism of commodity and money is destined to disappear. This in essence, points to the priority of use value over value and of commodity product over money."[46]

[43] Ibid., p. 330 et seq. The constant features of socialist commodity relations are, in our view, mingled with specifics, deriving from direct economic management, also in one of Eörsi's earlier works (*A szocialista polgári jog alapproblémái* [Fundamental Problems of Socialist Civil Law], Akadémiai Kiadó, Budapest, 1965), which results in some underestimation of the general significance of commodity relations under socialism and particularly of their impact on civil law. On the other hand, we think that Világhy, influenced also by the transitory characteristics of the full-scale operation of indirect economic management, places undue emphasis on the role played by commodity relations in the basic institutions of civil law (See op. cit., fn26).

[44] The possibility of relying directly on political economy for a definition of the subject-matter and concept of civil law is raised by Eörsi: op. cit. in fn43, particularly p. 62 et seq.; cf. Sárközy: op. cit., p. 10.

[45] Cf. Brus: op. cit., p. 112.

[46] Cf. Szabó: op. cit., p. 331 et seq.

(iii) The social ownership of the means of production enables the state to modify in a planned manner the proportions of social production and those of prices, including calculated and lasting shifts in proportions of value. Certain social preferences (considerations of cultural policy or distribution of income) justify long-term restrictions on the operation of the law of value also with respect to consumer goods and still more with respect to investments.[47]

Wider scope for cooperation between contracting parties is connected with these features of socialist commodity relations, "...thus there is no need for external legal means to inject cooperation into commodity relations as it is intrinsic to them. In essence, law (with all its active backlash effect) does not but reflect this phenomenon."[48] The greater emphasis laid on use value is reflected in the civil law principle of satisfaction of needs, and in the concrete application of this principle to the fulfilment of contract; namely in the requirement of striving for real performance. Eörsi points out in clear terms that a constant element of the socialist character of commodity relations consists in that "the transmission belt between social needs and contracts is not profit interest. This is the case since as under the system of direct economic management strict compulsory planning has detached it from the satisfaction of needs, and, in the constrained situation produced by the lag of capacity behind effective demand, has raised it to the rank of a new general principle."[49] This belief which we share does not derogate from our thesis that the "use-value orientation" of socialist commodity relations as a permanent feature basically independent of the prevailing system of economic management is likewise reflected in the contractual relationships of socialist economic organizations, and primarily in the rules on performance. This is indicated by the semblance of "exceptions"[50] designed to augment the buyer's right of withdrawal under the new system of management, for the right of withdrawal does not allow for any exception to the requirement of meeting needs, but is a necessary conclusion drawn from the removal of rigid plan discipline, which under the system of direct management was at times detached even from needs, precisely with a view to ensuring a fuller satisfaction thereof.

[47] Cf. Brus: op. cit., pp. 120, 138, 155 et seq., 167, 233.

[48] Sárközy: op. cit., p. 60; cf. Vékás, Lajos: *A szerződő felek együttműködésének elvi alapjai a szerződéses termeltetés jogviszonyaiban* (Theoretical Bases of Cooperation between Contracting Parties in Legal Relationships concerning Contract Delivery of Agricultural Products), Jogtudományi Közlönv. XXII, 1967, p. 599 et seq.

[49] Eörsi: *A reális teljesítés elve a gazdaságirányítás új rendszerében* (The Principle of Specific Performance under the New System of Economic Management), Jogtudományi Közlöny, XXII, 1968, p. 341 et seq.; op. cit. in fn6 p. 232 et seq.

[50] See the wording of Art. 23 of Government Decree No. 10/1966. (II. 14) and in particular of Art 1 of Government Decree No. 2/1970. (II. 3.); Art. 35, para. I, of Government Decree No. 44/1967. (XI. 5.); Art. 33, para. 3, of Government Decree No. 32/1967. (IX. 23.); Art. 553 of the Polish Civil Code; and in a rather restricted scope, Art. 170 of the Czechoslovak Economic Code.

The requirement of cooperation and the legal guarantees for real performance in subordination to the satisfaction of needs serve to exemplify the projection of the socialist features of commodity relations to the sphere of law. Here we do not go into details because, as has often been noted, the main features of the effect of commodity relations are strongly motivated by the methods and instruments of the prevailing system of economic management. Moreover, the utilization of commodity and money relations themselves is a function of the adopted system of economic management.[51] Therefore we shall consider first the major relationships between economic management and contracts, and in this context, the principal features of linkage between socialist commodity relations and contracts.

3. Economic management and contracts

We have more than once observed that the concrete range and significance of the operation of commodity and money relations, which are objectively and inevitably postulated by socialist economic and social conditions, as well as the corresponding spread and role of commodity contracts in a socialist system of the economy may vary by period and country. This realization has long been confirmed by historical experience, and the changing models of economic management witnessed within the past ten to fifteen years in the European socialist countries can be helpfully relied upon for exploring the deeper implications of this phenomenon as well.

(a) An analysis of existing experience reveals in the first place that the play of commodity and money relations in socialism is considerably influenced by the form of socialization of appropriation, namely the form of social ownership. As was previously discussed, separation of the ownership of the means of production and labour in a socialist economic and social system is but relative as a result of the socialization of the means of production. The history of the international development of socialism shows that this general feature of the socialist mode of production allows for different ways and means of uniting social property and production groups (ownership and labour).[52] Such differences are of great relevance to the sphere of action of commodity relations and to the use of commodity contracts.

[51] A similar position was taken in our study written in 1971 on a partly empirical, partly intuitive basis (Vékás, Lajos: *Economic Management and the Law of Contracts.* Acta Juridica 15 [1973], pp. 417 to 437), but today the theoretical substantiation of our final conclusions appears to be inadequate and needs to be improved upon.

[52] Cf. Eörsi: *Állami tulajdon – állami vállalat* (State Property – State Enterprise), Acta Fac. XII, Budapest, 1970, p. 42 et seq.

If we disregard the exceptional and transitory economic system of war communism, which was forced upon by special circumstances, the historical experience of the European socialist countries enables us to distinguish two basic variants of uniting social property and production groups.

One is the Yugoslav solution,[53] in which group ownership is the only transmission belt between social appropriation and labour. Under this system we cannot speak of state ownership as a dir*c*t proprietary expression of the all-social aspect. Although in Yugoslav theory no right of ownership except the "right of use *in rem*" is recognized, even in respect to enterprises and other economic organizations, because the state direction of the economy or the "penetration of commodity relations with public law elements is said to exclude the possibility to recognize the formula of commodity property. . ., (in reality) the Yugoslav enterprise's right of use *in rem* is a virtual embodiment of commodity property" – writes Sárközy.[54] Sárándi is also right in stating that the Yugoslav theory of "subjectless right of social ownership" is in essence nothing else than "reluctance to bring property within the scope of property law".[55] It may therefore be said that, in effect, the Yugoslav solution means "full identification of ownership and group in the whole of the national economy (not only in the cooperative sector)".[56] Thus, in this system of economic management appropriate to the socialist mode of production, the division of labour between economic organizations is coupled with economic separation of a proprietary nature: the means of production are in group ownership, the production collectives being linked together as owners. The economic organizations thus separated are interconnected with the help of commodity and money relations, which results in a broad utilization of, and places great importance on, commodity contracts. The proprietary character of economic separation is a natural breeding ground for commodity relations and hence the Yugoslav form of social ownership allots a highly important role to civil law contracts.

Until now the other socialist countries of Europe, including Hungary, have relied on a different variant for connecting social property with production groups. Under this approach, separation of group ownership is applied only to cooperative farms (kolkhozes), and the proprietary in-

[53] On the Yugoslav concept of social ownership, see Gams, A.: *Osnovy stvornog prava* (Bases of Property), Belgrade, 1968, p. 94 et seq.; *Right of Ownership within the Framework of State Property,* Archiv za pravne i drustvene nauke, Nos. 3 and 4 of 1962; Finzgar, A.: *Fundamental Problems of Socially Owned Goods under Property Law,* Archiv za pravne i drustvene nauke, Nos. 1 and 2 of 1965. Among high-standard summaries in Hungarian, see Sajó, András: *Az állami szocialista tulajdon és az állami vállalat* (Socialist Property of the State and the State Enterprise), in: *Polgári Jogi Tanulmányok* (Studies in Civil Law), I, Budapest, 1970, ELTE Sokszorosító, p. 364 et seq.; Sárközy: op. cit., pp. 126 et seq.

[54] Sárközy: op. cit., pp. 129, 127.

[55] Sárándi, Imre: *A társadalmi tulajdon változásai* (Changes in Social Ownership), Acta Fac. XII, Budapest, 1970, p. 14 et seq.

[56] Eörsi: op. cit. in fn 52.

dependence of state economic organizations, first of all state enterprises, is not recognized on the premise that state ownership is one and whole.[57] So the real and concrete extent of economic separation amongst state economic organizations is basically dependent on the form of economic management, and therefore the actual role of commodity and money relations in a socialist economy is likewise determined by the prevailing system of economic management particularly in economic relationships within the sphere of state property. This is why the nature and function of contracts under such an economic system may be said to depend primarily on the given form of economic management.

The foregoing shows that the close interrelationship of commodity relations and contracts to economic management is clearly manifest above all in relationships between enterprises separated within the sphere of united state property. At the same time the case of Sárközy for bringing the form of socialization of property (the form of social ownership) into relationship with the system of economic management appears to be convincing to us.[58] Furthermore, it should be pointed out that an important role in leaving scope for the action of commodity and money relations, and in changing the significance and function of contracts may be played by economic management also in the event that group ownership is recognized in a wide area: in Yugoslavia "it was the economic reform of 1965 that really allowed. . .enterprises to make use of the possibilities inherent in the principle of social self-management but exploited earlier in a rather formal way".[59]

(b) In the first decades of socialist construction economic science found it evident that economic management based on the social ownership of the means of production could be of one form only: direct guidance through more or less detailed plan instructions. However, practical economic activity in the European socialist countries led to the recognition that the pattern of objective economic and production relations includes surface aspects that are not determined by the form of ownership of the means of production, and are consequently susceptible of change in an economic system based on the social ownership of the means of production. Indeed, they do change by necessity, due to the development of production relations induced by the growth of productive forces.

These aspects are present at the points of contact between the economic basis and the social superstructure. Therefore they are considerably influenced – subject to the primacy of the economic structure – by political, legal and other elements of the superstructure. These economic

[57] This concept is clearly reflected in positive law, but theoretical approaches have become rather divergent since the introduction of economic reforms. For a summary account, see Sárközy: op. cit., p. 207 et seq.

[58] Sárközy: op. cit., Part II, particularly p. 155 et seq., 235 et seq.

[59] Ibid., p. 128.

and legal elements, which constitute the framework for actual economic processes, and determine the organizational and operational forms of economic activity, are reduced by Hungarian economic literature to the category of form of economic management or economic mechanism.[60] A most important attribute of the form of economic activity is economic management, in which the typical dynamisms of the basis are so closely interwoven with the constituent elements of the superstructure as to combine to act, primarily with legal institutions as a determinant factor.

We believe that this mixed nature (basis vs. superstructure) of the form of economic activity or economic management accounts for the significant role played by the institutional systems of these categories in determining the functions of legal institutions, including contract. This is why we deem it of particular importance to give proper weight in our inquiry to the relationships between the economy and law, namely to the institutions of the form of economic activity that serve as transmission belts.[61] Therefore we think that a simple mechanical superposition of the elements of commodity relations and contracts cannot be a satisfactory approach, as such inquiries are much too abstract and reveal anything of the concrete economic function of contracts. Adequate results can only be expected from an examination of the relationships between the form of economic activity and contract.

(c) The different forms of a planned economy based on the social ownership of the means of production (models of mechanism) are classified by economic science principally through delineation of the levels of economic decision-making. Brus points out that under a schematic approach all economic decision in a socialist system fall into three groups: the first includes fundamental macroeconomic decisions which, by their nature, should, as a rule, be taken at the central level; the second includes decisions which affect the structure of individual consumption under a given pattern of incomes and, apart from exceptional periods, should

[60] In economic literature there is no commonly held view concerning details of substance in the category of form of economic activity, but the general contours may be said to have emerged. See Hegedűs, András: *A tervgazdálkodás konkrét rendszeréről* (On the Concrete System of a Planned Economy), Közgazdasági Szemle, VII of 1960, p. 1242 et seq.; Szabó, Kálmán: op. cit., p. 23 et seq. Cf. Lakos, Sándor: *A közgazdaságtudomány néhány elvi kérdéséhez* (On Some Theoretical Questions in Economic Science), Társadalmi Szemle, XIX, No. 2 of 1964. p. 64; Erdei, Ferenc: *A társadalom vezetésének korszerű tudományos megalapozása a szocializmusban* (Laying a Modern Scientific Foundation for the Guidance of Society under Socialism), Valóság, VII, No. 4 of 1965, p. 24.

[61] In this context we see a great value in Sárközy's monography which proceeds from the thesis that "the law regulates property relations through the form (in the forms) of economic activity rather than directly, and is linked through them to material property" and regards as erroneous the thesis of direct linkage between property law and production relations (see op. cit., p. 78 et seq.). The aforementioned thesis of Sárközy that "the development of the forms of socialist ownership (including state ownership as the basic form of property) is fundamentally determined by the planned economic mechanism" follows from this concept (see op. cit., p. 143).

normally be decentralized and be implemented through the agency of the market; the third includes such other decisions as are in general very difficult to classify, although they are often called "timely economic decisions". The latter concerning the pattern and volume of production in particular branches and enterprises, the magnitude and composition of investments, the avenues of marketing and the sources of supply, smaller-scale investment projects, the concrete forms of remuneration, etc.). As a matter of fact, the solutions offered by the various models apply only to the last group of decisions, and are models of the operation of a socialist economy in so far as they must really be in keeping with the general principles of the system and differ from one another merely by the centralized or decentralized nature of decisions in the third group.[62] On these principles Brus distinguishes in the first place centralized and decentralized (at other times: direct and indirect) models of economic activity, mentioning the regulated and free market mechanisms as subvariants of the latter model.[63] Sárközy refers to "decentralized mechanism based on the dominant role of large cooperative farms and middle-level management organs and making limited use of plan indicators" as a third subtype of the indirect model.[64] The differences in categorization[65] arise from the varying emphasis placed on similarities and discrepancies according as may be warranted by the concrete aspects analyzed. In our view, differentiation between direct and indirect models is too abstract for a study of the role of contracts, while the subtypes of the indirect model blur essential differences. Therefore we find it practicable to distinguish four different models of mechanism: direct (plan breakdown), decentralized, planned market regulation, and free market regulation. It should be emphasized, however, that these are models, elements of which are blended in the practice of economic management, and the most that can be said of them is that any one system of economic management adopted in a given country at a given period tends to give prominence to the features of either this or that model.[66] Nor must we overlook alterations in a given model, namely the fact that the models are, even in this con-

[62] Brus: op. cit., p. 80 et seq.; cf. p. 95 et seq.

[63] For a detailed treatment of the centralized model, see Brus: op. cit., p. 83 et seq. and (for that of the decentralized model) p. 168 et seq.

[64] Sárközy: op. cit., p. 151 et seq.

[65] For different classifications of the models of economic mechanism, see Harmathy, Attila: *A gazdaságirányítási rendszer reformja és a szállítási szerződések szabályozása a szocialista országokban* (Reform of the Systems of Economic Management and Regulation of Delivery Contracts in the Socialist Countries), Állam- és Jogtudomány, XII of 1969, p. 24 et seq.; Világhy, Miklós: *A gazdasági jog kérdései egy kelet–nyugati kerekasztal-értekezlet napirendjén* (Questions of Economic Law on the Agenda of an East–West Round Table Conference). Gazdaság- és Jogtudomány, IV of 1970, p. 392 et seq.; Eörsi: op. cit. in fn52, p. 42 et seq.

[66] A mingling of elements in the models of economic mechanism is emphasized by Brus: op. cit., pp. 101 et seq., 223 et seq.; Sárközy: op. cit., p. 146 et. seq.

text, mere schemes or simplifications that are warranted or dictated by needs.[67]

(d) Considering that until now Hungary has relied mainly on the direct mechanism based on compulsory plan instructions, and on the mechanism of planned market regulation, next we shall examine the function and significance of commodity and money relations and those of contracts under these two models of management.

(i) In the model of economic management based on compulsory plan instructions commodity relationships do not play an active role in enterprise decisions and fulfil an essentially formal function even in the implementation of mandatory plan targets. Accordingly, the system of direct economic management assigns a basically passive role to commodity and money forms in the sphere of the national economy.[68] This is manifested among others in that scales of value expressed in monetary terms do not serve as a basis for economic decisions, but are used only for cost–benefit assessment in view of the aims set and the methods of production employed.[69] Additionally in that a balance in the public sector is ensured not so much through categories of value in terms of money, but through stocks allocated directly or in kind.[70] This does not, of course, mean that the use of commodity and money forms has no relevance under the system of direct economic management based on plan breakdowns. The recording of cost and benefit is itself of great significance, but in addition, commodity and money forms are particularly important in the exercise of control over the implementation of central decisions, while playing some part in economic stimulation. Still, on the whole, state enterprises operating under a system of compulsory plan instructions have a rather narrow scope for managerial independence. Their economic separation which hardly makes allowance for particular interests of their own is essentially limited to a scope absolutely required by the division of labour. All this is reflected in legal regulation as well: the theoretical substantiation of the independent juristic personality of state enterprises encountered a great deal of difficulty for a long time,[71] with the primary emphasis placed on the aspect of obligations[72] and on the relativity[73] of juristic personality. The artificiality and the restricted scope of economic independence, enjoyed by economic organizations managing detached parts of the united

[67] The changes in the direct models based on plan breakdowns are emphasized by Sárközy: op. cit., p. 149.

[68] Cf. Brus: op. cit., p. 103.

[69] Ibid., p. 158.

[70] Ibid., p. 100.

[71] On the backgrounds to Venediktov's theory of dual collective, see Világhy, Miklós – Eörsi, Gyula: *Magyar polgári jog* (Hungarian Civil Law), I, Tankönyvkiadó, Budapest, 1965, p. 132 et seq.

[72] Cf. ibid., p. 305; Art. 171, para. 2, of the Hungarian Civil Code.

[73] Cf. ibid., p. 134 et seq.; for a detailed theoretical discussion, see Eörsi: op. cit. in fn43, p. 189 et seq.

state property under the system of plan breakdown, are, of course, also manifested in the *inter se* relationships of state enterprises. The aspect of linkage is similarly artificial, externally induced and combined with elements of administration by the state as owner and public ministry. The true organizer of production turnover between enterprises is, depending on the degree of detail in which plan indicators are established, the plan which, broken down and legally binding, sets limits to relationships between economic units in terms of subject, object and content alike. It is direct tools (breakdown of plans), not commodity and money relations, that are used to ensure the distribution of live and dead labour and the harmony between the structures of production and needs.[74] Thus, in this sphere of relationships, commodity and money are formal and passive in nature, with contracts playing a subordinate role. The argument that contracts between state organizations "mean a form of commodity relations without commodity nature" is correctly interpreted in this sense.[75]

(ii) In the mechanism based on planned market regulation, commodity and money relations assume an active role in the sphere of state property as well, with the action of commodity relations brought to the surface, reinforced and extended by economic management. Commodity and money relationships – the market mechanism (within a planned and regulated framework) – are also relied upon for influencing enterprise decisions, particularly as regards the *inter se* relationships between enterprises.[76] A basic condition for it lies in strengthening and giving substance to the economic independence of state enterprises and their juristic personality expressive of it.[77] With the abolition of the breakdown of plan targets the dictated character of production turnover between enterprises disappears, and the obligation to make contracts thereupon becomes an exception (though is not entirely removed in view of the imbalances between demand and supply). Thus the independece of economic organizations manifests itself in the aspect of linkage as well: their will, including their contracts, are influenced not so much by direct means as by indirect economic regulators. This is coupled with an endeavour to maintain a balance between relationships in terms of value. All these combine to expand the links between contracts of the public sector and commodity and money relations. The closer links between commodity relations and contracts are evidenced by commodity relations that come into play in a

[74] Cf. Brus: op. cit., p. 112.

[75] Eörsi: op. cit. in fn10, p. 330. On the economic background to this problem Károly Földes writes: "There may be periods in which economic methods do not leave any room for this necessity (namely the categories of commodity relations – L.V.) to come into play" (op. cit., p. 176).

[76] Cf. Brus: op. cit., p. 159 et seq.

[77] For a new concept of state enterprises as subjects at law, see Sárándi, Imre: *Az új gazdasági mechanizmus és a jog* (The New Economic Mechanism and Law), Jogtudományi Közlöny, XXIII, 1968, p. 72; Eörsi: op. cit. in fn6, p. 199 et seq.

wider area (trade in means of production, technological development, new-product innovations, etc.), and owing no less to the legally guaranteed utilization of the possibilities offered by the freedom of contract, with a higher degree of reality and efficiency.[78]

At the same time Eörsi is correct in pointing out that under planned market conditions national economic contracts are all commodity contracts and are all linked with commodity relations in one way or another. However, "there are nevertheless contracts where the classical commodity-money exchange does not take place, (or) the parties do not stand at the two opposite poles of commodity relations, (or) have no or only secondary and minor conflicts of interests typical of commodity relations".[79] It is very important to stress this because the scientific recognition that the legal regulation of contracts cannot be explained merely by commodity relations, nor by neglect of its fundamental linkage with these, has been substantiated by practical experience gained in the application of the regulated market mechanism.

The growing significance of contracts on the national economic plane is shown primarily by the active part they play in the harmonization of production and needs, and by the important direct function they fulfill in the implementation of planned guidance. Under the system of direct economic management, contracts as civil law frameworks for plan targets brought down to the enterprise level do not play an active role either in ensuring planned implementation or in organizing production turnover and cooperation between enterprises. The function they are assigned is not independent, but is reduced to signalling the shortcomings or distortions of planned guidance.[80] By contrast, under regulated market conditions, the plans of enterprises rest not the least with contracts, which, given the volume of orders covered by them, act as a most important factor in, and provide a basis of information for, enterprise planning, whereby their pragmatism serves as a guarantee and precondition for plan fulfilment. As demonstrated, there is an inverse relationship between enterprise plan and contract, when the system of direct economic management is contrasted with the regulated market mechanism. Whereas in the former case the conclusion of contracts is determined and delineated by enterprise plans based on plan breakdown, in the latter case the enterprise contracts, oriented by national economic plan targets and regulators and

[78] Eörsi: op. cit. in fn6, p. 224 et seq.

[79] Ibid., p. 229.

[80] On the relationship between the planning and contractual systems under direct management, see Eörsi: op. cit., in fn11, pp. 115 et seq., 251 et seq.; György, Ernő: op. cit., p. 92 et seq. On planning procedures in the regulated market mechanism, see Kálmán, György: *A népgazdaság központi irányításának jogi eszközei* (Legal Means of Central Economic Management), in: *Jogi kérdések az új gazdaságirányítás köréből* (Legal Questions of the New Economic Management), Közgazdasági és Jogi Könyvkiadó, Budapest, 1967, particularly p. 108 et seq.

other centrally applied instruments or indirectly influenced through the market mechanism, are essential components of planning. Thus, in the regulated market mechanism, contracts may indirectly, through the implementation of enterprise plans, make an active contribution to the fulfilment of the national economic plan as well. This implies further that in the planned regulated market mechanism there is no type of contract that may be said to serve better than another the realization of plan targets. In theory, all national economic contracts are destined to subserve plan fulfilment and none can be accorded priority in this respect. Hence any distinction between plan-implementing and "market" contracts is of a historical value only.[81] They partly serve in classifying contracts under the system of direct economic management, and partly in differentiating between them under the system of direct management and in the regulated market mechanism, as in the latter all national economic contracts are plan-implementing and market-oriented simultaneously.

This aspect brings us to the next topic: how the differing role of commodity and money relations, the differing system of economic management tends to influence the pattern of contractual relationships in the sphere of the national economy, and what scheme of systemization is warranted by such difference in respect of contracts of socialist organizations and those of citizens?

4. Contracts between economic units as a system apart

As we have anticipated our position in the introduction to this chapter, the nature and significance and the corresponding legal regulation of contractual relationships between socialist organizations have a close and objective linkage with the prevailing system of economic management. We think that our detailed analysis of the operation and effects of commodity relations under socialism, and of the influence exercised on them by the system of economic management has buttressed and proved our introductory thesis grounded on more or less empirical facts. Related studies make it also possible for an optimal systemic arrangement of contracts between socialist organizations to be brought into relationship with the models of economic management.

(a) The contracts of state economic organizations under the system of direct economic management are marked by a function assigned to them in the implementation of mandatory plan targets, by subordination to

[81] For this distinction, see Csanádi, György: *A szerződések szabályozása a magyar jogban* (The Regulation of Contracts in Hungarian Law), Gazdaság- és Jogtudomány, IV, 1970, fn.3 at p. 454 et seq.

plan breakdowns, by a vague and formal commodity character. These fundamental features and their surface symptoms, or legal reflections (like the obligation to make contracts, and other provisions of administrative law, compulsory types of contract, peremptory regulation), cause the contracts of the public sector to be first separated from the rest of contracts, and then to be united as a system apart. According to Eörsi, three stages of development may be distinguished in this process.[82] In the first stage, the plan-implementing contracts are formally fitted into contract types established by kind of performance under the traditional civil law approach (delivery contract into sales contract, building contract into contract of *locatio conductio operis,* etc.), although there is less and less room for the integration of new elements into the traditional frameworks. In the second stage, a new quality is generated by the proliferation of increasingly different features: the contracts of delivery, building, design, etc. form a separate type as distinct from the "archetype" and come to be recognized as independent types of contract. In the third stage, the most important contracts of state enterprises are caused by circumstances with their primary role of plan fulfilment as the motivating factor of separation to be integrated at a new level, precisely in the complex of these circumstances, and to form the class of plan contracts. This is, of course, a simplified, abstract scheme of the process reflecting the substance without details,[83] and still less presenting the shifts of emphasis on approaches to codification in the different socialist countries, an aspect which we shall discuss later. The fundamental *differentia specifica* of contracts thus separated lies in their special relationship to plans, in their direct plan-implementing role, which is conspicuously manifest in the case of contracts covering collateral plan targets (contracts of delivery, building, design, etc.): "the distinctive features of plan contracts manifest themselves most vividly and most plainly in the conjunct or congruent aspects of the plans of the two parties".[84]

The systematic separation of contracts between state enterprises under direct economic management is a natural and direct concomitant of their differences in function or substance. The first sign of systematic separation which, if we may add, is not inevitable, since it is not necessarily associated with the special relationship to plans but partially with the lack of elaborate dogmatics, and is more or less transitory. It is the erosion of the dividing line between the traditional bounds of typification. The essence, the root of the phenomenon, is undoubtedly to seek in the preponderance of administrative elements – the plan-implementing role instead of civil-

[82] Eörsi: op. cit. in fn11, p. 78 et seq.

[83] Ibid., p. 79 et seq.

[84] Ibid., p. 95. On the "not entirely passive" role of plan contracts, see Eörsi: op. cit. in fn10, p. 327.

law attributes – in the contracts of the public sector under the system of direct economic management. Therefore these features come into play also in the choice of the abstract level of systemization, while the traditional civil-law criterion – the nature of performance – takes on at least a secondary importance. This phenomenon may be illustrated by the Hungarian legislation of 1951 on delivery contracts,[85] which irrespective of the nature of performance, defined as delivery contract any agreement which has been entered into either for delivery of goods, or "for other performance of an economic interest", for the purpose of realizing plan targets, with a time-limit set for subsequent fulfilment. This is provided that at least one of the contracting parties is a state organ or state enterprise. The primacy of administrative law elements over the civil law aspect, and the disruptive effect of the plan-implementing function on the types of contract are clearly in evidence in spite of the rather wide exceptions allowed by the said regulation (agreement concerning immovables, contract for production, lease, tenancy, loan, loan for use, insurance, carriage by train, agency, commission, etc.). This arrangement was doubtless influenced by the economic law approach[86] and no less by the crudeness of a new dogmatics, but the decisive cause, the objective basis lies in the functional separation of contracts within the public sector. This is demonstrated by the new regulation of 1955,[87] which, though it limited the concept of delivery contract to forward delivery contract subject to plan, served as the underlying law of the contracts of *locatio conductio operis*, building, design and forwarding as well as some contracts of carriage between socialist organizations. This situation remained unaltered by the entry into force of the Civil Code, although it laid down supra-type rules common to plan-implementing contracts and formulated at a higher level of abstraction. The said regulation on delivery contracts invariably remained (until the 1961 Code of Investments) to be the underlying legal material governing the class of contracts concluded between socialist organizations and bearing the character of *locatio conductio operis* (building, design).

The direct plan-implementing role of contracts between state enterprises, the preponderance of this function is likewise manifest in the sectoral delineation[88] of contract types as another form of systemic separation in the mechanism of direct management. Under Hungarian legislation concerning economic management based on plan breakdowns, no organizations other than socialist ones bound by the obligation to draw

[85] Decree No. 206/1951. (XII. 8.) of the Council of Ministers. For its appraisal, see Csanádi: op. cit. in fn10, p. 11 et seq.

[86] Cf. Eörsi: op. cit. in fn11, p. 81 et seq.

[87] Decree No. 50/1955. (VIII. 19.) of the Council of Ministers.

[88] See Sárándi: op. cit., p. 74; *Les formes juridiques du trafic de produits entre les organisations socialistes,* Annales Universitatis Scientiarum Budapestinensis, Sectio Iuridica, XI. 1969, p. 120. For a fuller discussion, see Vékás: op. cit. in fn51, p. 169 et seq.

up plans could logically be subjects of delivery contracts directly serving for plan fulfilment. Such contracts could not be made by cooperative farms or groups either as parties placing orders or delivering goods.[89] At the same time the strict subjection to plan of state enterprises and other economic organizations of the state prevented them, again logically, from using contracts other than those falling into the type of plan contracts for the realization of plan targets and for the determination of mutual obligations involved in those targets.[90] The law explicitly ruled out the possibility for them to make, as producers, contracts for production and for bulk delivery of produce.[91] All this is an indication that the civil-law approach slipped into the background: the decisive element in the choice of contract type was not the economic objective to be attained or the nature of performance as an expression thereof, but the sectoral position of contracting partners; more specifically the disparate nature of management, namely the element of administrative law. Under the system of direct economic management, the proprietary element is very strong in the guidance of the economy by the state[92] which tends to reduce the scope of autonomy enjoyed by state economic organizations. The most important and most conspicuous earmark of this is the breakdown of plans, which in turn raises a barrier between the contracts of state enterprises and those of cooperatives: the former are allowed to make plan contracts only for the realization of plan targets, but the latter – because of their different planning procedure[93] – are ruled out of such contracts.

[89] Decree No. 50/1955. (VIII. 19.) of the Council of Ministers is not logical in allowing industrial cooperatives to conclude delivery contracts (para. 1 of Art. 1). It is to be noted that, obviously for lack of clarified theoretical bases, the regulation of 1951, in delimiting the scope of subjects in delivery contracts, was content to provide that one of the contracting parties shall be a state organ.

[90] E.g. Art. 1, para. 3, of Decree No. 50/1955. (VIII. 19.) of the Council of Ministers.

[91] Art. 2, para. 2, of Government Decree No. 24/1960. (V. 10.).

[92] On the separation of direction by the State as proprietor and as public ministry, see Világhy: *A népgazdaság ágazati irányításának lényege és eszközei* (The Essence and Means of Sectoral Direction of the National Economy), Állam és Igazgatás, XXI, 1971, p. 346 et seq.; *Gazdasági reform és polgári jog* (Economic Reform and Civil Law), Acta Fac. X, Budapest, 1968, p. 47; Eörsi: *A magyar gazdasági mechanizmus jogi aspektusai* (Legal Aspects of the Economic Mechanism in Hungary), Gazdaság- és Jogtudomány, IV, 1970, p. 435 et seq. The strong relativity of the separability of direction by the State as proprietor and as public ministry is emphasized, very logically in his own concept, by Sárközy: op. cit., p. 247 et seq.; cf. Eörsi: op. cit. in fn6, p. 38 et seq.

[93] The practical distortions of the adopted planning procedures ignorant of the proprietary character of cooperatives are disregarded in this context. On this point see Sárándi: *A termelőszövetkezeti demokrácia vagyonjogi alapjai* (Foundations of Cooperative Farmers' Democracy in Property Law), Állam és Igazgatás, XVI, 1966, p. 245 et seq.; *A gazdaságirányítás új rendszere és a termelőszövetkezetek szerződéses kapcsolatai* (The New System of Economic Management and the Contractual Relationships of Cooperative Farms), Jogtudományi Közlöny, XXI, 1966, p. 354 et seq.; Vékás: *A mezőgazdasági termékek szerződéses felvásárlása fejlődésének néhány alapvető elméleti tanulsága* (Some Basic Theoretical Lessons Offered by the Development of the Contractual Purchase of Agricultural Products), Acta Fac. X, Budapest, 1968, p. 328 et seq.

(b) Against this background, the next question concerns the kind of codification best suited to the national economic plans in the model of direct economic management. The answer depends basically on the extent to which the legislator intends to express the differences between these contracts in functions, contents and systems or on the ways and means of having the remaining features common to the rest of contracts reflected in codified law. Of course, a given arrangement may also be influenced by other circumstances or secondary aspects. According to Eörsi, the concrete form of planning, and, in particular, the use of so-called ministerial contracts work in the direction of separation renders the integration of these more difficult, during the existence of a civil code at a time when plan contracts had been legislatively covered.[94]

A variety of solutions are theoretically possible and, as mentioned earlier, nearly all variants of codification have been applied in practice by the different socialist countries of Europe. The approach under economic law (German Democratic Republic) and the separate economic code (Czechoslovakia) give maximum prominence to the distinctive features of contracts in the socialist sector, and rely on them as the general principle of codification. Furthermore, while accepting the undeniable drawbacks of repeating the rules, they fully ignore the affinity which these contracts show to those of citizens. The separate set of principal rules on plan contracts may be included among the general rules on contracts, either arranged under a separate chapter (Polish draft civil code)[95] or projected by subject-matter to the whole of the general part (partly the Polish Civil Code).[96] The Hungarian Civil Code opted for a fourth approach, that of arranging the most important general rules on plan contracts under a separate chapter inserted among those dealing with the types of contract. We agree with Eörsi in that this approach places the greatest emphasis on the common civil-law features of contracts: "Where civil-law relationships are regarded as pivotal and the impact of administrative elements on legal solutions is seen merely as an influencing factor, the arrangement of plan contracts is shifting towards the special part of the law of obligations."[97]

As seen today, in a "historical retrospect", the real specifics of national economic contracts under the system of direct economic management are found to have actually strengthened the tendency towards separation. Yet we think that full separation under the economic law approach is overemphatic of differences, and is entirely ignorant of common features. The result is undue duplication of legal material in the model of direct economic management, and still a greater deficiency of that approach is

[94] Eörsi: op. cit. in fn11, p. 90.
[95] Eörsi: ibid., p. 89.
[96] This was proposed also by Vasilev during the preparation of the Bulgarian Civil Code (see Eörsi: ibid.).
[97] Ibid.

seen in the difficulty it creates for achieving the uniformity of codification even in the period following the system of economic management based on plan breakdowns. Meanwhile the commodity character of national economic contracts has strengthened and the cohesive homogeneous elements of civil law have come to predominance in the contractual system. The objective factors of differentiation exercise by themselves a very strong effect, and their artificial reinforcement (by a separate judicial organization, a separate code, or both) brings about a situation in which the specifics deriving from the system of direct economic management outlive their source and continue to strengthen the factors of separation when the common features have become the objective dominant factors at work. Today, when we are fully aware of the effect exercised by economic management on the contracts of socialist organizations, the kind of codification giving maximum prominence to the specifics of the plan breakdown model – a mechanism of economic guidance *par excellence* – cannot be deemed to be the most appropriate solution.

Nor is, in our view, the approach of the Hungarian Civil Code borne out in every respect by subsequent appraisal. As has been stressed in the early part of this chapter, the Hungarian Civil Code deserves great credit for its success in avoiding, by the inclusion of plan contracts in the special part, a complete severance in two parts of the contractual system of the civil law. Even so, the objective differences were noteworthy, and the separate organization of arbitration committees as a serious sociological factor likewise served to strengthen the tendency towards separation. Thus, without a conscious effort for unity in the Code, it would have been still more difficult, after the introduction of the planned regulated market mechanism, to express the common civil-law features indicated by the specifics of commodity relations which came to be reinforced in national economic contracts. Yet this is but a subsequent verification of the Code's concept. We maintain that at the time of its elaboration, under the system of economic management based on plan breakdowns, the structure of the Civil Code did not express adequately the real specifics of the contractual system in the socialist public sector. The abstraction as embodied in the concept of plan contract really differentiated by "the legal characteristics of performances" [98], but was expressed not on the plane of the specific of contract types but at a higher level nearer the general. This logical flaw is a reflection of the sociological fact that, in reference to its actual role, Chapter XXXV of the Civil Code virtually fulfilled the function of a special "second general part". It was the "general part" on the plan-implementing contracts of state organizations – embedded in the special part. As noted earlier, the real general part – which contained the rules of Chapters XVII to XXVIII on the general aspects of contracts – was not

[98] Ibid., p. 90.

operative in respect of the national economic contracts under the system of direct economic management. Strict plan discipline did not allow room for the application of some of these rules, while other rules were not "needed" by the plan-implementing contracts of enterprises as they were regulated by provisions of administrative law and were subjected to administrative restrictions. They were, in addition, neither geared to, nor intended for, national economic relationships since these were subject to direct guidance. Accordingly, it was of no use that the legislator "prudently" included the plan contracts among the contract types. The lack of objective cohesion was felt in practice. Under the system of direct economic management, in the mechanism based on plan breakdowns, their separate treatment in the special part was merely a thin umbilical cord, in the form of a "supra-type" abstraction, between the civil law of contract and the national economic contracts.

The foregoing makes it clear that, in our view, the best way to follow, with respect to the common rules on contracts between state organizations under the system of plan breakdowns, would have been to include them among the general rules on contracts while arranging them not in a separate chapter, but as far as possible, in a manner to ensure that the general longer-term features of these relationships, that are not attributes of a given mechanism, came into play in respect of other contracts as well. Such an approach of codification would have been best able to express, under the system of direct economic management, the common features of all contracts in addition to emphasizing the differences, while being the simplest way of creating (precisely thereby) an environment for contract law in a future mechanism. We admit that at the time the Civil Code was framed there was not enough experience to rely upon for developing such an arrangement. A more solid dogmatic basis for the contracts of the socialist sector was lacking, and the haunting spectre of economic law was undoubtedly an added disturbing factor, but, most of all, there was in our view not a realization that the system of direct economic management based on plan breakdowns. Therefore the legal characteristics reflective of it are not attributes of a single conceivable economic mechanism, and contractual system resting on social ownership, are far from being inevitable and permanent concomitants of the socialization of the means of production. They are specifics of the economic model and contractual system of a rather short period of transition. We feel that the Polish Civil Code of 1964 had a better intuition of it, or possibly that its solution was perhaps more than intuition, since at the turn of the 1950's and the 1960's, the new theoretical approach of the Polish economic science was gaining ground.[99] Moreover, disputes about the economic mechanism were getting under way in other socialist countries as well.

[99] The oft-quoted book of Brus was written in 1960.

5. Reintegration of the contractual system

As shown by practical experience and scientific analyses, the category of plan contracts is deprived of substance by the abolition of the system of direct economic management based on plan breakdowns.[100] The most important factor making for the notional abstraction of plan contracts, namely the enterprise plan when mandatorily broken down by operation of administrative law, ceases to exist. In addition, the economic and legal specifics tending towards the separation of contracts between economic organizations of the state are fading out, and the common features derived from commodity character and from the system of economic management governed by uniform principles become more marked in the planned regulated market mechanism. It is natural that, under the system of direct economic management based on plan breakdowns and administrative intervention, there should be an objective possibility and justification for a category expressing the common features of contracts between state enterprises, and it is as much natural that this category should disappear in the regulated market mechanism.[101] This holds true whether the concept of plan contract is used or not (as is the case in some socialist countries).

(a) We are usually less emphatic about the fact that when a change in the system of direct economic management occurs the outdated abstraction separative of plan contracts is accompanied by essential changes in the types of contract classed in that category.[102] A largely transformed economic function can be found behind the types of one-time plan contracts that continue to be used with the same designation in the regulated market mechanism. As a matter of fact, the transformation of economic function is larger than is indicated by the changes in legal regulation itself, although the formal aspects of normative regulation are themselves reflective of very important changes. It will suffice to refer to an example regarding the deregulation of the obligation to make contracts and to enforce claims, or to the right of the party making the order to withdraw from delivery contracts and from contracts of *locatio conductio operis.*[103] Also, as noted above, the new economic function of contracts

[100] For shifts of emphasis mainly on a positive solution, see Eörsi: op. cit. in fn6, p. 134 et seq.; Világhy: op. cit. in fn26, p. 461 et seq.; *Gazdasági reform és polgári jog* (Economic Reform and Civil Law), Edition cited in fn92, p. 57 et seq.; Nizsalovszky, Endre: *Az állami vállalatok forgalmi viszonyainak új alakulásához* (New Pattern of Economic Relationships between State Enterprises), Állam- és Jogtudomány, XI of 1968, p. 531; Csanádi: op. cit. in fn10, p. 14 et seq.

[101] The deprivation of substance of the category of plan contracts is graphically demonstrated by Chapter XXXV of the Hungarian Civil Code. Most of its relevant rules had to be repealed during the reform of economic management, but not even the rules which were formally retained, either in their original or amended versions, are applied in practice any more.

[102] See in particular Harmathy: op. cit. in fn10; cf. the works cited in fn100 and Vékás: op. cit. in fn51, p. 165 et seq.

[103] The impacts of the reform of mechanism on the law of contract are expressed most plastically perhaps by Government Decree No. 44/1967. (XI.5.) on Contracts of *Locatio Conductio*

may be illustrated by the radically changed relationship between contracts and plans.

The considerably greater number of contract types used by enterprises for economic transactions in the regulated market mechanism is basically associated with the changed relationship between enterprise plans and contracts.[104] In this economic model, the few types of contract that were used on a compulsory basis for the realization of plan targets handed down under the system of direct economic management are not sufficient any longer. This is the case because the economic organizations have to make arrangements mostly individually for the procurement of the necessary means of production and raw materials as well as for the sale of their products. Furthermore, with the plan breakdown by enterprises abandoned, the obstacles to cooperation, association and collaborative arrangements between enterprises in pursuit of economic goals are removed.[105] The more or less total release of channels for production turnover and cooperation, and the near total abolition of the compulsory use of contract categories for that purpose, are natural corollaries of the change in economic conditions and requirements.[106] Among the

---

Operis between Enterprises. Cf. Harmathy, Attila: *A vállalkozási szerződések új szabályozásáról* (On the New Regulation of the Contracts of *Locatio Conductio Operis*), Magyar Jog, XV, 1968, p. 3 et seq.

[104] For a more detailed discussion, see Csanádi: op. cit. in fn10, p. 17 et seq.; Vékás: op. cit. in fn51, p. 159 et seq. A widening scale of the applied types of contract may also be observed in the German Democratic Republic, where the decentralized form of indirect economic management has been adopted instead of the regulated market mechanism, while the contractual system is characterized by separation under the economic law approach. Cf. Eörsi: op. cit. in fn10, p. 334.

[105] Cf. Csanádi: Ibid., p. 23 et seq.; Világhy: *A társulási formák a mai jogban* (The Forms of Association under Contemporary Hungarian Law) Jogtudományi Közlöny, XXIII, 1968, p. 351 et seq.; Sárközy: *A szocialista szervezetek társulásai* (Associations of Socialist Organizations), Állam- és Jogtudomány, XIII, 1970, p. 308 et seq.; Harmathy: *Az együttműködési szerződésekről* (On Contracts for Cooperation), Állam- és Jogtudomány, XIII, 1970. p. 689 et seq.

[106] See Section III of Government Decision No. 1020/1967. (VII. 11.) in respect of agricultural products and Art. 1, para, 2, of Government Decree No. 25/1967. (VIII. 20.) in respect of industrial products. Cf. Eörsi: op. cit. in fn6, p. 219 et seq.; Világhy: *Gazdasági reform és polgári jog* (Economic Reform and Civil Law), edition cited in fn92, p. 59 et seq.; Sárándi: *Les formes juridiques. . .*, edition cited in fn88, p. 119 et seq.; Görgey, Mihály: *A szállítási szerződés szabályai módosításának egyes termékforgalmi összefüggései* (Some Aspects of the Amendment of Rules on Delivery Contract concerning Commodity Circulation), Döntőbíráskodás, IX of 1968, p. 128; Kálmán, György: *A szerződési rendszer az új gazdasági mechanizmusban* (The Contractual System in the New Economic Mechanism), Magyar Jog, XV, 1968, p. 217 et seq. For the partially compulsory use of types in domestic relationships between foreign trade companies, with restrictions relaxed by the practical applicability of "self-accounting" (delivery) contracts, etc., see Art. 1 of Government Decree No. 32/1967. (IX. 23.) and, for its reasons, Szász, Iván: *A külkereskedelm belföldi szerződéses kapcsolatai* (Domestic Contractual Relationships in the Realm of Foreign Trade), in: *Jogi kérdések az új gazdaságirányítás köréből* (Legal Questions of the New Economic Management), edition cited in fn80, pp. 247, 256. For the ratios of contract types used in domestic transactions between foreign trade companies, see *Jelentés a külkereskedelmi és a belföldi vállalatok közötti szerződéses kapcsolatok vizsgálatáról* (Report on Inquiries into the Contractual Relationships between Foreign Trade and Domestic Enterprises), MTA Állam- és Jogtudományi Intézete, Budapest, 1975, p. 26 et seq.

types of contract thus released, the delivery contract retains its dominant role[107] in the regulated market mechanism, but a significant role is also allotted to transactions of commission, sale and its subtypes; agency,[108] *locatio conductio operis* and its subtypes, society with its subvariants, etc. Preliminary contracts[109] are likewise a typical product of indirect management.

Similarly, the abolition of sectoral articulation in the contractual system of the national economy is an inevitable concomitant of the reform of direct economic management which abandoned the method of providing enterprises with compulsory plan targets. The types of contract became available to the turnover of both industrial and agricultural products. Cooperative farms may be subjects of delivery contracts either as parties supplying goods or placing orders.[110] State enterprises meanwhile may even as suppliers[111] enter into a contract for bulk delivery of produce, if these are the types of contract best suited 10 the economic goal or to the nature of performance. (It is not least the abolition of this artificial borderline between categories specifically established by the system of direct management, that leads us to ask whether there is an essential difference. A specific feature calling for the use of a separate contract type, between the principal contracts used for the marketing of industrial and agricultural products, the delivery contract and the contract for bulk delivery of produce.[112]

Consequently, in the regulated market model of economic management, the major change in the contractual system of the national economy, can be said to consist in that, by contrast to the system of direct management, the traditional logical order of contract types is reestablished, and that the replacement of administrative by civil-law elements enables the traditional continental pillars of the contractual system of civil law to become of relevance to economic relationships. This applies in the sphere of the national economy as well and comes to play a part in commodity and money relations that arise out of the social ownership of the means of production. This tendency is indicated alike by the "hollow-

[107] During the first two years of the regulated market mechanism in Hungary some 85 to 90% of the turnover of non-individual production items continued to be handled through delivery contracts in home trade, the metallurgy and mechine industry and the light industry.

[108] Cf. Sárközy, Tamás: *A beruházási szerződéses rendszer elvi kérdéseiről* (On theoretical Questions of the Contractual System in the Field of Investment), Gazdaság- és Jogtudomány, VI, 1972, p. 337 et seq.

[109] Cf. Veress, Bulcsú: *A gazdaságirányítás új rendszere és az előszerződések* (The New System of Economic Management and Preliminary Contracts), Jogtudományi Közlöny, XXIV, 1969, p. 333 et seq.

[110] Art. 1 of Government Decree No. 55/1967. (XII. 17.).

[111] Government Decree No. 54/1967. (XII.17.), para. 1, supbara. (a), of Art. 2.

[112] For a summary of arguments for and against the contract for production and for bulk delivery of produce as a separate type of contract, see Harmathy: op. cit. in fn10, p. 58 et seq.; Eörsi: op. cit. in fn6, p. 142 et seq.

ness" of the "supra-type" category of plan contracts, by the more varied spectrum of the contract categories used and by the elimination of sectoral limits between types.

(b) At the same time there are signs of the converse effects arising in the model of indirect economic management. We have in mind above all the application of "self-regulating" and standardized contracts under socialism as known to contemporary bourgeois laws.

It is pointed out by Eörsi that the essentially similar level of productive forces leads to similar arrangements under the laws of the two social systems. This is due to the fact that although the forces of production operate mainly through production relations, the similarities indicated by the forces of production are eroded, mostly but not entirely, by the contradiction existing in this sphere. To distinguish between the two effects is always artificial and difficult.[113] In the realm of law, a conspicuous example of the convergent effect exerted by the similar levels of productive forces is provided precisely by the appearance of "self-regulating" and standardized contracts: "The growth of productive forces had led to a mass of standardized terms and conditions, which in turn called into being a mass of standardized contracts in both systems of society."[114]

In a socialist national economy based on the common public ownership of the means of production, "self-regulating" or complicated individual contracts are resorted to mainly in the indirect planned market mechanism relying on commodity relations as well, a mechanism in which, as previously discussed, agreements between socialist economic organizations are effective transmission belts rather than mere legal forms of economic relationships. As noted in our discussion of contemporary bourgeois legal development (Section 3 of Chapter IV), the growth of productive forces, and their increasing complexity create more frequently situations in which an agreement between economic organizations entering into a contractual relationship, does not, because of its complex substance, fit into the system of typified contracts. Therefore the parties, instead of mixing or forcibly using outdated types of contract, set themselves to also "regulate" the details of their relationship. In the field of such complicated economic relationships that call for special skills the socialist civil law is also unable to be of optimal assistance, while the development of productive forces points beyond the traditional system of contract types in the socialist law as well.

[113] Eörsi: op. cit. in fn10, p. 399 et seq. The two other causes of similarity between the bourgeois and socialist laws is seen by Eörsi in the transitory character of the socialist state and in the convergent effect of the class struggle (see ibid.). Cf.Mádl, Ferenc: *Az összehasonlító nemzetközi magánjog elmélete. Egy kísérlet magyarázatokkal* (The Theory of Comparative Private International Law. An Experiment With Explanations), Állam- és Jogtudomány, XV, 1972, p. 497 et seq.

[114] Eörsi: op. cit. in fn10, p. 402; cf. ibid., p. 336.

Nor is the possibility ruled out of misusing standard contracts (blankets, model contracts) under conditions of socialism. Cases of misuse occurred even under the system of direct economic management. This is the case particularly in relationships between industry and agriculture, and despite the added constraints that did not allow the parties to depart, usually not even at concordant will, from the conditions established for contracts for production and for bulk delivery of produce.[115] We believe that the real categories of contract are more in keeping with the requirements of the regulated market mechanism than is the system of rigid law-like general conditions which are of doubtful value as a source of law.[116] On the other hand, however, this also tends to reduce the role of contract types, as can be seen in contemporary bourgeois laws. It does so while leaving scope in principle for misuse of economic superiority or monopolistic position. Still, in the case of "self-regulating" contracts, the socialist law is confronted in a relatively direct way just as the bourgeois law is, with situations produced by the development and complexity of productive forces; whereas in the case of standard contracts the effect of productive forces on the elements of the superstructure makes itself felt through the "filter" of production relations, and, therefore, socialist law is better equipped than bourgeois law to prevent misuse of standardized contracts. Herein lie the function of the social ownership of the means of production, and the significance of the fact that commodity relationships between socialist economic organizations are based on the socialized forms of property. It should nevertheless be emphasized that, as is also shown by real economic life experience, socialist economic and production relations only create a possibility for preventing, but do not automatically block the way to, misuse of blankets, terms and conditions of business and model contracts. It is therefore necessary, even under our conditions, to maintain control over standard contracts, and to keep them within manageable bounds by legal means.

A detailed discussion of this aspect would, however, take us far from our set purpose. Enough examples have been given to indicate the main developments which in certain areas of economic life have relevance, even under socialist conditions, and beyond the traditional contractual system, including in the forefront the traditional types of contract. Socialist law is also caused by the development of the forces and relations of production

[115] For a criticism of this situation, see Sárándi: *A felvásárlás jogi szabályozásának elvi kérdései* (Theoretical Questions of the Legal Regulation of Procurement), Jogtudományi Közlöny, XXI, 1966, p. 45 et seq. The test of the Civil Code as amended by Law-Decree No. 39 of 1967 (Art. 416, para 1) allows in general for departures from the terms and conditions of contract.

[116] Cf. Sárközy: *Szállítási alapfeltételek, illetve a szerződések szabályozásának jogforrási rendszere* (Basic Conditions of Delivery and the System of the Sources of Law Governing Contracts), in: *Jelentés a szerződések rendszerének vizsgálatáról* (Report on Inquiries into the Contractual System), edition cited in fn10, p. 423 et seq.

to seek "active adaptation".[117] These factors working towards renovation should similarly be considered in reviewing the contractual system of the national economy.

By and large, it can still be stated that in socialist law, the types of contract practically retain the same relevance which we have attributed to them in the contemporary bourgeois laws of the Continent. They are elements of systemization, chiefly of codification, and, under a not too rigid approach, a helpful guide to legal practice, while performing a significant didactical function. As can be seen, socialist transformations have not accelerated the process which was started by the pivotal recognition of the general binding force of contract, and which changed the function of contract types. It allotted them a smaller role in general. Although as noted, their significance in the major sectors of the national economy is diminishing or changing (few types, use of compulsory categories) in the sphere of relationships between state enterprises under the system of direct economic management. This is but a natural and transitory concominant. – We might call it a symptom of the decline of contracts in the said model of management, under which the elements of administrative law suppress, as a rule, the elements of civil law. As we have attempted to describe, the logical order of contract types under planned market conditions is reestablished. This is also the case in relationships that are within the sphere of the national economy where the types of contract perform a function similar to that in other spheres of contractual relationships.

(c) As we have attempted to demonstrate in the foregoing discussion, in the indirect, planned market mechanism of the economy, the contracts of socialist organizations are characterized, in addition to a functional renewal, by a general tendency towards integration into the traditional contractual system. We maintain that uniform regulation should, under such circumstances, be the point of departure for codification in devising an optimal arrangement for the contracts of the national economy and of citizens. While under the system of direct economic management described above the possibilities for variation differed only in the manner, form, and extent of separation – the very fact of (at least a relative) separation being a necessary concomitant of the economic and legal characteristics of relationships between state organizations –, the unity of the contractual system is a salient feature of the planned market mechanism, with variations used only for expressing aspects of detail in codified law.

The economic motive for integration in codified law is provided by the fact that, in the regulated market mechanism, economic management places great reliance on commodity and money relations in the socialist sector, and in the *inter se* relationships of state enterprises as well. In our analysis of the linkage between social ownership and commodity relations,

[117] On "active adaptation" see Eörsi: op. cit. in fn10, p. 413 et seq.

we have sought to present the distinctive features of commodity relations. However, we must sum up, by stating that the dominant feature is the unity of common elements, and the divergences are mere exceptions in the economic structure of the contracts of citizens and of socialist organizations.

A similar picture emerges from legal regulation: the civil-law approach is reinforced and the elements of administrative law are displaced in the sphere of national economic contracts as well. A very important sign of unification, is, as demonstrated the breakaway of contract types from the forms of property, their non-attachment to one or another sector, and the general restoration by codification of their function fulfilled in systematization. All these traits tend to accentuate the fundamental unity of the contractual system of civil law in the indirect, planned market mechanism of the economy.[118]

Also, the codification effort should naturally express the differences between citizens' contracts, and of socialist organizations. As these differences stem from various sources, their nature and legal qualification are also different. If the specific features arising from wholly eventual or unwarranted legal regulation are disregarded,[119] most of such differences are in the nature of civil law.[120] Therefore their legal expression is warranted within the unity only, often not in the code but in a lower source of law. These differences stem mainly from the fact that the contracts entered into within the sphere of the national economy, cover mass-produced and often standardized products of large scale production. Similarly the practicable approach of codification seems to be that primary emphasis should be laid on the common principles governing these contracts and on other more lasting features: blanket contracts, terms and conditions of business, principal rules on preliminary contracts, major exceptions concerning breach of contract, etc. As we have stated in our outline of economic models, differences between national economic contracts also result from the survival of features typical of the system of direct economic management into the planned market mechanism. In Hungary, for instance the 1968 reform retained the obligation to make contracts in a significant area of activity, and peremptory regulation remained more marked in respect of national economic contracts than of contracts between citizens, and so on.[121] The basic unity of the contractual system in the planned market mechanism makes it advisable for the specifics of the

[118] A uniform approach to the codification of contract law is proposed by Eörsi: op. cit. in fn6, p. 136 et seq.; Harmathy: op. cit. in fn10, p. 109 et seq. Compare also Világhy: op. cit. in fn26, p. 461 et seq.

[119] Cf. Eörsi: ibid., p. 139 et seq.

[120] Eörsi: ibid., p. 224.

[121] See Government Decree No. 25/1967. (VIII. 20.) on Production Turnover (Articles 2 to 8) and Decree No. 33/1975. (XI. 29.) of the Council of Ministers (particularly Art. 3).

said category not to be met by a separate treatment (e.g. among the general rules on contracts or under a separate chapter among the types of contract).[122] It does partly by incorporation in the body of general rules on contracts,[123] partly by a modification of the rules governing the different types of contract. A further discussion of this topic would go beyond the bounds of our study, therefore we shall mention but a few general principles. First of all, it seems necessary to have all types of contract revised with regard to their "thrust" for citizens. The very contract of sale, the commonest and most typical transaction of private persons from ancient time, should be made a still more suitable – undoubtedly auxiliary – legal channel than it is at present for production turnover between socialist organizations.

As pointed out by several authors,[124] the rules of the Civil Code on agency are almost completely unsuited to serve as general provisions governing transactions of agency between economic organizations in the planned market mechanism. Although after 1968, agency in the market, mainly in respect of investments,[125] has acquired a significant role also in relationships between socialist organizations. Transactions pertaining to other classes of contract (*locatio conductio operis,* commission and, in particular, society) have come to be preponderant precisely in the sphere of the national economy. Therefore the dominant factor in their regulation is the national economic model, with the necessary differences to be expressed by allowing exceptions in respect of contracts between citizens.[126]

6. Summary

Our analysis of the interrelationships between socialistic ownership and the contractual system has shown that the existence and role of contracts even under conditions of socialism are basically attributable to the persistence of commodity production. Since the socialist economic and social

[122] For the most systematic treatment of the arguments for separation within the Code, namely for the creation of the so-called economic contract, see Görgey, Mihály. *Szocialista gazdálkodásunk szerződési rendszerének alakulása* (Development of the Contractual System in our Socialist Economy), Jogtudományi Közlöny, XXIII of 1968, p. 434 et seq. For a detailed discussion of counter-arguments, see Eörsi: ibid., p. 136 et seq.; Vékás: *A szocialista gazdasági szervezetek szerződési szabályainak rendszertani elhelyezéséről (A "gazdasági szerződések" problémájához)* (On the Systemic Arrangement of Rules Governing Contracts of Socialist Economic Organizations [To the Problem of "Economic Contracts"]), Acta Fac, XVII, Budapest, 1975.

[123] For more detail, see Eörsi: ibid., p. 140 et seq.; Vékás: ibid.

[124] Széll, András: *A szerződéses gyakorlat új vonásai a beruházásoknál* (New Features of Contractual Practice in the Field of Investment), Döntőbíráskodás, XI, 1970, p. 176; Sárközy: op. cit. in fn108, p. 338.

[125] Csanádi: *Polgári jog* (Civil Law), Tankönyvkiadó, Budapest, 1969, p. 345 et seq.; Sárközy: ibid., p. 333 et seq. For the national economic role of contract of agency in the mechanism based on plan breakdowns, see Csanádi: *A megbízási jogviszony* (The Contract of Agency), Közgazdasági és Jogi Könyvkiadó, Budapest, 1959, p. 157 et seq.

[126] Eörsi: ibid., p. 145; Harmathy: op. cit. in fn10, p. 111 et seq.

formation, which is based on the social ownership of the means of production is of a transitory character, and emerges at a level of development of productive forces where the persistence of commodity production and, naturally within planned frameworks allowed by social ownership, the utilization of the law of value are an objective necessity, civil-law contracts have a role to fulfil in relationships within the sphere of the national economy as well. The intensity and scope of their function performed within the sphere of state property depend precisely on the extent to which the system of economic management relies on commodity relations, and assigns them an active role in micro-economic relationships between enterprises. This accounts for the notable difference in the significance of contracts under the system of direct management based on plan breakdowns and in the indirect planned market mechanism.

(a) This difference has a considerable bearing on the way in which national economic contracts can be incorporated in the contractual system.

Under the system of economic management which is based on plan breakdowns, and which assigns to commodity and money relations and consequently to contracts a subordinate, virtually passive role in the sphere of the national economy, the contracts made in this domain differ, both in economic function and in legal features, so much from the contracts of citizens, that the dominant factor is one of separation with respect to systemization as well. Such separation is stressed in varying degree, and expressed in varying form by the codes of the socialist countries.

In the indirect planned market mechanism, commodity and money relations are used intensively in relationships between socialist economic organizations, the consequence being a change in the function and legal character of contracts and the prevalence of common features in contracts of the national economy and of citizens. The differences are seen within the unity only, and all these elements combine to strengthen the tendency towards systemic integration.

(b) The foregoing supports our conclusion that due to the heavy dependence of such systems on the adopted form of economic management, differences in the contractual systems of the codes of socialist countries are likely to be produced also by objective factors. Together with others (customs, traditions of codification, etc.), likewise they make for relative divergences with regard to the systemic arrangement of national economic contracts. After a while, a concrete approach of codification itself becomes a significant objectivized factor tending to be rigid and tending towards maintenance of the existing system. For instance, were it to come to the adoption of a planned market mechanism, and given the Czechoslovak separation under the approach of economic law, reestablishment of the unity of the contractual system would prove more difficult than the elaboration of plan contracts was for the Hungarian Civil Code. The latter in which the memory of those contracts is still lingering in the concept of economic contracts.

The contractual system based on social ownership may thus be built on different variants, but viewed in an abstract way, none of these can be said to be better or more suitable than the other. From our viewpoint, an optimal arrangement may be approached from the form of economic activity, namely from the system of economic management.

(c) The function fulfilled in socialist civil law by the categorization of contracts as a traditional governing principle of the continental laws of contract is likewise related to reliance on commodity and money relations.

The system of direct economic management based on plan breakdowns – which, prevailing for shorter or longer periods in the European socialist countries, does not rely on commodity and money relations in *inter se* relationships of economic organizations – meets the traditional aspects of categorization by elements of administrative law, particularly in regards to the plan-implementing function of national economic contracts. It is not the least for this reason that the contracts of socialist organizations become separated with respect to systematic arrangement from the transactions of citizens, which are handled through traditional channels and are arranged by types of contract. It seems as if in this mechanism of management, the contractual relationships that are based on socialist ownership were to outgrow definitively the system of categorization which were essentially geared to the accustomed economic function and physical nature of performance. Instead, they were to form a more or less separate unity at a higher level of abstraction (plan contract, economic contract).

It appears to us that this actually existing but relative and chiefly transitory trend of differentiation, which stems more from the system of economic management based on plan breakdowns than from the social ownership of the means of production, is honoured to the maximum extent by the kind of codification adopting the approach of economic law. The Czechoslovak legislation carries this approach to the point of unsettling the traditional principles of categorization and creating a separate contractual system both in the Civil Code and in the Economic Code. It does so not only for purpose of separating the contracts of citizens from those of socialist organizations, but for the most part also in respect of contracts between citizens. In the case of sale it creates separate "types" by the character of contracting parties, giving separate treatment to the so-called retail sales and to sales between citizens.[127] In the case of contracts in the nature of undertaking it duplicates part of the rules by the object of transaction, distinguishing between "types" involving the

[127] See the Czechoslovak Civil Code of 1964, Articles 239 et seq., 399 et seq.

manufacture of a new thing and the repair and alteration of things.[128] Classification by subject-matter is, also in general terms, relegated to the background in comparison with separation by subjects. Under the unmistakable influence of the economic law approach,[129] the basic criterion used by the Czechoslovak Civil Code for classification deals with the obligor of the principal performance being a socialist organization.[130] The result of this approach is, amongst others, that it lacks provisions for certain types of contract between citizens (*locatio conductio operis,* commission, etc.).

In the planned market mechanism which relies on commodity and money relations, also in the sphere of the national economy and assignment of substantive role to civil-law contracts, legislation is able to draw again upon the traditional principles of contract categorization at a higher level (by making use of substantive innovations to enlarge the function of contracts in the national economy). It achieves on these principles the fundamental unity of the civil law of contract in codified law. The reform of the Hungarian Civil Code of 1977 and 1984 may be the proof of the feasibility of this theoretical approach.

[128] See the Czechoslovak Civil Code of 1964, Articles 257 et seq., 263 et seq.
[129] Eörsi: op. cit. in fn10, pp. 220, 393.
[130] See the Czechoslovak Civil Code, Article 222 et seq.

VI. THEORETICAL CONCLUSIONS

"Durch die ökonomischen Verhältnisse wird. . .auch das Privatrecht bestimmt, das ja wesentlich nur die bestehenden, unter den gegebenen Umständen normalen ökonomischen Beziehungen zwischen den einzelnen sanktioniert. Die Form, in der dies geschieht, kann aber sehr verschieden sein."

---

1. Principal features of the economic determination and relative independence of law in the development of the contractual system

Engels' well-known statement[1] which we quoted as the motto of this chapter is in effect the "dominant idea" of our entire study. However hard we would look we could not find a better illustration of the Marxist approach to the relationship between the economy and law in the historical development of the structure of contract law. This evolutionary history demonstrates that, on the one hand, political, legal, etc. development is based on economic development and, on the other hand, all these elements react to one another and to the economic basis. Thus the economic situation is not the only active factor, the cause; all the rest a passive effect. There is interaction on the basis of economic necessity, which ultimately comes to prevail at all times.[2] In this study we have sought to present, in their interlocking relationship, the "ultimately" determining role of economic conditions and the diversity of the relatively independent products of legal development which are governed by their own rules and are indicative of habits of human thought.

(a) Appraising the results of pre-classical and classical Roman law, one can hardly speak of a contractual system; yet the types of contract as the major components of the contractual systems in the continental laws and later date works of codification are progenies of that law.

Despite the fact that the course of development of several hundreds of years cannot be traced in all its aspects, the pattern of economic conditions can be stated to have been the main underlying cause of the changes creating the classical types of contract which gradually sprang from simple

[1] Engels, Friedrich: *Ludwig Feuerbach und der Ausgang der klassischen deutschen Philosophie,* Berlin, 1962 (Marx – Engels Werke, Dietz Verlag, Band 21), p. 301.

[2] Engels: *Brief an W. Borgius,* Berlin, 1968 (Marx – Engels Werke, Dietz Verlag, Band 39), p. 206.

forms and partially from delictual roots. The decay of the closed subsistence economy, and the advance and widespread use of commodity and money relations bring home even in a historical retrospect of millennia, the objective economic and social demands which private law had to meet. It would nevertheless be incorrect to put the appearance and expansion of commodity and money relations simply in the same category with the emergence of private law contracts.[3] This is not because commodity exchange predated by far the emergence of law and particularly of private law, but mainly for the reason that commodity relationships did not take on the legal form of contract for a considerable length of time. The ancient ceremonial and often sacral "transactions" were superseded very slowly and gradually, and the delictual or even criminal law approach, as we call it today, was long to relax its hold. We can take almost as fact that the agreement of the parties – the soul of private law contract in the classical sense – was not confined, even in the early stages of legal development, to an interconnection by law of isolated commodity producers, but had a part to play in other areas such as international relations. Moreover, there is reasonable ground to believe that transmission of commodity relations was not the first function by which agreement came to acquire legal relevance.

Thus, historically speaking, commodity relations and contract can in no way be conceived of as identical notions. This is evidenced by the evolution of Roman private law, the most advanced law of simple commodity production. It is also borne out by the subsequent results of legal development. The special close linkage between commodity relations and private contract law consists in that the contract is a legal form that is best able to give an adequate expression of the common act of will required for the mutual appropriation of the products, turned into commodity, of isolated producers. This is what – neither less nor more – is meant by Marx's thesis that quoted in the first chapter: "This legal relationship which takes the form of contract is, whether or not legally developed, a relationship of will wherein economic relations are reflected. The substance of this relationship of law or will is expressed by economic relations themselves."[4]

Additionally, the historical development of contract law and, with it the contractual devices of Roman private law convincingly demonstrate that the most suitable legal forms, those of contract, are practically enforced

[3] Such mechanical superposition of economic and superstructural elements was challenged by Engels, who mindful of the complex interrelations and interactions between the two spheres stressed: "*Sonst wäre die Anwendung der Theorie auf eine beliebige Geschichtsperiode ja leichter als die Lösung einer einfachen Gleichung ersten Grades.*" Engels: *Brief an Joseph Bloch,* Berlin, 1967 (Marx–Engels Werke, Dietz Verlag, Band 37), p. 463.

[4] "*Dies Rechtsverhältnis, dessen Form der Vertrag ist, ob nun legal entwickelt oder nicht, ist ein Willensverhältnis, worin sich das ökonomische Verhältnis widerspiegelt.*" Marx, Karl: *Das Kapital,* Berlin, 1962 (Marx–Engels Werke, Dietz Verlag, Band 23),p. 99.

by the preponderance of commodity relations. The sacral features disappear or at least become much less rigid; the ceremonial forms are adjusted to the practical needs of economic transactions; the legal consequences of a punitive nature are eliminated; the range of actionable contracts is widening; etc. Of course, all this takes place by stages, with digressions and roundabout ways, setbacks and blunders, but in the end commodity and money relations receive recognition and sanction in the most adequate legal form, that of contract: *"Es ist eine Wechselwirkung aller dieser Momente, worin schließlich durch alle die unendliche Menge von Zufälligkeiten (d.h. von Dingen und Ereignissen, deren innerer Zusammenhang untereinander so entfernt oder so unnachweisbar ist, daß wir ihn als nicht vorhanden betrachten, vernachlässigen können) als Notwendiges die ökonomische Bewegung sich durchsetzt."*[5]

Investigators of legal development and its moving causes cannot dismiss with indifference the intermediary elements, nor even the "random" factors, but on the contrary, can only complete the picture with as full a presentation as possible of such aspects. This is why we have found it necessary to also trace the development threads of the forms of legal thinking which evolve in relative independence of the changing pattern of economic conditions.

We can be certain that even if allowance is made for the eventualities of other conditions the commodity relations of Rome, which developed into a world empire during the short period of a few centuries, would by all means have achieved one form or another of the necessary legal recognition and protection by the early imperial period. It therefore seems to us equally certain that the concrete approach "opted for" – the legal recognition accorded to the classes of contract at a given level of the "specific", namely the types of contract – is inseparably linked up with the degree of development attained by the Romans' way of legal thinking and can be related most directly to the actions of the formulary system. We repeat that legal thinking is itself basically conditioned by the development of economic and social relations. With the growth of commodity and money transactions, for instance, there was an obvious increase in the number of litigations (with shifts occurring primarily in the content of disputes) and of legal problems, all of which generated changes in legal thinking. Still, the very fact that during the period of commodity and money relations expansion and of the actual emergence of contract law, in the last two or three centuries B.C., the Roman proceedings became dominated precisely by the formulary action. It was so apt at grasping the "specific", it shows a relationship to the main features of the concrete stage of economic development that is "so remote or untraceable as to be regarded as non-existent or negligible". The Roman economic and

[5] Engels: op. cit. in fn3.

social conditions in the late republican and the early imperial period could not have been thought of without a relatively developed law of contract, yet the concrete forms of its evolution, particularly the established principles governing the classification of contracts, cannot be related direct to the existing level of economic and social development. They are accounted for by legal thinking factors enjoying a relative independence thereof. (It would be a "game" even transcending the bounds of hypothesis to ask how the contractual system of the continent would have developed had Justinian's "mania" of seeking for the classical not bequeathed to posterity the types of contract well conservable in the *actiones*. Or even had the full manuscript of the Digests not been unearthed at the end of the 11th century, when commodity and money relations were gathering renewed momentum, but perhaps some 500 years later.)

A sign of the relative autonomy of legal thinking is also seen in the failure of Roman law to have arrived at the general concept of contract, although in the *stipulatio* it had actually devised the legal form by which to reach that stage. This is one of the consequences of the Romans' way of legal thinking which was so "adverse" to definitions and systemization. It stems from the same stock of approach under which the types of contract or the corresponding forms of action were devised and conceived independently of interaction between them. The spread effect of legal consequences was hardly recognized even in cases where their functional interplay was rather strong. Quoting Kaser all this goes to show that Roman private law was developing through practice and can only be understood from its casuistry.[6]

(b) The greatest "enigma" of interrelations between the economy and legal development is undoubtedly presented by the common law. The same holds for the evolution of contract law. It is no accident that Max Weber,[7] the best qualified opponent of the Marxist concept professing the fundamental economic determinism of law, is so bent on making references

[6] Kaser, Max: *Das römische Privatrecht,* I, München, 1955, p. 399. It is stated by György Lukács, relying on investigations by Max Weber, that "even the Roman law, representing a stage of legal evolution most similar to the capitalist line of development but being nevertheless precapitalist in the modern sense, is characterized by too empirical, and concrete traditional limitations... The entirely systematic categories which provided the very first pillars for achieving an all-embracing generality of legal regulation came about in the course of modern development". Lukács: *Történelem és osztálytudat* (History and Class-Consciousness), Magvető Kiadó, Budapest, 1971, p. 339.

[7] It is impressively stated by Peschka that "Weber misunderstands the Marxian thesis of the economic determinism of law, and replaces it by a vulgar-materialist concept in so far as he starts from the assumption that the Marx legal theory of law is influenced and determined exclusively by economic conditions and that – what is inseparable from this – the Marxian concept of law recognizes only the direct economic conditionality of law, ignoring the indirect effects exercised on law by economic factors and processes". Peschka, Vilmos: *Max Weber jogszociológiája* (The Legal Sociology of Max Weber), Akadémiai Kiadó, Budapest, 1975, p. 125.

to the peculiar institutions of common law. He refers to its distinctive features indicative of considerable differences from many aspects of the development of continental law.[8] One could say the "enigma" is twofold: first, it is more difficult to unravel the development of the English law of contract in and by itself, for the tangle of its legal forms conceals a more hidden world of economic interrelations, and, second, the large degree of difference from the development of continental law calls for an explanation, as well. The main clue to both aspects of the "puzzle" is provided by a Marxist interpretation, correctly understood and not vulgarized, of interrelations between the economy and law.

The most striking feature of the development of common law is the aspect of continuity which is formally ensured by the peculiar method of "law-finding" through judge-made precedents, but which rests on the underlying condition of continuous economic and social development based on compromises. As noted earlier, the decisive specific of capitalist development in England is seen by Engels in the compromise concluded between the burgeoning middle class and the ex-feudal landowners. Engels also stresses that in England the continuity of pre- and post-revolutionary institutions and the compromise between landowners and capitalists were expressed in the continuity of judicial precedents, and in the religiously strict preservation of the feudal forms of the law.[9] As can be observed, the basis for the conservation of feudal legal forms was laid by this special and early class compromise. Here again, the factors at work are naturally deeply entrenched and are so entangled as to be barely capable of unravelling. Regardless of whether they concern the concrete threads of development of the common law of contract, the feudal substratum, or the legal devices used for meeting the needs of capitalist development. The intertwining effects of sociological phenomena; e.g. the role of a strong society of lawyers, which emerged at a relatively early stage, the specifics of the legal system; e.g. non-reception of Roman law, early appearance of a united law, case-law approach, procedural approach, etc. and other circumstances let alone aspects leading us into the world of poetic phantasy like the implications of the sea and seafaring life for English mentality provide a rather complex background to an analysis of the development of common law.[10] While these influences and their relative independence cannot be disputed in the majority of cases, the decisive element is that of continuity, the economic and social compromise which

[8] Weber, Max: *Rechtssoziologie*, Neuwied, 1960, particularly p. 284 et seq. Examples to show that the types of contract lead only such differences as are negligible from the viewpoint of the economic system are taken by Weber from the Roman law (ibid., p. 79; cf. pp. 95, 122 et seq.).

[9] Engels, Friedrich: *Socialism*, Special introduction to the English edition of 1892, p. 97 et seq. Cf. Eörsi, Gyula: *Comparative Civil (Private) Law*, Akadémiai Kiadó, Budapest, 1979, p. 114 et seq.

[10] Eörsi: op. cit.

served to promote the conservation of legal forms and the evolution of society alike.

It is precisely the development of contract law at the common law that shows most clearly that the demands of economic conditions even break through such legal forms as stand far from them and are apparently imperfect or almost unsuitable. What else can be the explanation for the fact that the common law, which is still averse to thinking in abstract terms and more so to devising and applying more general categories, has found ways and means to lay down sanctions for breach of contract on a general plane earlier than the most advanced legal systems of the Continent have? There emerges here an experience similar to that derived, *mutatis mutandis,* from the development of the Roman law of contract: concrete solutions may be motivated by myriads of "accidents", but the economic and social requirements are inevitably satisfied. The form and chiefly the details of a solution are subject to the influence of many eventualities: who would tell why the legal form of the general recognition of redress for breach of contract was not found in covenant, for instance, but in trespass and partly in deceit, namely assumpsit and its delictual roots? The common law also could not remain for long indifferent to the pressure of the economy and "had" to come by one road or another to the general sanctioning or legal recognition of agreements (with consideration).

The emergence of the common law of contract is at the same time well illustrative of the fact that the law is a form of economic relationships, showing at that a special interrelation between content and form: content may undergo profound modifications without any essential change in form. A rather interesting picture presents itself in the course of development during which the feudal (or at least embryonally feudal) categories of the English law of contract, following the changing pattern of economic and social conditions, evolved into a private law capable of meeting the demands of capitalist development. Engels wrote regarding this process: "They may largely preserve, as they did in England in accord with the whole process of national development, the forms of old feudal law and give them bourgeois substance, and may even bestow clearly bourgeois meanings upon feudal terms."[11]

We see examples of the relative independence of legal development, of the play of immanent factors of the legal system, in the common law having "omitted" the categories of contract, these important ingredients of the continental contractual systems which had assimilated the Roman law, and having arrived, in the absence of them, at the general recognition of the legal relevance of contractual agreements by skipping, as it were, the plane of the peculiar "specific" expressed in them. Our hypothesis

[11] Engels: op. cit. in fn1.

through which we seek a relationship between non-classification of contracts under the continental legal concept, and the general sanctioning of breach of contract at a relatively early period, is perhaps not without foundation. At any rate, the most concrete analysis of economic conditions,[12] the appraisal of the identical and different features of economic and social development in England and on the Continent, cannot by itself provide an explanation for the fundamental divergences of the contractual systems at the common and continental laws. As what we have here is a typical problem which is ultimately clarified only by economic development. Further, consideration of the internal relatively independent factors of the legal system is also indispensable and at times even insufficient for clarification.

The differences between the common law of contract and the contractual systems in the continent, as well as the reason for these differences, corroborate the main Marxian concept of society: "It is always the direct relationship of the owners of productive facilities to the direct producers – with the given form of this relationship being of course always in conformity with the existing degree of the mode of labour development. Hence it is with the social productive force of labour – in which the innermost secret, the hidden groundwork. . .of the entire structure of society resides. This does not prevent the same economic basis – same in respect of its main conditions – from displaying innumerable variations and degrees of manifestation that result from an infinity of different empirical circumstances, natural amenities, racial patterns, external historical influences, and so on, which are explicable only by an analysis of such empirical circumstances."[13]

(c) The primacy of economic factors and the relative autonomy of legal development are illustrated equally by the historical process leading up to the continental recognition of the general binding force of contract.

Available data indicates that in most areas, the classical Roman law of contract was able to satisfy the needs of simple commodity production, however advanced it might have been, without recognizing the general binding force of contract. The gaps in the closed system of types were filled for the most part by the general applicability of *stipulatio,* and where impossible the post-classical law adopted innovative devices to serve as auxiliary expedients (*praescriptis verbis actiones*). In addition to underlining the significance of insufficient economic pressure, we had to point to the play of other factors within the law. At the given level of develop-

[12] Peschka for instance, rightly claims that Max Weber's concept of legal sociology fails to take into account the concreteness of capitalist economic conditions that gave rise to different systems of law. . ., thus causing the final economic determinism of legal systems to melt away (in Weber's approach). Op. cit., p. 131.

[13] Marx: *Das Kapital,* Berlin, 1962 (Marx – Engels Werke, Dietz Verlag, Band 23), p. 799 et seq.

ment of the Roman society, state and law, the requirements for legal certainty could hardly allow for legal consequences to be attached to informal agreements, while the dominant thought of the day, which was typically analytical rather than conceptual, did not favour in theory the kind of abstractions as a contract. The weakness of legal thinking in terms of abstraction, acquired decisive significance, particularly in the Western Roman vulgar laws, which had already recognized the actionability of all written agreements in the way of *stipulatio.* However, they failed to reach the stage of conceptual generalization, whereas Justinian's codification is a truly graphical illustration of a relative time-lag between the development of society and law. The imperial code basically summarized and revived the classical law of contract with its principle of *nudum pactum* and closed system of types, although under the pressure of prevailing social conditions it recognized some significant postclassical "incongruities". (This otherwise admirable piece of codification on the abstract plane – this value-saving deed which laid the basis for the private law of continental Europe, might not have been very different in its time, from the social rootlessness of inorganic receptions in the 20th century.[14]

Economic and commercial requirements, the progress of legal thinking and considerations of legal certainty, are intertwined in the medieval development of continental law. The latter which arrived at the recognition of the general binding force of contract. The decisive significance of economic and business requirements is directly shown by the fact that the practice of general sanctioning of agreements had first developed before the *curia mercatorum.* The plea of *nudum pactum* in transactions between merchants ceased to be tolerable as early as the 14th century. Protection for the security of economic relationships is expressed in the theory of *pactum geminatum* with its typically medieval, transitory nature. An example, impressive enough to delight the mind of the relative autonomy of legal thinking, is provided by canon law, built as it was on principles of moral theology but was later carried over to temporal jurisdiction; the complex theoretical armory which helped the nature law of the 17th century to carry to final victory the pinciple of general legal recognition of contract is also a good example. On the other hand, it cannot in any way be regarded as "accidental" that a theoretical justification for the satisfaction of the primordially legal needs of commerce, of capitalist development, of the bourgeoisie be "found" by this precise theory: namely, the ideology of the surgent boutgeoisie.[15] This is added evidence of the interrelation between the economy and legal thinking, one that is enigmatic in details but unambiguously clear in its fundamental aspect.

[14] Eörsi: op. cit., pp. 198 et seq., 563 et seq.

[15] Cf. Szabó, Imre: *Hugo Grotius és a burzsoá jogbölcselet* (Hugo Grotius and the Bourgeois Philosophy of Law), in: Hugo Grotius: *A háború és béke jogáról* (On the Law of War and Peace), I, Akadémiai Kiadó, Budapest, 1960, particularly pp. 71 et seq., 74 et seq.

(d) The socialist background to the hold of traditions in maintaining the basically unchanged character of the bourgeois contractual systems is provided by the constant elements of economic conditions primarily by the continuing predominance of commodity relations. Even so, the contractual systems of the bourgeois codes, geared as they were to the economic and social conditions of the classical age, have been eroded by the monopoly capitalist transformation. Signs of obsolescence are similarly demonstrated by the categories of contract, the traditional pillars of the contractual system.

It is only on the surface that the problems of mixed contracts can be deemed to be a matter of exclusively legal relevance or rather of legal practice. This is the case because lying behind the apparently sole legal causes of primarily legal difficulties (more exact synchronization of facts and legal consequences, appearance of peremptory rules, etc.) are the contradictions working between the monopoly capitalist economy relying on modern productive forces, and the codes resting on the principles of classical capitalism. Economic transactions and most of contractual relationships became more complex and unable to simply fit into the changed cloak of contract types. The question of what jurisprudence mainly in Germany, has "added" to the objective basis underlying the complex problems of contracts, and what is fact and what is "overplay", or where the line between "reality" and "poetry" is drawn, are a matter of legal thinking, the deep underlying causes of which lie elsewhere.

The strain between modern productive forces and the traditional law of contract is reflected in the ramifying problems concerning the terms of standardized contracts and in the "self-regulation" of individual contracts cutting across boundaries of categories. The difficulties of keeping standard contracts within manageable legal limits are related to the impact of productive forces reaching the domain of law through the prism of production relations. This explains why the problem is of varying relevance in the capitalist and the socialist law, and why the possibilities of solving it differ in principle in the bourgeois and socialist systems of law. The nearly identical levels of productive forces give rise to identical problems whose solutions may be made either easier or more difficult by production relations. Yet the legal means of dealing with them – which again reveal the separate life of legal forms – may nevertheless be similar or even identical.

(e) The development of the socialist contractual system shows mainly that the nearly identical levels of productive forces, the existence of commodity and money relations provide some objective basis for traditionalism which makes for the adoption and utilization of existing legal forms and methods of systematization. At the same time, the contradiction between the social ownership of the means of production, and the persistence of commodity relations is clearly reflected even today in the difficulties of systematization encountered in obtaining systematic arrangements of contractual relationships between socialist organizations.

It is an interesting experience that the contracts made on the basis of citizens or private persons personal property, fit, almost without exception, the civil law arrangements that follow the main contractual systems of the bourgeois codes of private law. Whereas contracts made between socialist organizations on the basis of social property cause difficulties of arrangement. In the case of transactions between private persons, the types of contract offer a quite satisfactory solution regarding both systematization and legal practice. The existing problems are neither greater than, nor – in their primarily legal manifestations – very much different from, those faced by bourgeois laws (atypical and mixed contracts, standardized transactions, etc.).

With respect to contracts between socialist organizations, a lot of hard thinking is still going into deciding whether the socialist legal systems should place emphasis on socialist ownership or on the commodity character of contracts in elaborating a systematic arrangement. We believe that the problem lies in asking the wrong question. The approach that is overemphatic about the choice of focus, declaring it to be the watershed for systematization, suffers from the basic flaw that it tacitly presupposes an (initially) antagonistic or at least sharp contradiction between social ownership and commodity relations. In point of fact, several decades of building a socialist economy and society have demonstrated that in reality there is no antagonism of this kind, and that social ownership and commodity relations are not mutually exclusive categories. This being so, we think that the general criterion for systematization can only be to the extent to which commodity characteristics as the common economic attributes of contracts manifest themselves *in concreto* in the contracts of socialist organizations. This is the decisive determinant of the essential specifics of legal regulation, much like administrative controls or their scope, applicability of contract types, differing by the nature of performance, as categories of systematization, etc. Furthermore, since the concrete operation of commodity aspects – the utilization of commodity and money relations in the socialist sector – is basically conditioned by the adopted – naturally non-voluntary – model of economic management, it appears that the fundamental role in the systematization of contracts by the socialist civil law is likewise played by the essential type orientation of economic management. Furthermore, considering that the system of economic management follows diverse models in the socialist countries, the differences between contractual systems and works of codification can be reduced to the play of objective factors as well.

2. Dialectics of the "individual–specific–general" in the historical development of the contractual system

One may observe a special dialectical "play" of "the individual-specific-general" in the various phases of development of the contractual system. The interesting "hide-and-seek" of the categories of the individual-specific-general has peculiar surprises in store for the investigator, especially in a parallel application of ontological and gnosiological approaches and the comparison of the results obtained by the two methods.

(a) In the development of Roman contract law it is no longer possible to detect the stage at which the law bestowed legal relevance on a spate of disputes and unsettled problems individually by recognizing the legal effect of "individual" facts of life. The beginnings of legal development were in all certainty characterized by this approach in Rome as well, even if not exclusively, for under the influence of other laws the application of legal remedies started to move early on towards a degree of relative generality.

At any rate, the relatively long road travelled by ancient Roman law towards expressing the legal recognition of economic "transactions" on the plane of "the specific" (in the forms of *mancipatio, nexum,* etc.) is a striking feature of development. It may be natural for these "transactions" to have recognized the "specific" criteria for obtaining legal relevance and remedy in aspects corresponding to the general level of law, namely in formal ceremonial externals. The formal, ceremonial, procedural aspects (*in iure cessio*) constituted a *differentia specifica* serving as a measure of differentiation. This in turn implied that the ancient "transactions" were not in need of separation by substance (economic function, legal effects). If for no other reason their substance rendered them usable as transmission belts for a rather broad range of economic and legal objectives (*nexum* in its original form, *mancipatio* owing to the ingenuity of its artificial extension, which had been started by the ancient law), and thus, in both substantive and objective terms, they represented "the specific" shifting towards "the general", and "embracing" several of the contract types that were to emerge at a later date.

It is highly characteristic of the insignificance of the substantive aspects of differentiation and integration, that while *nexum* was originally of a more general character and was later reduced to the ancient transaction of loan, *mancipatio* had a reverse "career". It served initially for cash purchase and was later assigned a more general role as a ceremonial purchase transaction which the civil law of antiquity destined for acquisition not only of property but also of other rights of dominion (servitude, husband's authority, *mancipium*) known to civil law.[16] What actually mattered was form, or ceremony (due to peasants' mistrust generated by the lack of mass-scale economic operations, by fear of non-enforcement of law)[17] and the substantive aspects of economic goals achieved by operation of law were relegated to the background. The absence of substantive subtleties from the law is best evidenced by the complete lack of the later contract-law approach in the "transactions" of ancient Roman law. We have therefore dealt with them only in light of their actual economic function (transfer of ownership of things, money, etc.), in a way of presenting them as a prefiguration of contract law.[18]

Special mention is owed to the fact that the ancient procedure of *legis actio* with its formal rigidity was favourable to a more general and less selective kind of legal remedy and consequently was not, even in principle, very much suited to provoke a differentiation of the forms of "transactions" on the basis of some sort of a substantive "specific".

The lack of substantive differentiation between the forms of "transactions" – their overgeneralization was unable to meet the requirements of more intense economic relationships. Separation on the plane of the "specific" close to the "general" was not a suitable means of law for a more adequate transmission of increasingly complex commodity and money relations. Chiefly the formulary system – the forms of procedure based on *legis actio* – were too rigid and general. The growing complexity of economic relationships required more balanced legal solutions, called for the legal categories to be narrowed in scope, and for the substantive aspects to be given greater emphasis. The types of contract were destined to meet this demand.

From our viewpoint it would nevertheless be incorrect to be led by the development of the Roman law of contract to the conclusion that legal development was moving from more general categories back to more narrow ones, and still less that it returned from "the general" to "the specific". This is not even indicated by the objective facts of evolution, and it is by no means a valid claim that the types of contract were, so to speak, concretized from the general by some conscious effort. As previously stated, although on a plane nearer the "general". the "transactions" of ancient law were themselves an embodiment of the "specific", and the types of contract did not emerge from them, nor led by them but rather along a new path on practically new principles. The ancient law "transactions" made abstractions in external, formal elements as as-

[16] Marton, Géza: *A római magánjog elemeinek tankönyve. Institúciók* (Textbook of the Elements of Roman Private Law. Institutes), Tankönyvkiadó, Budapest, 1963. p. 148.

[17] Ibid., p. 10. *"Die Form ist die Feindin der Willkür, die Zwillingsschwester der Freiheit"* – writes Jhering: *Geist des römischen Rechts*, II/2, 1923, p. 471.

[18] A similar view is expressed in the manuals of Roman law we have drawn upon in this study (Kaser, Marton, Brósz–Pólay).

pects reflecting the level of legal development in their time, and expressed through them the "specific" as a separating factor. In like manner, the categories of contract were differentiated on a level appropriate to their time; namely by substantive elements, by aspects (nature of performance) embodied in economic goals that had achieved legal relevance and expression. This is not to say, of course, that an important part was not played by forms in the formulary action, which squeezed the types of contract into rigid legal forms, and elevated them from the transactions and usages of daily life to the domain of law.[19] On the contrary! They were of utmost importance, especially from the standpoint of actionability or legal recognition. Yet the formal aspects had no bearing on the "choice" of the "specific", the *differentia specifica.* The ancient "transactions" and the types of contract were thus placed at relatively different points on the plane of the "specific", and what was more important to the further development of contract law, relied on different elements. We see the moving cause behind the career of contract types precisely in the fact that the abstract plane of the "specific", expressed in them was, at least for a long period of time; optimal, neither too wide nor too narrow. It proved to be very suitable for perceiving the "individual", the particular. Over and above this, types of contract were separated by reference to such a criterion of commodity relations – namely the legally relevant nature of performance, the economic goal – which in essence is still capable today of a systemic channeling (by codification) of contractual relationships, of their differentiation which served to facilitate legal practice.[20]

A separate treatment is warranted by *stipulatio,* which of all lucky children of contract Roman law, was a transaction capable of the most ingenious and most varied applications. The main reason for its nearly unlimited applicability is seen in the fact that it gave legal force to the meeting of minds, the most essential aspect of agreements in everyday transactions, in its simplest possible and at the same time most abstract element. *Stipulatio* practically served as an objective meeting point for the "individual" in the transactions of daily life, and for the "general" invested with legal relevance. Thus, in *stipulatio*, Roman law came, again objectively, very close to a general recognition of the legal relevance of agreement. When *stipulatio* reached its full development and when it was largely freed from its ancient sacral features (which occurred rather early!), its limitations to the legal recognition of agreement (e.g. formal

[19] The advent of categorization amid the facts life, and the subsequent emergence, through long centuries, of legal terminology from the usage of everyday language are graphically and persuasively presented in a discussion of the development of lease and of the terminological separation of sale from lease by Kaufmann, Horst: *Die altrömische Miete,* Köln – Graz, 1964, primarily p. 17.

[20] The inadequacy of *locatio conductio* in comparison to modern requirements and its causes, have been discussed above. The core and substance of present day problems in connection with contract types will be treated at the end of this chapter.

requirements, the need for two *stipulationes* for the making of an agreement) were less significant than its advantages (chiefly its abstract nature free from *causa*). Therefore we are also inclined to accept the view that *stipulatio,* in so far as its practical effect was concerned, did not lag too far behind the objective situation which had emerged with the recognition of the general binding force of contract. It is a different matter that Roman legal thinking failed to encompass the conceptual generality already inherent in *stipulatio,* that its development did not reach that point, which is of course a very important aspect. Still, a totally different result is obtained by an ontological and gnosiological approach to *stipulatio.* The institution of contract actually existed (or *quasi* existed) in Roman law, but the Romans were far from its recognition conceptually and even more so scientifically.

It is interesting that, apparently, Roman law did not come any closer to such recognition, even in the period when mainly in the post-classical law, the strict forms of *stipulatio* were being gradually relaxed to the point at which all formal requisites except setting in writing were replaced by deed. This was the case despite the fact that at this stage of legal development, practically all contracts put into writing were already actionable, as we have discussed. The "only" thing lacking was the recognition, and its declaration, that a pact or agreement is legally binding if drawn up in the prescribed form. Since Roman law did not reach that stage, the difference between the concrete generality of *stipulatio* and the abstract generality of contract subsisted all along. We cannot repeat often enough that this detracts nothing from the value of the stupendous results achieved by the Roman law of contract. Having developed the substance of contract types is a truly admirable accomplishment.

We feel that the way the Roman law grasped the "individual-specific-general" bears out what we have already stated, namely that legal development does not follow the order of logical categories, and that it can hardly be squeezed into them, and that it is wedded to them over a long historical time-horizon, at the most and in its tendency only.

At an early stage of development of Roman law, the peculiar categories of the "specific" represented by the formal elements of contractual patterns, had been found coexistent with the actually "near-general"; while the types of contract delineated by the substantive "specific" had also emerged in the pre-classical age. This was so that the only task left for the continental laws of contract was to find the way to the "general" from the types so remarkably framed.

The development of the common law of contract is also highly instructive from the point of view of our subject.

The process which was under way in the 12th and 13th centuries – the period in which writs were isssued – provides an insight into a stage of development of a legal system at which a concrete case became the concern of the law virtually in its individuality. The "individual" was receiving legal recognition practically in the absence of any kind of abstraction. The slow process of abstraction was taking place through a selection and improvement of writs, with a peculiar result that was entirely different from those achieved by the evolution of Roman law. Whereas the contract types of Roman law (or their *actiones*) were differentiated by the economic goals of contracts as expressed in legal forms, the medieval English forms of action were essentially distinguished by the physical nature of the thing in litigation (land, movable thing, money, etc.).

It is all the more surprising that from this level of legal development, based as it was on a primitive abstraction, the common law of contract managed to reach the "general", which was capable of meeting the demands of economic conditions. Finally it came to the general sanctioning of breach of contract as early as the beginning of the 17th century. Meanwhile we think that the common contract law cannot be said to have evaded, so to speak, the stage of development through the "specific". This is due to the fact that there is no doubt that contractual actions (or actions of a contractual function), despite the low level of abstraction manifest in them, were themselves a peculiar embodiment of the "specific", which, however, was to be found on a plane different from that signalled by the Roman types of contract. Given their original forms of abstraction, the actions were more similar to the abstractions which, based on form and having a more general character, were represented by the "transactions" of ancient Roman law. However, they were of a "specific" character nonetheless. Not even a law based on a system of precedents can do without appropriate levels of abstraction, and not even the road travelled by the common law of contract was leading directly from the "individual" to the "general".

The question may thus arise as to whether the common law, by its general sanctioning of breach of contract and by its elaboration of the action of assumpsit, has also arrived at the category of contract on the conceptual plane. We cannot, of course, speak of a scientific concept, but we think we can, by all means, speak of the recognition of contract in its general, abstract essence. In this respect the English contract law at the turn of the 16th and 17th centuries together with its consideration theory, was absolutely superior not only to the fully developed Roman law, but also to the continental laws of contract as they existed at the time of the Slade's Case. It was stated in principle, in connection with this famous precedent itself, that, as discussed, a mutual enforceable agreement of two parties was to be sanctioned by law, and that pledge or promise was enough to support such sanction. This testifies, in our view, to a conscious recognition of the common core of agreements or contracts, namely to the fact that general sanctioning was an intendment of the law. It was due not less to this aspect of development that the common law of contract proved in practice more capable than the German BGB, for instance, for laying down sanctions for breach of contract on a truly general plane. At the same time it followed from the essential features of the entire development of common law that the English lawyers took little interest in formulating scientific concepts. The result was that – although the common law solved the general questions of contract much earlier and even placed them in the centre of contract law – the general concept of contract was given some sort of a scientific formulation only as a by-product of the consideration theory.

3. On the essence and present-day role of the types of contract

In the continental legal systems, including the Hungarian, categorization of contract has retained a highly important role to the present day. As we have tried to demonstrate, they have undergone major changes in function in the course of time, but have also preserved their relevance in current laws. We therefore feel it befitting to conclude our study on the crucial phases in the development of contract types by giving a brief summary account of their essence and modern-day function.

(a) In our search for the essence of contract types as legal categories we proceed from the recognition of legal theory that "specificity" is to be viewed as a specific conceptual element "determining the concrete setup of the realm of legal reflection".[21] After György Lukács,[22] Peschka states the following: "The category of both individuality and generality is unable to grasp concurrently the individual phenomena and essential generality of the socialistic relations calling for regulation in such a way as to eliminate both aspects while preserving them and thus ensure applicability of legislation to concrete, individual cases whereby it is not only related to a concrete individual phenomenon of social relations, but also act as a transmission belt, creating a form of transition to the essence or generality of social relations, by thus influencing and regulating conjointly the individual case in accord with the general as expressed in the content of the legal norm. . . The logical form constituting a transition from the individual to the general and from the general to the individual, linking the individual with the general, and serving as a point at which the individual and the general swing into each other is a category of specificity. . . Such

[21] Peschka: *Jogforrás és jogalkotás* (Sources of Law and Legislation), Akadémiai Kiadó, Budapest, 1965, p. 324 et seq.

[22] Lukács, György: *A különösség mint esztétikai kategória* (Specificity as an Aesthetic Category), Akadémiai Kiadó, Budapest, 1957, p. 92: "Movement from the individual towards the general and *vice versa* is always through the specific; this is a real transmission belt both in objective reality and in thought reflecting it with an approximate adequacy."

specificity of the legislative process, the legal regulation of social relations. . ., is embodied in the typical in the course of concrete legal reflection."[23] Thus, in general, legislation relies on the typical aspect of social relations for regulation. In the legal reflection process the typical appears in varying form according to the diversity of socialist relations, and is to be found at different logical levels, without reflection itself being removed from the plane of specificity. In the process of legal regulation, the diverse aspects of social relations are given normative substance in relatively separable areas of the broad spectrum of specificity, which, together with typicality, is a general characteristic of legal regulation or legislation.[24]

The question may be rightly asked as to what constitutes the specifics of contract categories in comparison with the general features of legal regulation. If a legal norm is commonly expected to give expression to the typical of a specific character in a particular set of social relations, what are the attributes of the norms relating to the types of contract under civil law? Is there any specific feature, by comparison to the general characteristics of legislation, in the rules of law that give normative form to the types of contract, and if there is one, what does it consist of? We maintain that the types of contract or their normative forms do have specific features, which are manifest in and arise out of the fact that the principal contract types of civil law, *a priori* the traditional forms of antiquity, express the "scientific type" rather than simply the decisive typical that appears in legal reflection. This view of ours is buttressed by the development of the continental legal systems as well. A two thousand years span, during which the fundamental types of contract – conceived in the actions of the Roman formulary system, disentangled from their procedural pupa, and provided with a dogmatic armory in the centuries of *usus modernus,* which were also permeated with the theory of natural law in the 17th century and crystallized in the science of the Pandects – finally became the most important ingredients of the contractual systems of the codes. It allowed them sufficient time and scope to develop into categories at the level of scientific generalization.

The main feature of the scientific category, the main criterion for delimiting it from types of a different nature, is a higher degree of generalization. György Lukács writes on the artistic, aesthetic type that it "cannot rise. . .even to the scientific generality of type",[25] and Peschka holds the following view: "Scientific generalization seeks to define the

[23] Peschka: ibid., pp. 324 et seq., 334, 337.

[24] On the philosophical concept of type, see Lukács: ibid., p. 217: "By type we mean a concentrated summation of those definitions which are called into life objectively and necessarily, by the definite concrete place they occupy in society, primarily in the process of production. . . The concept of categorization is subordinate to that of the general set of laws. In both life and science. . . it is directly of a specific nature. . ., with the aspect of generality to predominate (in it), even though the aspect of specificity remains its indispensable feature."

[25] Ibid., p. 221.

pure category, to condense the typical traits of a particular set of social relations or of a social phenomenon in one class through generalization of the highest degree. It is only in the rarest case that the generality of this scientific type is necessary for and attainable by legal reflection. . . The decisive category in legal reflection is characterized by the fact that it seldom rises to the scientific generality of class, but nevertheless comes close to it and tends towards it."[26]

(b) We think that part of the problems in the legal field is in applying the rules on the types of contract to concrete facts arises precisely from this feature of contract categories, namely from the higher degree of generalization indicated by the nature of the scientific type.

The scientific generality of contract categories is clearly of use to shaping the contractual system, particularly to systemization in works of codification, and to evolving the didactics of contract law. However, it is not without problems in legal practice.

For an understanding of this question we must revert again for a moment to the traits of specificity in legal reflection. We agree with Peschka's view, which we quote on this point too: "In the process of legal reflection the expression, by means of categories of socialist relations as the substance of legal norms is always in keeping with the specific nature and structure, and the aims and purposes of legal regulation. Therefore social relations as the substance of legal norms are always reflected in the types by these not emphasizing the pure category condensing a given set of social relations, but the stronger or weaker characteristics of the typicality of the particular social relations or situation and the attitude of the participants therein, while keeping in mind the said requirements as that of facilitating the process of realization of what is emphasized as determinant by the legal norm, namely the success of regulation. Already at this point of reflecting the social content by selecting and emphasizing the typical features all is pointing to the direction of normative as manifest in the final formulations by the law. . . In the process of legal regulation the expression, as the substance of legal norms, of the typical of a set of social relations or of a social situation to be regulated is achieved not by simply adopting the scientific type or the typical covering the given aspect of social relations. It is also by making it the substance of legal norms."[27] True, given their economic and social function and nature, the rules of civil law do not generally use as closed concepts as, for instance, the norms of criminal law. Nor is it disputed that the categories at the level of scientific generalization are given normative substance not only through the classification of contracts under civil law but that similar solutions can be met with in other areas as well.

[26] Peschka: ibid., pp. 338, 339.
[27] Ibid., p. 339.

With respect to the basic types of contract (sale, *locatio conductio operis,* agency, etc.) it should nevertheless be stated that the scientifically elaborated types have received normative substance or legal character in a much too direct form, in their scientific generality. The main explanation for this is to be found precisely in the evolutionary process of the basic types of contract, notably in the fact that more than one of the present-day codes on the continent have devised systems of categorization, defining and delineating their concepts, exactly in the form perfected by the science of the Pandects. It is hardly accidental that the problems in legal science concerning the types of contract have emerged chiefly in the application of the rules of these codes. (In our view, the fact that the rules on contract types are introduced by a definition of some kind (as in the German BGB) or by a formulation of the normative character (as in the Hungarian Civil Code) makes no theoretical difference in this context.)

The concrete roots of the judge's dilemma are seen in the fundamental contradiction existing in that the normative concept of the said traditional contract types was defined in the codes generally of the scientific type, whereas the legal consequences were formulated in relation to the typical of a much narrower compass. More specifically, such consequences are no longer applicable except to a narrower scope covered by the type in contrast to the concept. In the application of law there often arises a conflict between the conceptual generality of contract types, and the relatively narrow scope of legal consequences. The judge is virtually enticed and invited by the general definition of type to subsume a concrete case, but his attempt to apply the rules governing details often proves futile, as these rules express, at least in part, a different type. In other words, a concrete contract, in the last analysis, shows itself to be atypical in relation to the given category, although at the outset it appeared typical when viewed only in the conceptual scope of the given category. A concrete transaction is covered by the concept of contract category at the level of the scientific category but it is not the case for the legal consequences that are built on a narrower cross-section of specificity. Peschka is right in pointing out that "even if. . .the scientific category, condensing as it does a given set of social relationships or a social situation, becomes in its purity. . . the substance of a legal norm, it acquires its real meaning always in conjunction with other provisions, parts and places of regulation".[28]

This discrepancy between the concepts of contract categories and legal consequences derives from our standpoint from the fact that the facts of life have developed in complexity since the formulation of the rules which are mainly still patterned after traditions, and while the original abstraction of concepts would be still able to cover the new incidents of

[28] Ibid.

social relations, economic and social developments have often outgrown the diameter of the rules governing partial aspects. Thus, as a result of the legacy of long-standing historical traditions and of the adoption of old approaches and devices, legal consequences express for the most part an earlier level of economic and social relations. As has been repeatedly pointed out in previous chapters, most of the concrete rules relating to contract categories are formulated even in the current codes "with an eye" mainly to transactions between the one-time small contractors of capitalism at its phase of free competition, or between citizens of socialist countries contracting on the basis of personal or private property, that is to say to the facts of life manifested in those transactions.

Legal formulation as the peculiar relative generality of legal reflection is in vain if the rules are not or only hardly applicable to contracts made under conditions of modern-day productive forces and amid modern socio-economic relations. The "individuality" of an aspect of current relations can hardly be covered by the "typical" of relations "kept in view" by the legislator. The attribute of specificity, indicated as intrinsic to legal reflection, that "in a sense it represents the whole area of transmission, a range of real and concrete motion. . ., which appears to be wider or narrower according to the subject-matter or goal of cognition"[29] is of no avail. It cannot be suited to remedy each and every legislative anachronism. The elasticity of the typical of legal reflection is able to synchronize the legislative type with the "individuality" of concrete facts for very long and on a rather broad scale. The scope of action of specificity "may be widened by the perfection of cognition. . . if it extends the context to include aspects not known before to have a role in the relationship of an individuality to a generality, and may narrow it in so far as it is capable of rendering several intermediate determinants, which were regarded before as independent of one another, subordinate to a single determinant".[30] But this flexibility, this quality of specificity as a transmission belt, is also unable to "correct the trajectory" whenever required by the application of the rules on contract types to every instance of difference between the "individuality" of the concrete case and the legislative type. This is impossible even in case of the most ideal of legal practice, and still more so in situations where – and these are the typical – the process of judicial law-seeking on the Continent, enfeebled and dependent on the "crutches" of statute law, is rather prone to establish atypical elements and facts. In the case of contract categories this problem is accentuated by the fact that, due objectively to the often archaic character of relations "kept in view" by the regulation of categories, a concrete agreement contains facts

[29] Lukács: ibid., p. 93.
[30] Ibid.

atypical in nature. Moreover, it is to be regarded as an atypical contract in its entirety.

From the foregoing it becomes clear that, in our view, to be regarded atypical not only are the types of contract specifically not covered by regulation to be regarded atypical, as is commonly held in Hungarian literature as well,[31] but that this category also includes transactions which, though in some of their – perhaps main – aspects share the features of a given regulated type, cannot, in their concrete essence, be credited with the basic nature of the given type. Nor for the same reason, can they be brought under the rules thereon. On this point we are more inclined to accept the arguments of Larenz rather than the commonly held view, when he means the latter category by atypical contracts, although we must admit, he does not mention (at least explicity) the transactions that are commonly deemed to be atypical, that is to say are entirely unregulated.[32]

We do not, of course, claim that all difficulties encountered in the application of rules of types of contract, stem from the contradiction of regulation here described. This we think to be the principal problem in the case of ancient contract types. In the case of newly emerged categories the handicaps in legal practice are often due exactly to unfounded categorization, the creation of too narrow types, and a shift of the "specific" towards the "individual". However, in view of a close relationship existing between this problem and historical development, we have found it appropriate to attempt an explanation of the causes behind the contradictions residing in the rules on the basic traditional types of contract.

(c) The contemporary laws of the Continent, both capitalist and socialist, adopt different approaches in expressing, though not in a uniform manner, the said contradictions of the contractual system.

As noted in Chapter IV, the crisis phenomena of categorization, including the problems of standard contracts, are likewise closely related to the regulation of contract types, which is not always equal to modern requirements.

The proliferation of subtypes of certain contracts may also a reflection of meeting this problem. A growing number of subtypes receive normative formulations particularly in the case of sale and *locatio conductio operis.*

The lack of solution in the socialist contractual systems also stems in part from this same source. For instance, as we have argued in Chapter V, in the indirect economic mechanism based on planned market regulation,

[31] Villányi, László: *Kötelmi típusok. Vegyes szerződések* (Types of Contract. Mixed Contracts), in: Szladits, Károly (ed.): *Magyar Magánjog* (Hungarian Private Law), IV, Budapest, 1942, p. 2; Világhy, Miklós – Eörsi, Gyula: *Magyar polgári jog* (Hungarian Civil Law), II, Tankönyvkiadó, Budapest, 1965, p. 8.

[32] Larenz, Karl: *Ergänzende Vertragsauslegung und dispositives Recht*, Neue Juristische Wochenschrift, 1963, p. 740.

it is theoretically possible to integrate the contracts of citizens and socialist organizations into a unified system. However not all types of contract are susceptible to a single homogeneous regulation. In this case the formulation of exceptional rules (or, if you like, the establishment of subtypes) is called for on the "model" of the basic type. Formulation of differing rules or "modelling" (e.g. in the case of *locatio conductio operis,* agency, society, or perhaps commission, not to mention the full separation of delivery contract) is required not by the various forms of ownership, but because not even the classes of contract that may be reduced to a common denominator on the plane of scientific abstraction in the definition of concepts can always be regarded as homogeneous for a formulation of legal consequences and partial rules. Here again, the core and substance of the problem lies in that the set of social relations encompassed by the conceptual generality of the scientific type is not sufficiently homogeneous to be amenable to uniform regulation (e.g. mass and serial production, or individual manufactures on the one hand and narrow scope of market conditions typical of the traditional manufacture on the other).

A common feature of solutions mentioned here as an example (standard contracts, subtypes, "modelling" with establishment of general rules allowing for exceptions) is the aim at a breaking down or a relative narrowing of the much too general concepts of type by legislative action (subtypes, "modelling") or by "quasi-legislative" means (standard contracts).[33] The main problem with these solutions is in finding the right proportions and emphasis. Excessive restriction of the scope of types is liable to create, in an apparently paradoxical way only, the same problems for legal practice as presented by the contradiction between the more general concepts of type and the relatively narrower diameter of legal consequences, namely the proliferation of atypical elements and agreements. In addition, the often repeated advantages of categorization in systemization and didactics tend to be reduced by the establishment of unwarranted or ill-advised contract types. Consequently there is no need for new types of contract to be recognized where legal practice can be reasonably assisted by the creation of subtypes or by "modelling".

[33] In contemporary Western legal theories, serious arguments have been advanced and even whole doctrines have been devised, though not without any adverse critical reaction, to support the claim that the said similar problems of legal practice should be solved by means of "law-finding" (by analogy or under a typological concept of legal norms, etc.). See, *inter alia,* Engisch, Karl: *Die Idee der Konkretisierung in Recht und Rechtswissenschaft unserer Zeit,* Heidelberg, 1953, enlarged edition in 1968; *Logische Studien zur Gesetzesanwendung,* Heidelberg, 1963; Kaufmann, Arthur: *Analogie und "Natur der Sache", Zugleich ein Beitrag zur Lehre vom Typus,* Karlsruhe, 1965; Larenz, Karl: *Methodenlehre der Rechtswissenschaft,* Berlin, 1969; Leenen, Detlef: *Typus und Rechtsfindung,* Berlin, 1971; Wolff, Hans Julius: *Typen im Recht und in der Rechtswissenschaft,* in: *Studium Generale,* V, 1952, p. 195 et seq. A fuller critical appraisal of thsese very interesting and instructive ideas, however, is outside the scope of our study's principal subject matter.

All in all, the analysis and appraisal of the crucial phases in evolutionary history lead us to conclude that the idea of types and typification of contract is an indispensable guide to the contemporary continental contractual systems as well. We would be able to subscribe to an opposing viewpoint only if we failed to consider the evolutionary process of the continental contractual systems, as well as its results and lessons, and if we were also ignore the sociological substance of the legislative and "law-finding" mechanism in the continental countries.